THE END OF THE CHINESE CENTURY?

Also by Bertil Lintner

*Great Game East: India, China and the Struggle
for Asia's Most Volatile Frontier*

THE END OF THE CHINESE CENTURY?

HOW XI JINPING LOST THE BELT AND ROAD INITIATIVE

BERTIL LINTNER

HarperCollins *Publishers* India

First published India by HarperCollins *Publishers* 2024
4th Floor, Tower A, Building No. 10, DLF Cyber City,
DLF Phase II, Gurugram, Haryana – 122002
www.harpercollins.co.in

2 4 6 8 10 9 7 5 3 1

Copyright © Bertil Lintner 2024

P-ISBN: 978-93-6213-559-9
E-ISBN: 978-93-6213-219-2

The views and opinions expressed in this book are the author's own
and the facts are as reported by him, and the publishers are not in
any way liable for the same.

Bertil Lintner asserts the moral right
to be identified as the author of this work.

All rights reserved. No part of this publication may be reproduced,
stored in a retrieval system, or transmitted, in any form or by any
means, electronic, mechanical, photocopying, recording or otherwise,
without the prior permission of the publishers.

Typeset in 11.5/15.5 Adobe Garamond at
HarperCollins *Publishers* India

Printed and bound in India by Replika Press Pvt. Ltd.

This book is produced from independently certified FSC® paper to ensure
responsible forest management.

CONTENTS

Introduction vii

1. A New Silk Road? 1
2. Ruler of the East 26
3. The Great Golden Peninsula 56
4. Collision Course on the Roof of the World 92
5. The Indian Ocean 123
6. Pearls of the Pacific 154
7. Whose Asia-Pacific Century? 185

Acknowledgements 209
Notes 211
Index 213

The detailed notes pertaining to this book are available on the HarperCollins *Publishers* India website. Scan this QR code to access the same.

INTRODUCTION

IT WAS MEANT TO BE EVEN BIGGER AND GRANDER THAN AMERICA'S Marshall Plan, which helped rebuild Europe after World War II. First unveiled by the Chinese President Xi Jinping during a visit to Kazakhstan in October 2013, China pledged to invest US$1 trillion—and according to some sources as much as US$8 trillion[1]—in the construction of roads, railways, bridges, ports and other infrastructure projects across the globe. Originally called the One Belt One Road (OBOR), it became the Belt and Road Initiative (BRI) and was going to create a new and, according to Xi, a more just world order.

For President Xi personally, the BRI was also an attempt to secure a place for himself in the history of China, and even the world. Mao Zedong destroyed the old, corrupt order and managed to unify China. Deng Xiaoping, once derisively branded a 'capitalist roader' by Mao, lived up to that moniker and laid the foundations of a modern economy. Mao's austere socialism gave way to Wild-West capitalism, which led to a dramatic increase in living standards but also to economic inequality between the newly rich—and some became immensely rich—and those who had benefitted less from Deng's free-market reforms. Xi wanted to make China great again and turn the country from being merely an economic growth engine into a global political and military force, which would eventually overtake the United States as the world's most powerful nation.

More than 150 countries and about thirty international organizations signed up to reap the benefits of the BRI. But when representatives of those nations met in Shanghai in October 2023, the mood could hardly be described as upbeat and optimistic. Ten years after Xi's speech in Kazakhstan, it had become clear to many that the BRI was not a Marshall Plan. China had not been providing the signatories with aid and expertise. It was all about loans that sooner or later would have to be repaid. China's promises of prosperity had brought debt and distress to countries such as Laos, Sri Lanka and Pakistan. Portugal and Italy had decided to leave the BRI altogether and had begun to reassess their overall relationship with China. In Europe, the European Union refused to bail out Montenegro from its loans from China.[2] The Philippines President, Ferdinand Marcos, Jr, was conspicuously absent from a meeting in Beijing in October 2023, which was meant to mark the tenth anniversary of the BRI. He and his government have terminated a series of Chinese-initiated infrastructure projects, and will instead be working with Japanese and Western corporations.[3]

A railway in Kenya, which was opened with much fanfare in 2017, turned out to go no further than to the middle of the country. Kenya has also been left servicing loans totalling around US$ 4.7 billion, mainly borrowed from Chinese banks.[4] The railway was meant to continue to Uganda, but that country was already struggling to repay its debt. So, six years later, the railway ends abruptly in an empty field in the Rift Valley, some 350 kilometres from the Ugandan border. The entire project has not only been a fiasco but also the target of lawsuits, criminal investigations over corruption and resentment by environmentalists and displaced workers in the trucking industry.[5]

A China-funded high-speed railway connecting the Indonesian capital with Bandung found it hard to attract passengers because the distance is only 143 kilometres. To make sense, the railway should have connected Jakarta with other metropolitan centres on Java, such as Surabaya or Yogyakarta.[6]

In Central Asia—where Xi first unveiled his plan—favourable public opinion towards China is waning. Opinion polls conducted in Kyrgyzstan,

Kazakhstan and Uzbekistan show increasingly negative views on China, and at the same time, and not by coincidence, Chinese investment has dramatically increased there. Here, as well as in other countries where Beijing has launched BRI projects, Chinese investment comes with Chinese workers—making employment opportunities for local workers are few and far between—and all those countries are now also heavily in debt to China.[7]

While questions are being raised about the economic as well as political reliance on China and the BRI, China itself has encountered serious challenges since the project was launched. The first was the 2019–20 Covid-19 pandemic. China was the first country to experience an outbreak of the disease, and responded with drastic measures that had a crippling impact on its economy. Entire cities, including the financial hub of Shanghai, were closed down. It is not known exactly how deeply the pandemic has affected China's economy, but no country, no matter how developed and economically powerful, could possibly go through what China did during and immediately after the pandemic without serious consequences.

It has also become clear that the Chinese real estate market is in serious trouble. As the American journalist Linette Lopez reported for *Business Insider* on 15 October 2023: 'China has a population of 1.4 billion, but it has built housing for a population of 3 billion, according to expert estimates. Many of the mega-developments became empty monuments of Beijing's insatiable desire for growth. In Shenyang, farmers have taken over a development of empty mansions for cattle grazing.' According to Lopez, 'Country Garden, China's largest real-estate developer, is on the brink of collapse. In a sign that Beijing has grown tired of this game, Xu Jiayin, the chairman of Evergrande, another embattled real-estate behemoth, has been detained by authorities.'[8] Money-starved provinces are forced to ask for bailouts, which the central government doesn't want to, or can't, provide.

Then came the wars in Ukraine and the Middle East. Proposed trade routes through Central Asia to Europe were disrupted, and China's main economic activity became the export of military material, especially drones, to Russia—even as Chinese companies providing the Russian war machine with weapons risk being sanctioned by the European Union.⁹ Russia may be a lucrative market for the Chinese, but it cannot compare with what could have been achieved if there had been a smoother relationship with European nations.

China's standing is not only a question of the impact of the pandemic, Ukraine and threats of sanctions. Many foreign companies have discovered that it was, after all, not as profitable to invest in China as they had originally thought. According to the Economist Intelligence Unit, 'Anxieties around geopolitical risk, domestic [Chinese] policy uncertainty and slower growth are pushing companies to think about alternative markets.'¹⁰ Major foreign companies have not yet closed down their entire operations in China, but rather than reinvesting in China, many are moving their profits to safer jurisdictions. Even official Chinese data shows that foreign businesses have been pulling out their assets from the country at a faster rate than they have been putting them in.

The most extensive and detailed study of the BRI in the Pacific has been done by Carol Li in a paper for the University of Hawai'i at Mānoa. According to her study, China's state-owned policy banks and state-owned commercial banks accounted for 80 per cent of the total BRI funding in 2018, and the main part of that came from two state-owned policy banks, the China Development Bank, which has provided US$ 196 billion in loans, and the Exim Bank, which has supplied more than US$ 145 billion to fund some 1,800 projects.

In addition, Li writes, China's four major commercial banks—the Bank of China, the Industrial and Commercial Bank of China, the China Construction Bank and the Agricultural Bank of China—together contribute approximately 46 per cent of the BRI Funds, and that the government's Silk Road Fund, which was established in 2014 exclusively to focus on the BRI projects, has over US$ 40 billion in assets. Li concludes: 'The BRI's fragmentation contributes to difficulty in tracking investments and outcomes, and thus the lack of transparency.'¹¹

But most of the countries that are supposed to benefit from the BRI schemes are not in a position to repay the loans they have been compelled to take from those banks, which has led to what is termed a 'debt trap' situation. China has bartered unpaid loans for equity—as has been the case in Sri Lanka and Laos, for instance—and thus gained considerable economic and, therefore, also political influence in those countries. But loans that cannot be repaid mean billions of dollars have been flowing out of China. Much of that money is not coming back, and whatever equity the Chinese government has gained in exchange for non-performing loans cannot compensate for the losses in terms of hard currency. In short, the BRI is a recipe for financial disaster.

A major weakness in the actual implementation of Xi's BRI is that there is no central governmental body that oversees the projects, and it is not clear which ministry or ministries are responsible for them. Yuen Yuen Ang, a professor of political science at the Centre for Chinese Studies at Michigan University, argues that the modus operandi for the BRI is 'typical in China, where the central government often issues broad directives and expects lower-ranking officials to figure out how to fulfil them.'[12]

The hallmark of such communist-style mass campaigns, Ang argues, is that 'everyone pitches in with frenzied enthusiasm and little coordination. Vast resources and human capital are mobilized toward one goal. Banks, businesses and officials across the country participate en masse, rather than dividing up responsibilities, as local governments rush to meet what they see as their superiors' wishes.'[13]

According to Ang's excellent analysis of the BRI, 'top officials still haven't defined what constitutes a BRI project or who qualifies as a participant in the initiative. As a result, every investment project, whether public or private, profit-making or money-losing, honest or dishonest, claims to be part of the bandwagon.'[14] When everything seemed to be on track back in 2018, *The New York Times* had reported that attempts were being made to win friends with grandiose schemes, including plans for an indoor ski slope near the beaches of Australia's Gold Coast, a spa with Chinese medicine in the Czech Republic and cultural centres and amusement parks in the Philippines, Indonesia, Vietnam, Italy, Hungary and Serbia.[15]

The Chinese system, where political ambition takes preference over robust fiscal policies and sound economic management, is starting to break down. It would, however, be a serious mistake to believe that Xi and his ruling inner circle would abandon their plans to make China great again. What we are likely to see is a downscaled version of the original plan. The new focus will be on countries and markets closer to home, primarily China's northern neighbour Russia, Southeast Asia, the Himalayan region and the small and vulnerable island nations of the Indian and Pacific Oceans. But even there, China cannot expect friction-free relationships. Xi himself has warned China to prepare for 'great struggles' on the road to glory.[16]

The 'Chinese Century' never materialized. Instead, we have to contemplate the painful adjustment to a China rife with seemingly unsurmountable domestic problems, and what that means for the regions of the world that Xi is still determined to try to dominate.

1

A NEW SILK ROAD?

THE FIRST, CURIOUS NAME OF XI'S PLAN—ONE BELT ONE ROAD—alluded to the opening of a new, proposed overland 'Silk Road Economic Belt' connecting China with Europe through Central Asia, and a 'Maritime Silk Road' that the Chinese claimed existed in ancient times across the Indian Ocean. But the name was modified to the Belt and Road Initiative (BRI) in 2016, as the Chinese government had come to the conclusion that the emphasis on the word 'one' was open to misinterpretation.

In the media and at conferences, the project was also referred to as 'the New Silk Road' and as such represented a modern version of the 'Silk Road', an ancient trade route that, according to *National Geographic*, was 'used by traders for more than 1,500 years, from when the Han dynasty of China opened trade in 130 BCE until 1453 CE, when the Ottoman Empire closed off trade with the West.'[1] The route stretched for 6,437 kilometres, *National Geographic* asserted, supposedly from the then Chinese capital Xian all the way to Rome. The aim of China's new 'Silk Road' was to restore the country's old glory as a global, benevolent trade nation.

In a 2016 article, Yang Minghong, a Chinese scholar at Sichuan University in Chengdu, tried to point out the differences between the Marshall Plan and China's BRI, arguing that the former was 'closely connected with the Cold War' and enabled the US to 'intentionally penetrate its political ideology to the European countries through economic aid and development.'² There is no question that one of the aims of the Marshall Plan, which launched after the devastation of Europe in World War II and during the initial stages of the Cold War, was to consolidate the resistance of Western Europe's democracies to the growth of a totalitarian Soviet-controlled bloc in the east. But to claim that the US tried to impose democracy in Europe's democracies, among them West Germany, which had been a democracy before a dictatorship took over in the 1930s, is absurd. The BRI, in contrast, Yang argues, is a benign international aid plan 'that will not promote the development of the Cold War pattern' but will be based on 'an open, inclusive and balanced regional economic cooperation architecture that benefits all.'³

But the combination of interests—Xi's dream of making China great again and the not particularly well-hidden agenda of aiming to dethrone the US from its position as the world's leading superpower—nevertheless shows that there are elements of a new 'Cold War' in Xi's plan for a different world order. The inevitable outcome of the BRI will be a divided world where superpowers are competing for influence, and smaller nations are being crushed between the strategic interests of mightier countries. In other words, the new 'Cold War' is not that different from the old one; only the players, motivations, means and methods are no longer the same. Complicating matters even further, there are new superpowers emerging, primarily China's regional archrival India, which may enjoy a friendly relationship with the US but should by no means be seen as an unwavering US ally.

The first problem with Xi's initiative is that not everyone in Asia and the Pacific, the main targets of the BRI, shares his vision of a China-dominated future. Countries such as Laos, where China built a high-speed railway, and Sri Lanka, where a new deepwater port was opened, soon found out that Chinese aid is actually loans that have to be paid back, thus forcing them into what came to be called 'debt traps'.

When China pushed for an 873-kilometre high-speed rail link connecting the new line from the southern Chinese province of Yunnan via Laos with Thailand's eastern seaboard, the government in Bangkok did not reject it outright, but found ways to stall the plan. If implemented, it would enable China to link up with the rest of Southeast Asia and as far as Singapore, which is a stated BRI goal for the region.[4] The Thais, it seems, prefer to work with Japan, which offers better quality for its infrastructure projects and is less controversial in today's geostrategic context.

Not even in the former Soviet republics, through which the old so-called 'Silk Road' allegedly passed, is Chinese investment that welcome. According to a number of opinion polls carried out from 2017 to 2021, respondents in Kazakhstan and Uzbekistan show an increasingly negative view of China.[5] Kyrgyzstan has remained more consistently anti-Chinese. In all those now independent republics, anti-Chinese sentiment has grown in pace with increased investment from China. Locals apparently feel exploited by what they see as greedy Chinese investors who show little or no understanding of local culture, values and social norms.

Opposition to China's forays into weaker countries in the region has been outrightly violent. In July 2021, nine Chinese engineers and four locals working on a hydropower project in northern Pakistan were killed and many more injured when the bus they were travelling in fell into a ravine following a road-side explosion.[6] That project, part of the BRI, also includes the construction of a network of roads and pipelines between Pakistan and China.

A month later, a suicide bombing targeted a vehicle carrying Chinese workers in Gwadar, where China is involved in the construction of a massive port project. No one died in that attack, but, in April 2022, a suicide bomber killed three Chinese nationals working at the Confucius Institute, a China-funded cultural centre, in the southern Pakistani city of Karachi.[7] The China–Pakistan Economic Corridor, which links ports in Pakistan with China's road networks, is a vital link of the BRI and Gwadar is one of China's main projects in the Indian Ocean region.

The China–Myanmar Economic Corridor, another BRI priority in the region, is also in jeopardy—thousands of demonstrators gathered outside the Chinese embassy in the commercial capital Yangon to protest what they saw as Beijing's support for a hugely unpopular military coup on 1 February 2021.[8] Chinese flags were burned; and when the military crushed the anti-coup protests with lethal violence, pro-democracy activists sought refuge in Myanmar's rugged frontier areas—including those adjacent to China—where they resorted to armed struggle against the junta that had seized power.[9]

Then, in January 2023, Fiji, a strategically important nation in the Pacific Ocean, took bold steps to end its cooperation with China. A police training and exchange agreement with China was scrapped and the commissioner of police and the supervisor of elections, who were seen as being close to China, were dismissed from their respective posts.[10] Prime Minister Sitiveni Rabuka told the *Fiji Times* why they had been sidelined: 'Our system of democracy and justice system are different [from China's] so we will go back to those that have similar systems with us [i.e., Australia and New Zealand].'[11] China has, however, been more successful in the Solomon Islands and Samoa. In April 2022, China signed a security agreement with the Solomon Islands that, according to the Chinese foreign ministry, will 'promote social stability and long-term peace and security'.[12]

A leaked draft agreement included a provision that would allow China to send armed police and military personnel to the Solomon Islands, as well as base its navy ships off the coast of the islands.[13] Not surprisingly, the agreement caused alarm bells to go off in the traditional Pacific Ocean powers: Australia, New Zealand and the US. In July that year, Solomon Islands' Prime Minister Manasseh Sogavare met Australian Prime Minister Anthony Albanese and New Zealand Premier Jacinda Ardern in separate bilateral meetings on the sidelines of the Pacific Islands Forum in Fiji, where concerns were raised.[14]

US President Joe Biden also chimed in. Sogavare was invited to the White House in September and, in a bid to counter China's growing influence in the Pacific, Washington announced that it would reopen its embassy in Honiara, the capital of the Solomon Islands.

Less is known about the agreement China signed with Samoa in May 2022, but according to a press release issued by the Samoan authorities, China provides infrastructural development support to various Samoan sectors and there would be 'a new framework for future projects', which were 'to be determined and mutually agreed ... Samoa and the People's

Republic of China will continue to pursue greater collaboration that will deliver on joint interests and commitments.'[15]

Despite those successes, it is obvious that China also sees dangers ahead for the BRI. Beijing must have noticed how the BRI has been received and perceived in other countries in the region. Wang Yiwei, a Chinese scholar and former diplomat, identifies five such potential risks in an English-language book promoting the BRI.[16] The first two are natural and environmental risks. Natural disasters such as landslides could be a problem when roads are built in mountainous areas. Extensive mining may affect the environment and result in pollution, for which China could be blamed. Although Wang does not mention it, rising sea levels around low-lying islands such as the Maldives and some of the Pacific Ocean nations would come under those types of risks as well. Number three on Wang's list concerns threats posed by what he calls 'extremist forces'. He mentions Islamic militants and unidentified 'armed groups in Southeast Asia' as forces that could pose a threat to the BRI.

The only armed rebel groups in Southeast Asia would be ethnic insurgents in Myanmar; Muslim and communist forces in the Philippines; and Muslim separatists in southern Thailand. Those in Myanmar would be of specific concern because they operate in the economically important China–Myanmar Economic Corridor, which provides China with direct access to the Indian Ocean.

Number four on Wang's list is the 'threat of non-governmental organizations'. According to Wang, NGOs supported by the West could accuse China of 'plundering resources of related countries and damaging the ecological environment. And with that accusation as an excuse, various NGOs are able to mobilize the masses to boycott.'[17][sic]

Fifth and last on Wang's list is 'maritime security risk'. He mentions piracy off the coast of Somalia as the main problem, which was the pretext for China to establish its first military base abroad. The Chinese naval base in Djibouti on the Horn of Africa may be more suited to guarding the entrance to the Red Sea and on to the Suez Canal than combating Somali pirates, who have not carried out any major attacks in recent years.[18]

China's concerns about potential threats to the BRI, its military aspirations and its determination to become a global superpower should be seen in the broader context of China's 'third revolution' under Xi and the ideological underpinnings behind the thought of making China great again. In the beginning, there was Marxism, and with the advent of Vladimir Lenin and the Russian revolution it became Marxism-Leninism. When Mao was added to the pantheon of communist leaders, Marxism-Leninism and Mao Zedong Thought were the preferred ideologies of true believers in the revolutionary gospel.

The 'Communique of the Seventh Plenary Session of the 19th Central Committee of the Communist Party of China (CPC)', which was issued on 14 October 2022, went a step forward and stated that the Party now follows 'the guidance of Marxism-Leninism, Mao Zedong Thought, Deng Xiaoping Theory, the Theory of Three Represents, the Scientific Outlook on Development, and Xi Jinping Thought on Socialism with Chinese Characteristics for a New Era.'[19] Exactly what that means is not entirely clear, but the emphasis should be on the New Era. Xi's campaigns at home aim to turn China into a single nation-state that will lead the world into a common future free of Western decadences like democracy, civil rights and individual freedom—and that involves a lot more than just dethroning the US from its position as the world's leading superpower.

But a global superpower also has to be a strong, unified nation at home, and that is why Xi has introduced policies that diverge sharply from China's, until recently, relatively tolerant tradition of, at least in theory, accepting ethnic diversity. After the communist takeover in 1949, at least fifty-five ethnic minorities besides the Han majority, which makes up 92 per cent of China's now 1.4 billion population, were recognized by the central authorities. Among them were Uighurs, Kazakhs, Tajiks and other Turkic groups in the west, Tibetans in the south, Mongols in the north, Koreans in the northeast and various ethnic minorities in Yunnan, including Yi, Bai, Hani, Zhuang and Dai. In recent years, the government has begun to promote a more pan-Chinese identity known as 'zhonghua minzu', which relates to nation-building and race rather than the old term 'zhongguo renmin', or simply 'the Chinese people'. The Han, or

Mandarin, language previously known as hanyu has become guoyu, 'the national language'.[20]

Regardless of what the Chinese authorities are saying today, the notion of China as a monolithic nation-state is a new phenomenon. The old emperors did not truly rule over the outlying areas of their perceived realms and were in many cases content with collecting annual or even irregular tributes from local rulers in Tibet, today's Xinjiang, Yunnan, parts of Mongolia and elsewhere. No centrally directed governance existed in any of those territories up until the late nineteenth century, and even then, only tenuously. It was only after the first republican revolution in 1911–12, which overthrew the last imperial dynasty, that the new rulers made attempts to turn China into a more modern state with a functioning central government and fixed borders. Sun Yat-sen, the founder of the Chinese republic, sought mostly unsuccessfully to establish 'five races under one union', and he identified those races as the Hans, Manchus, Mongols, Tibetans and Huis or Muslims.[21]

In the beginning, Mao's communists were even more lenient when it came to the question of ethnic minorities. The CPC's 'state constitution' of 1931 stipulated 'the right of self-determination of the national minorities in China, their right to complete separation from China, and to the formation of an independent state for each national minority.'[22] The constitution went on to say that 'all Mongolians, Tibetans, Miao, Yao, Koreans and others living on the territory of China shall enjoy the full right to self-determination, i.e., they may either join the Union of Chinese Soviets or secede from it and form their own state as they may prefer.'[23]

This policy was abandoned as soon as the communists seized power, but ethnic rights were still recognized and China consisted of several autonomous regions as well as autonomous counties on an even more local level. It could be argued that this was a showcase system where the Hans were the dominant force, while leaving space for learning non-Han languages and the preservation of local cultures. But now even that pretence is gone, as the country is, in the words of American China scholar James Millward, becoming 'zhonghua-ized'.[24] This is not happening without significant local resistance in areas such as Tibet, Xinjiang, Inner

Mongolia and the Korean-speaking provinces of Jilin, Heilongjiang and Liaoning. The resistance, in turn, could threaten national unity and cause instability, which would undermine Xi's grand plans for a strong new China, among them, of course, the BRI.

It is also important to remember that the very historical example from which the BRI got its name, 'the Silk Road', is a myth—and it is a myth that is so universally believed and accepted that few historians and other writers have even thought of questioning it. One of those who has is Warwick Ball, an Australian-born archaeologist who has worked extensively in the parts of Central Asia through which the supposed 'Silk Road' ran. He writes in his book, *Rome in the East: The Transformation of an Empire*: 'The existence of the "Silk Road" is not based on a shred of historical or material evidence. There was never any such "road" or even a route in the organizational sense, there was no free movement of goods between China and the West until the Mongol Empire in the Middle Ages'[25]—and that had nothing to do with desert caravans carrying silk across some of the most inhospitable terrain on earth. Ball writes: 'The greatest value of the Silk Road to history is as a lesson—and an important one at that—at how quickly and how thoroughly a myth can be enshrined as unquestioned academic fact.'[26]

No historian disputes the fact that there was trade between China and Rome dating back to ancient times, but it was never direct and did not to any large extent involve silk. According to British historian Susan Whitfield: 'There was no "Silk Road". It is a modern label in widespread use only since the late twentieth century and used since to refer to trade and interactions across Afro-Eurasia from roughly 200 BCE to 1400 CE. In reality, there were many trading networks over this period. Some of these dealt in silk, yarn and woollen fabric. Others did not. Some started in China or Rome, but some in Central Asia, northern Europe, India or Africa—and many other places. Journeys were by sea, by rivers and by land, and some by all three.'[27]

The term 'Silk Road', or rather *Seidenstrassen* in the German language plural, was coined by Ferdinand von Richthofen, a nineteenth-century German geographer. He had made seven expeditions to China from

1868 to 1872 and first used the term in an article titled 'Über die centralasiatischen Seidenstrassen bis zum 2 Jh. n. Chr.' for the academic journal, *Verhandlungen der Gesellschaft für Erdkunde zu Berlin* in 1877.[28] The term was then used only by Albert Hermann, another German academic, in a lengthy essay published in 1910 entitled 'Die alten Seidenstrassen zwischen China und Syrien', or 'the old Silk Roads between China and Syria'.[29]

So the road was not to Europe. The whole concept of such a road to wherever it went might well have been forgotten had it not been for Sven Hedin, one of von Richthofen's students at Friedrich Wilhelm University (now the Humboldt University) in Berlin. Hedin, a Swedish explorer, followed literally in von Richthofen's footsteps with travels in China and Central Asia, and published a book in Swedish in 1936 and in English in 1938. The Swedish edition was called *Sidenvägen* and was published by Albert Bonnier Förlag in Stockholm, but it was E.P. Dutton's English version, *The Silk Road*, that became an international bestseller.[30]

From then on, 'the Silk Road'—now for the first time in the title of a book in English and in the singular—became the accepted term for the concept, which, for instance, was described as 'a global superhighway where people with new ideas, new cultures and new religions made exchanges that shaped humanity' by the BBC in a series of programmes aired in 2022.[31] It is supposed to be 'the first superhighway that carried goods and ideas between Europe and China. Covering 5,000 miles, passing through thirteen countries and crossing some of the most dramatic landscapes on the planet.'[32] The distance '5,000 miles' is more than 8,000 kilometres, so here the 'Silk Road' is even longer than *National Geographic*'s very precise figure of 6,437 kilometres.

And what 'thirteen countries'? Ideas may have been exchanged because we know that Nestorian Christians ventured as far east as China, and the Venetian merchant Marco Polo travelled east and brought back tales of exotic cultures and beliefs. But it is doubtful whether Marco Polo went all the way to China and, as he claimed, befriended Kublai Khan, the founder of the Yuan dynasty. It is more likely that Marco Polo based his stories on what he had heard from Persian and Arab merchants he had met in Central Asia, which he undoubtedly did visit. Critics point to serious omissions in Marco Polo's tales. Every European who went to China at that time and later would mention the Great Wall, tea drinking, chopsticks, how the Chinese language was written in characters instead of letters and women with bound feet. Marco Polo did not. And no Chinese or Mongol records mention a European called Marco Polo, although he claimed he had served for several years at the court of Kublai Khan.[33]

Marco Polo also never wrote anything. He related his stories to Rustichello da Pisa, who wrote *The Travels of Marco Polo* while they were together in prison in Genoa in the early fourteenth century. No original copy of the book has been preserved but there are about 150 different versions that have been reproduced by other writers in various languages. Whatever the case, *The Travels of Marco Polo* did have an impact on European perceptions of China. He described a country with a sophisticated civilization and not the home of barbaric savages, which was the main theme of other contemporary travellers such as the Italian diplomat Giovanni da Pian del Carpine and the Flemish missionary and explorer William of Rubruck. But how important were Marco Polo's tales compared to what happened later in history, when sea travel made contacts easier, Asian and African countries were colonized and exploited by Western powers—and, at the same time, translations of Eastern religious and philosophical works reached the West?

A more nuanced view of those exchanges is presented by the American historian Valerie Hansen in her book, *The Silk Road: A New History*. She states that the 'road' was actually 'a stretch of shifting, unmarked paths across massive expanses of deserts and mountains. In fact, the quantity of cargo transported along these treacherous routes was small.'[34] Much of the traffic was local, and while China was the earliest country to produce silk, it did not dominate the trade. 'Silk,' Hansen writes, 'is even more misleading than "road", inasmuch as silk was only one among many Silk Road trade goods. Chemicals, spices, metals, saddles and leather products, glass, and paper were also common. Some cargo manifests list ammonium chloride, used as a flux for metals and to treat leather, as the top trade goods on certain routes.'[35]

The Iranian scholar Khodadad Rezakhani writes in his excellent book, *The Road That Never Was: The Silk Road and Trans-Eurasian Exchange*: 'The popularity of the concept of the Silk Road has also resulted in a proliferation of output from all walks of scholarship and art ... However, one seldom finds works dedicated to the actual history of the region. Urban sites along the Silk Road are commonly described as "oases", whose main importance and raison d'être seem to have been the Silk Road itself. This would then run contrary to the reality, the existence of ancient cities and centres of civilization millennia before any supposed "opening of the Silk Road".'[36]

Samarkand in today's Uzbekistan was the hub for that trade, but few of the routes mentioned by Hansen and Rezakhani originated in China and few, if any, of the traders were Chinese. Spices, cloth, precious stones, metals and other goods from India, the Arab world and Persia were far more consequential for the economy of the Roman Empire than any trade in silk with China.[37] Much of that trade was also by sea, a much easier way to travel in those days. Central Asia was a lawless mess where banditry was widespread and the geography so unfavourable that if theoretically any overland trade had occurred between China and Rome, it would have taken as much as three years to complete the journey—in one direction. Philip Bowring, a Hong Kong-based journalist and researcher, wrote in 2017: 'The first Roman known to visit China, in 166 CE, arrived by sea, landing in what is now northern Vietnam. The beginning of this trade underlined the fact that transport by sea was a fraction (one-seventh, according to the Romans) of the cost of going by land, and was far less subject to wars and frontier taxes.'[38]

It is also questionable whether silk was that popular in the days of the Roman Empire. It was frowned upon by many because it was considered an inappropriate luxury item due to its sexually suggestive smooth and glitzy surface. Seneca the Younger (c. 5 BCE–65 CE) wrote in his work, *De Beneficiis*: 'I see there raiments of silk—if that can be called raiment, which provides nothing that could possibly afford protection for the body, or indeed modesty, so that, when a woman wears it, she can scarcely, with a clear conscience, swear that she is not naked. These are imported at vast expense from nations unknown even to trade, in order that our married women may not be able to show more of their persons, even to their paramours, in a bedroom than they do on the street.'[39]

Seneca was actually commenting on what the Roman lyric poet Horace had written before: 'The other [prostitute] throws no obstacles in your way; through the silken vest you may discern her, almost as well as if she was naked; that she has neither a bad leg, nor a disagreeable foot, you may survey her perfectly with your eye. Or you would choose to have a trick put upon you, and your money extorted, before the goods are shown you.'[40] Some Chinese silk found its way to Rome, and there were some who appreciated it, precisely because it was an expensive luxury item, but silk did not become more widely used until the Crusaders brought it from the Middle East to Europe in the Middle Ages. Silk was then produced mainly in the Italian states and exported to the rest of Europe. In the sixteenth century, France also became a major silk producer, using more modern technology.

The BBC's Sam Willis, an educated historian, travelled to towns and cities along the so-called 'Silk Road' when he was working on his documentaries. Through his works, it is established that these places exist and there is no doubt that trade was carried out between them in ancient times. But that trade was local and if any items made it all the way from China to Rome, it would have been through a multitude of local merchants buying and selling goods originating in a number of Asian countries.

The writer and analyst Akhilesh Pillalamarri argues that 'due to the great distances involved, it is highly unlikely that caravans travelled along the whole length of Eurasia. Instead trade continuously passed between middlemen and exchanged hands every few hundred kilometres—about 500 kilometres at most.'[41] The traders came from a multitude of countries, and very few if any would have been Chinese because, as Pillalamarri points out: 'The Chinese state dissociated itself with trade, and most trade was conducted in China by private initiative. The Tang Code of the Emperor Taizong (reigned 627–649 CE) viewed commerce as polluting and did not allow officials above the fifth rank (out of nine ranks) to enter marketplaces.'[42]

If had there been any significant trade in any kind of item directly from China to Rome, some Roman coins would have been found in China, but that is not the case.[43] According to Valerie Hansen: 'The earliest European coins unearthed in China are from Byzantium, not Rome, and date to the 530s and 540s. Vague rumours to the contrary, not a single Roman coin has turned up in China—in contrast to the thousands of Roman gold and silver coins excavated on the south Indian coast, where Roman traders often journeyed.'[44] Ball, however, mentions a recent discovery of sixteen Principate-era Roman coins in Xian that were minted during the reigns of Roman emperors in the first and third centuries CE.[45] But Helen Wang, Sinologist and curator at the British Museum in London, points out that although those Roman coins were found near Xian, they were deposited there in the twentieth century, not in ancient times, and therefore 'do not shed light on historic contacts between China and Rome.'[46]

Exactly why von Richthofen and Hedin settled on the term 'Silk Road' is not entirely clear. But von Richthofen's journeys to Central and East Asia were in part motivated by the search for coal to fuel the first Chinese rail network and, as American historian Nile Green argues in a 2014 article for *The Los Angeles Review of Books*: 'In a very real sense, the image of a road spun from gossamer threads of silk was the dreamy sibling of the smoke-belching railroad. In the decades when German and Russian engineers were designing China's first railroad—in German *Eisenbahn* or "iron road"—the appeal of a road wrought from the very opposite substance is scarcely surprising. If the Silk Road suggests interchange between East and West, then there was reciprocity in its very conception as Europeans ferried iron and coal to China and carried home dreams of a highway named for the softest stuff known to man.'[47]

In other words, 'the Silk Road' is not only of recent origin but also a Eurocentric misnomer, which nevertheless appealed to the Western notions of 'the exotic East'. Frances Wood writes in his book about 'the Silk Road': 'The Silk Road, or Roads, is one of the most evocative of names, conjuring visions of camels laden with bales of luxurious brocades and diaphanous silks in all colours of the rainbow.'[48]

In his poem 'The Golden Journey to Samarkand', James Elroy Flecker wrote:

> When those long caravans that cross the plain
> With dauntless feet and sound of silver bells
> Put forth no more for glory or for gain,
> Take no more solace from the palm-girt wells.[49]

Such romanticism has for centuries clouded Western views of the East. Instead of being a part of the world wrecked by poverty, despotism and lack of meaningful development, 'the East' became this dreamland of strange creatures, stunning landscapes and age-old rituals shrouded in mysticism. In Latin, *ex oriente lux, ex occidente lex*, 'from the East comes light, from the West comes law' is an old phrase that refers to the creativity of 'the East' (here meaning Mesopotamia and today's West Asia) and how it could, and should, be tamed by Western (Greek and Roman) law. There is, as one writer has pointed out, 'a lot of cultural bias and West European arrogance wrapped in those six words,'[50] but they reflect a long-established view of 'Eastern societies'—whatever that means—as being very different and more spiritual in nature than from those in 'the West' (whatever that means). The 'Silk Road' brand appealed to those romantic but distorted views of Asia, and this certainly helped sales of Hedin's book when it was published in 1936.

For Hedin, 'the Silk Road' was probably not meant to be more than a catchy book title. It is worth noting that the Swedish edition (but not those in English and later in other languages) had the subtitle: 'En bilfärd genom Centralasien', or 'A journey by car through Central Asia'.[51] And that is what Hedin's book is about; not a history of silk or the trade in silk. He also admits in all editions that 'The name "Silk Road" is not Chinese and has never been used in China.'[52] But after Hedin had made the name popular in English, it was adopted into Japanese (Shiruku Rodo), Russian (Shelkovyy Put), Farsi (Rah-i-Abrisham)—and Chinese (Sichou zhi lu).[53]

It is not clear when the Chinese began to use the term Sichou zhi lu—a direct translation of 'the Silk Road'—but it was most likely in the late 1970s or early 1980s, after the death of Mao Zedong and the ascendance to power of the market-oriented Deng Xiaoping. The 'Silk Road' in English was first used in China in 1989, when Beijing's Foreign Languages Press published a book by Chinese author Che Muqi entitled *The Silk Road: Past and Present*.[54] Since then, glossier books about 'the Silk Road' have been produced in China, like the coffee-table-like *Footprints of Foreign Explorers on the Silk Road*, which was published in Beijing in 2005 and supposedly 'Compiled by the information office of Xinjiang Uygur Autonomous Region of China'.[55]

It may sound surprising that China's current communist and supernationalist leaders would adopt such a Eurocentric and in many ways nineteenth-century colonial concept as 'the Silk Road', but as Swedish Sinologist Lars Ellström writes in his book, *The Road to Kashgar*, about a 5,000-kilometre, two-and-a-half-year long walk through China: 'The name "Silk Road" has probably stuck in the West because it has an—incorrect—impression that it was trade with Europe that was most important and partly because it is exotic and interesting. This is probably furthermore the reason why it is also used in China today: it is good marketing and contributes to tourism.'[56]

Today, promoting the BRI is more important than tourism, which explains why the Chinese authorities have invented a flurry of 'silk roads' criss-crossing the globe. The first mention of such a new 'silk road' even predates the BRI. Pan Qi, a former vice minister of communications, wrote for the weekly *Beijing Review* on 2 September 1985 that 'there was a road connecting western Yunnan with southeast and west Asia quite early in history: Zhang Qian, a Han Dynasty (202 BCE–220 CE) diplomat, helped open a southern "Silk Road" from Sichuan, and the artery was travelled for centuries.'[57] Zhang Qian may have written about trade routes to and from China, Central Asia and beyond, but none that stretched from Sichuan to Southeast Asia. According to Chinese researcher Tian Jinchen, Zhang helped establish 'a network of trade routes that linked China to Central Asia and the Arab world.'[58]

Again, there is no doubt that trade existed between China's southern regions and some parts of Southeast Asia in ancient times. But it involved tea from China to Southeast Asia and jade from the mines in Hpakant in what is now Kachin State in the far north of Myanmar to China as well as some precious stones. The trade was local and did not involve any central Chinese authorities. And it is worth noting that Pan Qi puts 'Silk Road' within quotation marks. In 1985, the Chinese had not yet begun to use it as a widely accepted term to demonstrate that China has been a major, global trading nation for millennia.

There may never have been a 'southern Silk Road' but the 'ambassador's road', sometimes called the 'tribute road', was real, although it could hardly be described as a highway even when it existed in the eighteenth and nineteenth centuries—long after the so-called 'Silk Road' was supposed to have brought goods and ideas between China, Central Asia and Europe. This road got its name because some Burmese kings and Shan princes paid tribute to the Chinese emperor, which, in today's China, has been interpreted as a kind of recognition of Chinese sovereignty over those regions. But tribute payment should be seen as a bribe or pay-off rather than a sign of acceptance of the authority of a higher power—take this and leave us alone. It was meant to keep the Chinese at bay, nothing else. Several Shan princes paid tribute to the Burmese kings for precisely the same reason.

More organized overland trade between southern China and Southeast Asia is a relatively new phenomenon, and did not happen because of any wisdom on the part of China's central government. In the mid-1850s, a Muslim community in Yunnan, known as Hui in China, Panthay in Burma and Jin Haw in Thailand, rose in rebellion against the emperor in Beijing. The fighting blocked Yunnan for nearly two decades, and the uprising was eventually crushed with a heavy loss of life. Tens of thousands of Yunnanese Muslims were butchered when Beijing reasserted control over the area, and many survivors migrated across the mountains into the north-eastern Shan states, now part of Myanmar. Deprived of land to cultivate, many of them became traders and, historically, they were excellent muleteers. The Panthay came to control much of the caravan trade in the region. Goods they transported as far south as Chiang Mai in northern Thailand (then the Lanna Kingdom) included salt, tea, minerals, precious stones, iron tools, brass bells and musk oil.

But the most lucrative commodity was opium from Yunnan, which was sold in the Shan states and Lanna in exchange for silver.[59] Vast quantities of silver were brought back to Yunnan by the mule caravans, and according to Thai researcher Chiranan Prasertkul: 'It is an irony that while silver currency in China proper was drained out through the foreign opium trade [to pay for opium from India before China grew its own], the silver specie of northern Southeast Asia were drawn into Yunnan through the very same kind of trade. The "silver crisis" spread through a very large area of the Southeast Asian hinterland and revealed the large scale of Yunnan cross-boundaries trade.'[60] As for the jade trade, few Chinese merchants ventured beyond the Hpakan mines and down to the Irrawaddy plain, where there was little trading interest at that time.

None of this seems to matter when the preferred BRI narrative is to depict China as a benevolent trading nation. After the 'southern Silk Road' came a 'southwestern Silk Road': 'The Southwestern Silk Route was an important point of contact between the two great civilizations of China and India, as well as a major conduit for the passage of East-West trade.'[61] *Travel China Guide* has a more elaborate description of this alleged trade route: 'The Southern Silk Road was mainly composed of West Route (Maoniu Route) and East Route (Wuchi Route). The West Route originated from Chengdu, wandered through Sichuan Province via Ya'an City, Maoniu (Hanyuan), Qiongdu (Xichang), and took traders to Myanmar (Burma) by way of Dali, Baoshan and Tengchong. Then its ancient trade route extended through to Juandu (India), Bangladesh and even Middle East. The East Route was very narrow and had [sic] only five-feet wide, so it was also called "Wuchi Route". It began from Chengdu, passed through Yibin, Zhaotong, Qujing and reached Kunming, where one branched road went to Vietnam and the other one wound to Dali, joining the West Route.'[62]

But there is more: the Maritime Silk Road, the revitalization of an alleged ancient Chinese network of trading routes across the Indian

Ocean, to Southeast Asia, South Asia, the Arab world and Africa. In reality, China paid only scant attention to maritime ventures in the past and, before modern times, had had no presence in the Indian Ocean since the fifteenth century, when an explorer and trader called Zheng He sailed his fleets to Southeast Asia, the Indian subcontinent, the Arab peninsula and even as far as the east coast of Africa. China's early communist rulers paid little attention to Zheng He, a Muslim eunuch from Yunnan, and stories about him and his travels also began to appear in the official media as China had started to shake off orthodox Communism in the late 1970s. Statues of Zheng He have since then been erected in a number of Chinese cities, among them Jinning, south of Kunming, the capital of his home province Yunnan, Nanjing and Shanghai—and, with Chinese assistance— even in Malaysia and Indonesia. Zheng He has been made into a symbol of modern China and its maritime ambitions and given a prominence he never had until quite recently. As the Canadian academic Timothy Brook has put it: 'The West had Columbus and the Chinese needed one.'[63]

There is no reason to belittle Zheng He's exploits. Over a period of thirty years, from 1405 to 1433, he commanded the largest fleet funded by the Ming emperor and undertook seven voyages across the seas. He brought gold, silver, porcelain and silk from China, and came back to China with exotic African animals like lions, giraffes, zebras and ostriches, which amazed the public.[64] But Zheng He's expeditions drained the emperor's resources, so, in the end, he decided to put an end to any such maritime ventures. Journalist and historian Bowring writes: 'The voyages [Zheng He's] were a triumph of logistics, but they were also inordinately expensive and did nothing to mitigate the security threats to China, which came from the north and west. Sensibly, the voyages were abandoned.'[65]

So it remained for 600 years—until Xi and his men decided to launch their 'Maritime Silk Road', ostensibly laid out and charted by Zheng He.[66] Consequently, Xi has missed no opportunity to fantazise about Zheng He and the fictitious 'Maritime Silk Road'. When Xi paid an official visit to the Maldives in September 2014, he stated that the island nation 'was an important stop along the ancient Maritime Silk Road.'[67] The purpose of

Xi's visit was to persuade the government of the Maldives to sign up for his BRI, which it subsequently did.

Historical records show that Zheng He was aware of the existence of the Maldives, but the description of the islands, as recorded by his interpreter and chronicler Ma Huan, is brief: 'Kings, chiefs, and people professed the Muslim religion. The people lived off fishing and cultivating coconuts ... the inhabitants knew nothing of rice.'[68] The Chinese seafarers noted that coconuts, cowrie shells and bonito fish were exported 'to foreign countries'.[69] But there is no suggestion in Ma Huan's annals that any of those goods were destined for China, or that Chinese goods were for sale on the islands. After that brief stop during one of Zheng He's expeditions, there is no record of any interaction, commercial or otherwise, between the Maldives and China until well into modern times.

The end of Chinese maritime ventures does not mean that no Chinese travelled on ships on the Indian Ocean, but they did so, as China's own records reveal, as individuals on Malay ships. According to Bowring, 'Chinese sailors were latecomers ... The seafaring history of the region at least for the first millennium of the current era was dominated by ancestors of today's Indonesians, Malaysians, Filipinos and (less directly) Vietnamese.'[70] This was not the least surprising given that during this era, Bowring argues, 'Malay people from what is now Indonesia were the first colonizers of the world's third largest island Madagascar, some 4,000 miles away. (The Madagascan language and 50 per cent of its human gene pool are of Malay origin.)'[71] Bowring also stated that, 'Malay seafaring prowess was later overtaken by south Indians and Arabs, but they remained the premier seafarers in Southeast Asia until the Europeans dominated the region.'[72]

The trade routes by sea were also more important than the long and hazardous routes over mountains and across deserts in Central Asia. Akhilesh Pillalamarri points out that, 'sea routes boomed during the ancient and mediaeval periods, and continue to do so.'[73] But 'there has never been one maritime road although there were more long-distance trips by sea than by land.'[74] It was not uncommon for Arab sailors to go from Basra in today's Iraq 'to Guangzhou in southern China. But like the land routes in Eurasia, there were also many local, overlapping trade routes, with terminal points in places like Ceylon and Srivijaya in Sumatra.'[75] According to Pillalamarri, not only Arab, but also Persian, Indian and Malay traders transported goods across the Indian Ocean. Chinese fleets were nowhere to be seen; that era ended with Zheng He's exploits in the fifteenth century.

But historical facts have not prevented writers such as Yang Minghong from claiming that some Chinese-initiated 'Maritime Silk Road' in history was 'a maritime trade network among the ports between East Asia and the coast of Africa. It started from Quanzhou and went across Southeast Asia, India and the Arabian Peninsula. It established a high degree of prosperity from the late Tang Dynasty [618–907 CE] and Song Dynasty [960–1272 CE], promoted the spread of trade, geographic knowledge and navigation technology.'[76] This, Yang argues, 'is the proof of the peaceful and friendly relations between China, South Asia and Southeast Asia and also reflects that China attached importance to the harmonious relationship with neighbouring countries ... this is completely different from the colonialist practice of Europe.'[77] There is not an iota of historical evidence to back up those claims, but they fit into Xi's policies of promoting the BRI along with the image of a friendly and benevolent China that has always enjoyed brotherly relations with its neighbours and nations further afield.

Xi himself expressed the same fanciful version of history in a speech when, on 14 May 2017, he opened the first 'Belt and Road' forum in Beijing: 'Over 2,000 years ago, our ancestors, trekking across vast steppes and deserts, opened the transcontinental passage connecting Asia, Europe and Africa, known today as the Silk Road. Our ancestors, navigating rough seas, created sea routes linking the East and the West, namely the Maritime Silk Road. These ancient silk routes opened windows of friendly engagement among nations, adding a splendid chapter to the history of human progress.'[78]

In the official Chinese propaganda, even Myanmar with its limited and mostly local trade with China has been elevated to a major conduit for goods going in all directions through that network of interconnected 'silk roads'. According to an article entitled 'How does the BRI bear witness to China and Myanmar friendship?', which was published on the *China Global Television Network's* website on 17 January 2020: 'In ancient times, Myanmar was a transportation hub of both the southwestern Silk Road between China, Myanmar and India and the Maritime Silk Road, bringing great convenience to trade between China, the Indian Ocean and the western world.'[79]

Apart from parts of the world where a few Chinese actually went as merchants or sailors on foreign ships, there is also supposed to be a 'Polar Silk Road', which, writer Fabio Tiburzi states, 'refers to the navigable Arctic Sea routes connecting three major economic centers, North America, East Asia, and Western Europe, via the Arctic Circle.'[80] According to some, there is even a Pacific Silk Road.[81] Places that were not anywhere near the ancient, alleged 'Silk Road' have also tried to take advantage of the concept's popularity. One such place is Hunza, where a sign has been erected saying: 'Old Silk Road to Hunza-Nagar'. A Pakistani journalist commented: 'That the classic Silk Road ever entered what is now Pakistan by way of Hunza is patent rubbish. But if people repeat the same falsehood a few times, let alone over decades, it becomes established truth.'[82]

The same could be said about most of the writings about 'the original Silk Road' and its modern offsprings, and von Richthofen and Hedin could not possibly have imagined what whirlwind of speculations, misrepresentations, fantasies and outright falsifications of history they were setting in motion when they came up with the terms 'Seidenstrassen' and 'the Silk Road'.[83] Perhaps the most bizarre of the 'Silk Roads' was the one invented by the Brazilian journalist Pepe Escobar when the Covid-19 pandemic hit the world in 2020: 'China rolls out the Health Silk Road: In the Belt and Road framework, China is supplying much of the world including virus-hit Europe with medicine and healthcare items.'[84] It did not take long for the recipient countries to discover that the Chinese Covid-19 vaccine was basically useless. Other 'healthcare items' also became scarce outside China as the pandemic caused the government in Beijing to place the entire country under lockdown.

Escobar's article appeared in the Asia Times, a Hong Kong-based website once known for carrying excellent material about politics, the economy and security-related issues in Asia. But in recent years—and especially since the Russian invasion of Ukraine in 2022—two of its directors, Uwe Parpart and David 'Spengler' Goldman, have turned it into a mouthpiece for Xi and Russian President Vladimir Putin.

Parpart and Goldman made names for themselves in the late 1970s and 1980s as contributing editors of the *Executive Intelligence Review*, the main publication of a movement headed by Lyndon LaRouche, a prominent conspiracy theorist who remained active until his death in 2019. Among LaRouche's most outrageous claims were that Queen Elizabeth II was the head of an international drug-smuggling cartel, and that the Oklahoma bombing in 1995 was the first strike in a British attempt to take over the US.[85] In 1997, the *Executive Intelligence Review* published a favourable review of the book, *La Face cachee de Greenpeace* ('the hidden face of Greenpeace'), which claimed that the global campaigning network for the protection of the environment is 'an irregular warfare apparatus in the service of the British oligarchy.'[86]

When almost the entire population in Myanmar in 1988 rose up against a dictatorship that had held the country in an iron grip for more than two decades, the *Executive Intelligence Review* and the Lyndon LaRouche movement were alone in defending the country's ruling military after its troops had opened fire on pro-democracy demonstrators, killing at least 3,000 people. According to the *Executive Intelligence Review*, the uprising was a plot instigated by the US and the UK to destabilize Myanmar.[87]

Lyndon LaRouche's widow Helga Zepp-LaRouche now heads the organization, which has adopted the more innocuous-sounding name the International Schiller Institute. She appears to be spending most of her time in China, where she takes part in government-sponsored conferences and television talk shows. An item on the institute's website describes her importance to China's BRI: 'Helga Zepp-LaRouche, founder and president of the International Schiller Institute, is right in the middle of the action in Beijing during the *Belt and Road Forum for International*

Cooperation. This comes after decades of leadership by Lyndon and Helga LaRouche for just this kind of mobilization for worldwide development. Since the 1990s, and Zepp-LaRouche's first participation in an international conference in China, where she called for a *"Eurasian Land-Bridge,"* she has become widely known as the *Silk Road Lady*.'[88] On the *Asian Times* website, Goldman, a.k.a. 'Spengler', has been promoting the concept of a 'Pax Sinica', or efforts by China to establish world peace.[89] Parpart's main contributions have been stories about Ukraine, how Russia will win the war and the follies of the policies of the West, which supports Ukraine.[90]

But the war in Ukraine is not going well for Russia and has disrupted all Chinese attempts to establish a 'new Silk Road' through Central Asia, which is of symbolic significance because it is, supposedly, the original route. The Covid-19 pandemic and Beijing's decision to take severe, but, as it turned out, ineffectual measures to contain the spread of the disease including shutting down the entire country for nearly two years, has also had a profound impact on the economy. It is becoming increasingly clear that there is no way China will be able to live up to the promises Xi made when he launched the BRI in 2013. A sixth threat to the BRI can now be added to Wang Yiwei's list: unexpected health crises.

China's domestic problems also became clear during the twentieth congress of the CPC, which was held in Beijing from 16 to 22 October 2022. Xi secured a third term as China's top leader.[91] Xi was re-elected and his proposals accepted unanimously by all 2,296 delegates with no abstentions. But as Bonny Lin and Joel Wuthnow pointed out in *Foreign Affairs* on 20 November 2022: 'The façade of a confident and robust Xi masked deep anxiety. Xi sees China hemmed in on all sides and facing intensifying security threats. This anxiety is driven by Beijing's perception of a hostile Washington, its problematic relations with its neighbours, and the fact that the Chinese People's Liberation Army still has a long way to go to become a force capable of fighting and winning local wars—never mind larger conflicts.'[92]

Gone, wrote Lin and Wuthnow, is the upbeat assessment from the previous 2017 party congress, which concluded that China enjoys a favourable external environment for development. Now, 'risks and challenges are concurrent and uncertainties and unforeseen factors are rising.'[93] Xi's report to the congress does not specifically mention the US, but his hints are clear. The US is the enemy because of its support for Taiwan and security arrangements with Japan, Australia, India and the UK—and that is a perception China shares with Russia, which is fighting a war in Ukraine against troops armed by the US and other Western democracies. The leaders of China as well as Russia feel that they are being encircled by the West, and share a common interest in resisting what they see as a threat to their national security interests.

When Xi met Putin at the opening of the Winter Olympics in China in February 2022, he emphasized the strategic relationship between China and Russia and their shared vision of a 'new international order based on their view of human rights and democracy.'[94] Xi reaffirmed that commitment when he met Putin in Moscow in March 2023.[95] Xi reportedly told Putin: 'Change is coming that hasn't happened in 100 years and we are driving this change together.'[96] But that 'new order' will be one built on myths and lies, like those about the multitude of newly created 'Silk Roads' and other rewritings of history.

At the same time, the China–Russia pact is more of a marriage of convenience than an equal, genuine partnership. The Chinese have not forgotten that old tsars stripped China of vast territories in the Far East in the nineteenth century, and now Russia is the weaker partner in a shaky relationship where China is gaining the upper hand. Chinese maps still show Chinese names for Russian cities like Vladivostok, Khabarovsk and Blagoveshchensk, and the Russians have not protested openly against that.

Furthermore, the leaders in Beijing are not unaware of their troubled relationship with several of their other neighbours. There are territorial disputes on land and on sea with India, Japan, Indonesia, Malaysia, the Philippines and Vietnam. Rising anti-Chinese sentiments in the Central Asian republics, Fiji and—among the public—in Myanmar, cannot have escaped the attention of Beijing's security planners either. Those concerns and economic setbacks, coupled with the effects of not having any proper organizational structure for the BRI, are likely to force China to downscale the BRI, and the most probable alternative to the grand, once-global plan will be projects in countries closer to home such as Myanmar, Laos, Pakistan and the Pacific-island nations. The war in Ukraine will also force China to focus on the resource-rich Russian Far East rather than trying to promote trade across Central Asia. Squeezed in the middle will be not only weaker nations but also local communities in those countries who will end up as pawns in a global power game over which they will have no influence.

2

RULER OF THE EAST

THERE WAS A TIME WHEN THE COMMUNIST GIANTS CHINA AND the Soviet Union were assumed to be the best of friends. But then, in the mid-1950s, Nikita Khrushchev came to power in Moscow and began talking about a peaceful transition to socialism in the capitalist countries and peaceful coexistence with the West. Equally bad from the point of view of the doctrinaire Chinese revolutionaries, in 1956, Khrushchev denounced Josef Stalin, the dictator who had died three years before. Stalin had been the Chinese leader Mao Zedong's hero and role model, the main supporter of the revolution that led to a communist takeover in China in 1949.

In the early 1960s, relations between Moscow and Beijing deteriorated even further, leading to a split in the international communist movement. More revolutionary-minded parties and movements sided with China, while the majority of the world's communists remained loyal to Moscow.

The conflict peaked during the Cultural Revolution in China, which lasted from 1966 until Mao's death in 1976. During that decade of intense turmoil in China, with Red Guards attacking suspected 'enemies of the people' all over the country, the revolutionary authorities in north-western China put up huge loudspeakers on the banks of the Amur river border, which blasted anti-Soviet propaganda twenty-four hours a day, year after year, to Blagoveshchensk on the other side. The Chinese condemned and denounced the Soviet 'revisionist renegade clique', which had betrayed true Marxism-Leninism. In 1969, there was even a brief border war over some disputed islands in the Ussuri river—a tributary to the Amur—near Khabarovsk. But the loudspeakers fell silent a long time ago and the days of outright hostility are over. Today, a completely different message, not old-style Maoist propaganda, emanates from across the Amur.

From Blagoveshchensk, people can now see a very different Heihe, with modern high-rise buildings and, at night, flashing neon lights. Trade is brisk and goods can now cross the river by truck—private cars are not allowed—on a 1,080-metre bridge that was built by a Russo-Chinese company and opened in 2022. Many individual merchants, though, still prefer to use the speedboats that shuttle back and forth between Heihe and Blagoveshchensk. But it is not an equal partnership. The Russian Far East as a whole has become a backwater, a source of raw materials for China's industries and a market for cheap Chinese consumer goods. Russia, once a superpower, and especially its remote far eastern cities like Blagoveshchensk, now hobbles along in the shadow of the much wealthier and more powerful China. The Chinese economy has grown from half the size of the Soviet Union's before it collapsed in 1991 to more than four times bigger than Russia's today.[1]

Before the Soviet Union disintegrated, the Far East was heavily industrialized. This began during World War II when numerous large plants and factories were evacuated from Ukraine and western Russia to more secure locations in the east. New heavy industries were established in the vicinity of Komsomolsk-on-Amur (the 'city of communist youth'), and at Khabarovsk and Krasnoyarsk, while coal and iron mines were opened up in the Amur river valley. Oil was brought by tankers from the Soviet-held northern part of the island of Sakhalin, and new railway lines were drawn between those new industrial centres.

For years after the war, the Far East also supplied European Russia and other republics with fish and crabs from the Sea of Okhotsk. The collapse of the Soviet Union with its state-controlled economy and the ensuing closure of most of those factories, mines and commercial enterprises coincided with China's transition from orthodox socialism to capitalism. The Chinese soon discovered the enormous potential of economic expansion into the Russian Far East. There was a huge, largely unexplored market for Chinese consumer goods, and natural resources that could be exploited. First came Chinese consumer goods which were more readily available and cheaper than those produced far away in European Russia—and soon even fruit, vegetables and other foodstuff began to flood the markets in towns like Vladivostok, Khabarovsk and Blagoveshchensk. From the Far East, timber and raw materials went south, across the border to China, and entire factories were dismantled and sold across the border as scrap metal. And the area's once famous seafood ended up exclusively in South Korea and Japan.

Chinese merchants came across the border to sell clothes, tools, toys, watches and electronic appliances. Many Chinese merchants also settled in the Russian Far East, or had a foothold in both countries. They were called 'Huaqiao' in Chinese, or 'sojourners', because they travelled back and forth. According to Russian academic Vladimir Portyakov: 'Russia's government policy of foreign market reforms, liberalized foreign trade, and facilitate[sic] travel for Russian nationals and foreigners created a breeding ground that rapidly swelled the influx of Chinese ... with domestic production in a deep slump and a slack in interregional industrial ties in Russia, its outlying regions and their businesses were compelled to look for closer relations with their foreign counterparts just to survive.'[2]

At the same time, Chinese contract workers came to work for Chinese-owned enterprises that had been established in the region, and they were actually preferred to local labourers. Anatolii M. Shkurkin, a Russian academic, expressed this in a paper on the Chinese in the Far East: 'Chinese workers are highly organized and disciplined at work. As compared with local inhabitants, they do not drink and do not demand any immediate payments except some obligatory minimum.'[3] The Chinese migrants were tolerated because they worked hard and took jobs that Russians were not prepared to do.

Documenting this migration with accuracy is problematic. Russia's Far Eastern Federal District is huge—6,952,600 square kilometres, but with a population of only 7.9 million in 2022, which has been declining steadily since the dissolution of the Soviet Union as many industries have closed and military installations, which were heavily manned and fortified during the confrontation with China, are no longer there. The exact number of Chinese working or living permanently or occasionally in the Russian Far East is a hotly debated topic and estimates vary from a few thousand to hundreds of thousands. No one can say for certain how many there are because Russia had no immigration legislation until 1992, when Boris Yeltsin, the first president of the Russian Federation, created the Federal Migration Service to implement policies that would prevent illegal immigration.[4] But then, and later, rampant corruption within that service and other governmental institutions have rendered any kind of legislation meaningless, and official statistics are, to say the least, unreliable.

But most importantly—if seen in the perspective of a possible significant demographic change—the provinces across the border, Heilongjiang, Jilin and Liaoning, which with parts of today's Inner Mongolia make up what is historically referred to as Manchuria, are home to more than 100 million people. There is no wonder that many Russians, and not only those who remain in the Far East, are worried.

Viktor Larin, a professor of international relations at the Russian Academy of Sciences, wrote in 2004: 'Within the past ten years, the territory has lost 10% of its population. And that is not the major concern; the most dangerous fact is that the major share of the local population is inclined to leave the territory of the Far East. According to interviews with Russian citizens in the Primorskyi Krai [the administrative unit around Vladivostok], two thirds of respondents (66%) are ready to leave Primorskyi Krai, should there be an option; among them, 25% would leave for abroad, others would go to other regions of Russia.'[5]

Even more alarmingly, Larkin wrote, 'most of them are young people, i.e. the most active population group.'[6] And he concludes, 'there is almost no hope that Russian people will move to the Far East. Only foreign migrants can provide for the economic development of this territory. Whether we like it or dislike it, whether we want or do not want it, no other way is available yet.'[7] Even President Vladimir Putin said during a visit to Blagoveshchensk in the summer of 2000: 'Unless we make real efforts to develop our Far Eastern areas soon, the ethnic Russian population will, within a few decades, have Japanese, Chinese or Korean as their native language.'[8]

There are some who disagree. Two Russian academics, Alexander Gabuev and Maria Repnikova, wrote in an op-ed for the *South China Morning Post*: 'Most Western media refer to alarming figures, some concluding there are two million Chinese, set to reach 10 million by 2050. The latest Russian national census in 2010, however, projected the number of Chinese residents at 30,000. Regional official and academic data we uncovered, in several research trips to the Far East since 2010, estimates the number of Chinese migrants as between 4,00,000 and 5,50,000. More than half are in the European part of Russia, where the labour market is bigger and more dynamic than in the east of the Urals. The most Chinese-populated Russian city is Moscow, not Vladivostok or Khabarovsk.'[9]

There may be more Chinese in Moscow than in Vladivostok and other Far Eastern cities and towns, but the Russian capital is not likely to become overwhelmed by Chinese migrants and merchants. The situation in the Russian Far East is far more delicate and potentially volatile—and not only because of the vast difference in the number of people who live there and across the border in China's northeast.

Historically, the Russian Far—or Wild—East is Russia's equivalent of America's Wild West. Russian eastward expansion began as early as the sixteenth and seventeenth centuries as peasants from impoverished European Russia were attracted by promises of free land. And then came the Cossacks, independent frontiersmen who staked out a life for themselves on the fringes of the Russian empire. They rode east to fight the Tatars, and to see whether the news they had received of a rich country full of precious furs and silver was true. As was the case in America, fugitives of all kinds and members of non-conformist religious sects also migrated to the new Promised Land.[10] In a sense, the Cossack represented the American pioneer, the Tatar the native American and the Russian army the US Cavalry. By the late seventeenth century, the European newcomers were as numerous as the indigenous Siberian tribes.

The number of Chinese living there is unknown as no proper census was ever conducted in the area.

Inevitably, the Russians clashed with the Chinese, who claimed the same territories. Delegations from Moscow and the Manchu court in Beijing finally met in the Siberian town of Nerchinsk in August 1689. Following several weeks of negotiations, the two powers agreed on 6th September that the border should run along the Argun, Shilka and Gorbitsa rivers and the crest of the Stanovoy Range north and east of the Amur river.[11] The Treaty of Nerchinsk was the first ever to be concluded between the Chinese empire and a Western power and the Russians agreed to halt their expansion south towards China proper. But the Russians continued undeterred with their conquest to the north and the east as far as the Kamchatka peninsula, dubbed the 'land of fire and ice' for its many active volcanoes and harsh climate.

In 1742, the Russians crossed the Bering Strait and reached Alaska. The biggest contiguous land empire in history was forming. The conquests continued and, in November 1856, the Russians established a new territorial unit along the Pacific coast, which they named the Maritime Territory (today's Primorskyi Krai). Russian sovereignty over all areas north of the Amur and east of the Ussuri, was eventually recognized by the Chinese authorities under the treaties of Aigun in May 1858 and Tianjin in June 1858. The Treaty of Peking, signed in November 1860, sealed the fate of those former Chinese territories, which were now officially under the rule of the Russian tsar.

But it happened with strong opposition from the then-emperor in Peking (now Beijing), Xianfeng of the Manchu Qing Dynasty (whose temple name was Wenzong.) The land that China lost to Russia in 1858 was called 'Outer Manchuria', or Wai Manzhou in Chinese. Xianfeng did not want to cede any part of his empire to the barbarians from the West, especially areas he considered part of Manchuria, the land of his ancestors. But, at the time, China was weak and had no bargaining power. The country was wrecked with civil strife and had suffered from humiliating defeats by Britain in two opium wars. The first lasted from 1839 to 1842 and led to the loss of Hong Kong, while the second was fought from

1856 to 1860 and resulted in the British acquiring more territory on the mainland opposite Hong Kong Island.

In 1859, the governor-general of the newly acquired Eastern Siberia, Count Nikolay Muravyov-Amursky, sailed along the Pacific coast and reached a spectacular, well-sheltered anchorage which was known to the Chinese as Haishenwai, or 'sea cucumber cliffs'. It was not more than a fishing village but the count described it as 'the best of all ports' and called it Vladikavkaz after a Russian outpost in the Caucasus. It soon became known as Vladivostok, 'ruler of the east', as more Russians settled there and the tsar wanted to show the rest of Asia who the new masters were. From humble beginnings, Vladivostok turned into a magnificent city and became the administrative centre of Russia's Pacific acquisitions. The Chinese, though, continued to call it Haishenwai.

Following the Russian conquests in the Far East, other towns in the region were also given Russian names. Khabarovsk got its Russian name after an early explorer—some would argue a Cossack—named Yerofey Khabarov, who had arrived there in the mid-seventeenth century and was among the first to encounter the Chinese and fight against their forces. Khabarovsk also grew into a major city in the mid- and late-nineteenth century as the area was opened for Russian colonization. The Chinese, however, call the city Boli. Blagoveshchensk on the Amur, which means 'the city of good news' in Russian, was given that name in 1858 after a church that was dedicated to the Annunciation, the biblical event when the angel Gabriel told the Virgin Mary that she was going to give birth to Jesus, the son of God. The old Chinese name for the place is Hailanpao. [12]

The Chinese never forgot those old names, and Vladivostok, Khabarovsk and Blagoveshchensk continued to be called Haishenwai, Boli and Hailanpao on many maps printed in China well into modern times. Under a directive issued in February 2023, those Chinese names are now even official in China. Sakhalin, which became entirely Soviet-controlled after World War II when the Japanese had to relinquish the southern half of the island, is now called Kuyedao in China and the Stanovoy Range, part of the border drawn in 1689, is referred to as the Outer Xing'an Range. [13]

Nor have the Chinese forgiven the Western powers, including Russia, for taking advantage of their country's weakness in the nineteenth century and forcing them to sign what they regard as 'the unequal treaties'. It is in a historical context a very odd term, as treaties under which one nation has to make concessions to another are never 'equal'; whether it is about Sweden ceding Finland to Russia in 1809 or Mexico giving up vast tracts of territory to the US at various times in the nineteenth century or Germany losing lands to Poland and the Soviet Union after World War II. Treaties ending a conflict always reflect the power of the winning or superior nation and, therefore, are by nature 'unequal'. China is the only country in the world which, much later and officially, seeks to 'rectify' what was agreed upon when such treaties were signed.

The Chinese have also not forgotten how their ancestors were treated in the Russian Far East. Tens of thousands of Chinese remained in the Russian-occupied territories. The Russian empire's census of 1897 showed a total of 42,823 Chinese in the Primorskyi (Primorye) region alone.[14] But only those who were married to Russians were entitled to Russian citizenship and they also had to become Christians. The vast majority of the Chinese in the Primorskyi region and elsewhere in the Far East were either descendants of original inhabitants or workers who had been brought in from China to clear forests, work in gold mines or do other menial work—and to take part in the construction of the last stretches of the Trans-Siberian railway. The construction commenced in European Russia in 1892 and the Amur river line north of the Chinese border was completed in 1916. There was now a continuous railway line all the way from Petrograd (St. Petersburg) to Vladivostok with a total length of more than 10,000 kilometres.

The participation of Chinese labourers in the construction of the Trans-Siberian railway has been overlooked by most Western historians, as has been the fact that Chinese workers were used to repair railways as far away from their homeland as Murmansk in north-western Russia. Some were even sent to work on the frontline in World War I, and as many as 7,000 Chinese could have been killed by German bullets while working as coolies for the Russian troops.[15] There are estimates that the total number of Chinese workers recruited by the pre-revolutionary, tsarist government could have been as many as 500,000.[16] In the Primorskyi region, the Chinese population, which consisted of permanent residents as well as seasonal settlers, increased from 47,390 in 1906 to 68,355 in 1908.[17]

Thousands of Chinese also lived in other cities and towns in the Far East, and they had little to do with their Russian neighbours. Languages and cultures were too different and many Russians did not accept them as equals. The worst and most racist incident occurred in the Blagoveshchensk area in 1900. A Chinese secret society called Yihequan, or 'the Fists of Righteousness and Harmony', began attacking foreigners and signs of foreign influence all over China. Dressed in brightly coloured clothing and wearing headbands with Chinese characters and religious amulets to protect them from 'foreign bullets', their battle cry was *'Sha! Sha!'* (Kill! Kill!). Entire Christian families, including children, were hacked to death with swords.

The Boxer Rebellion, as it became known because of the word 'fist' in the name of the chaotically organized bands of mostly young fanatics, spread as far north as Heihe, and even to the Chinese communities living near Blagoveshchensk on the other side of the river. Some local Boxers fired handguns and hit the city jail. A rumour spread that they were going to use a cannon as well, which the local Russian press irresponsibly reported, and anti-Chinese riots broke out in Blagoveshchensk.

At the time, many Chinese, mostly workers and traders, lived in an enclave called Trans-Zeya, a 10 kilometre wide and 60 kilometre long area on the banks of the Amur. Cossacks and Russian settlers attacked that place and killed anyone they could lay their hands on. Mobs robbed Chinese homes, and the local administrator, Lieutenant-General Konstantin Nikolaevich Gribskii, issued an order saying that all Chinese—20,000 of them—had to gather at one place near the city to be deported to China. Around 6,000 Chinese showed up and were marched to the banks of the Amur. But there were no boats waiting for them. Instead, Russian soldiers and civilians pushed them into the river knowing that few of them could swim. Shots were fired, and those who were not killed by bullets drowned in the river. Chinese residents who did not show up to be counted that day suffered the same fate a few days later. The total death toll is not known but is conservatively estimated at 7,000. But not all Russians were xenophobic bigots; some Russian families hid their Chinese servants in their homes when the mobs ran amok.[18]

The status of the Russian Far East came into question after the Bolshevik revolution in 1917. On 25 July 1919, the Russian communist diplomat Lev Karakhan issued a manifesto, which aptly became known as the 'Karakhan Manifesto' or the 'Karakhan Declaration' renouncing tsarist acquisitions and relinquishing the special, extraterritorial rights the Russians—like other foreigners—had enjoyed in China. The move was made as Vladimir Lenin's Bolsheviks were advancing into Siberia and the Far East, where tsarist forces were still active and a bitter civil war was raging.

The Bolsheviks saw the Chinese as one of 'the oppressed people of the East' and wanted them to be an ally against the tsarists and the Western forces that supported them.[19] But as the Bolsheviks seemed to be winning the war, such promises were largely forgotten later on. Nevertheless, it was too early to incorporate this far-flung and still potentially volatile region into the new communist state that was emerging from the ruins of the Russian empire. The compromise solution was the proclamation on 6 April 1920 of the Far Eastern Republic, a buffer state between Bolshevik Russia and the Chinese and other powers in the area such as the Japanese, the Czechs and other Western forces who were fighting on the side of 'the Whites' against 'the Reds'.

The President of the new republic was Alexander Mikhailovich Krasnoshchyokov, a Ukrainian who had once worked with the revolutionary leader Leon Trotsky. Krasnoshchyokov emigrated to the US after the first, failed revolution in 1905 and settled in Chicago where he became active in the Industrial Workers of the World (IWW), or 'the Wobblies', a militant American trade union movement formed in the early 1900s. Krasnoshchyokov returned to Russia in 1917, joined the Bolshevik forces and went to fight in the Far East. Recognized by Lenin in Moscow as an independent state, the Far Eastern Republic gradually acquired a semblance of authority over its territory, which encompassed the former Transbaikal and Amur Oblasts as well as Primorskyi Krai, a huge area stretching from land to the north of Mongolia all along the Chinese frontier down to the Pacific coast.[20]

The Japanese withdrew from the Far East in October 1922, and on 9th November the Far Eastern Republic was absorbed into the Russian central state and became part of the the Soviet Union when it was proclaimed on 30th December that year. Like many other revolutionary veterans, Krasnoshchyokov was arrested during Stalin's purges in the mid-1930s, sentenced to death for alleged 'espionage'—a common accusation levelled against Stalin's opponents and rivals—and executed on 26 November 1937.

The Chinese who survived the Blagoveshchensk massacre, along with other Chinese and Asians, were moved from their homes during those turbulent years in the 1930s. In 1932, the Japanese had set up a puppet state in Manchuria, which they called Manchukuo, and consequently Stalin thought all Asians were potential fifth columnists for the Japanese. Unlike the ethnic Koreans in the Russian Far East who were relocated to Uzbekistan and other Central Asian republics and eventually did quite well, thousands of Chinese perished in labour camps in Siberia or were executed on the spot. Some Chinese, however, took part in communist-initiated development programmes in Vladivostok in the 1930s, and those who were especially trusted by Soviet communist party officials had to study socialist ideology and underwent training for future revolutionary work in China.[21] But the once thriving Chinese communities in the Russian Far East were no more.

The ethnic cleansing of the Far East culminated in the late 1930s and the Russification of the area could continue without hindrance. Criminals had been deported to the Russian Far East since tsarist times and the Bolsheviks continued sending political opponents there after the revolution in 1917. Many had no choice but to remain there after serving their sentences, and so contributed to the growth of the ethnic Russian population of the area. More convicts were sent to Siberia and the Far East during Stalin's Great Terror in the 1930s. During 1937–38 alone, an estimated seven million people were banished to labour camps, and of those at least a million were executed while tens of thousands died of overwork, disease and starvation. There may have been similarities between the American Wild West and Russia's Wild East, but Siberia and the Far East were no Colorado or Wyoming.

The vast majority of the prisoners were, of course, political and Russian, but the treatment of the ethnic Chinese in Russia, and especially the old atrocities that were committed even before the Soviet Union was established, have never been forgotten in China. After the split between China and the Soviet Union in the early 1960s, the Chinese authorities set up an academic group to collect information about the Blagoveshchensk massacre, which showed the breakup of relations may not have been caused solely by disagreements over ideology. To the Chinese, Russia and the Soviet Union and now again Russia, has always been an imperialist power that grabbed land from China when the country was down on its knees and in no position to defend its interests.

Although the issue is not brought up when officials meet to discuss bilateral affairs, the data and exhibits about the killings in 1900 can still be seen at a museum in Heihe. And despite the official rhetoric, it would be a serious mistake to believe that China and Russia have become friends. China has not given up its policy of rectifying 'the unequal treaties' it was forced to enter into in the nineteenth century. That does not necessarily mean that China seeks to annex 'Outer Manchuria', but it has become economically integrated with the Chinese provinces across the Amur and the Ussuri. After the collapse of the Soviet Union, most trade is no longer conducted between the Far East and European Russia in the west but between Russia's eastern domains and China to the south.

Boris Yeltsin, who served as independent Russia's first President from 1991 to 1999, was too weak to do anything about it even on the rare occasions when he was sober. His main, and some would argue only, achievement when it came to relations with China was to sign an agreement with then-President Jiang Zemin to settle the sovereignty dispute over some islands in the Ussuri, the scene of the brief war in 1969. Yeltsin's successor Putin, who has served as Prime Minister and President and has always been the strongman of Russia since 1999, has done his utmost to rectify imbalances between the Russian Far East and the rest of the country. His words of warning in 2000 about what languages would be spoken in the Far East in the future was only the beginning. In 2012, he announced that economic development of the Far East was 'a national priority of the entire twenty-first century.'[22]

Kandy Wong, a journalist from Hong Kong, argues that Putin's 'pivot to the east' policy aims to develop Russia's vast, resource-rich Far East in collaboration with China, while also tapping the economic potential of Asia.[23] That grand scheme is part of Beijing's incongruously named 'Polar Silk Road', and it is clear that China is in the driver's seat. In 2018, Chinese President Xi Jinping paid a visit to Vladivostok and signed a six-year cooperation agreement on investments in sectors such as agriculture, tourism and infrastructure. The Russian Far East is also rich in natural gas, gold, coal, diamonds and timber—resources that China wants to extract in order to keep the development momentum of its own north-eastern region.

According to Wong's report, a Russia–China investment fund was formed as early as 2012 'to provide up to US$724 million in finances for development of northeastern China and the [Russian] Far East.'[24] Putin, on his part, declared that 'the Far East must catch the "Chinese wind" in the sails of its economy.'[25] According to Wong: 'As of last year [2021], Chinese investors are backing fifty-eight projects with a total of US$2.4 billion in priority development territories, while a large number of Chinese traders operate in the free port of Vladivostok. The [Russian Ministry for the Development of the Russian Far East and Arctic] had previously stated that China accounted for 73 per cent of all foreign investment in the Far East.'[26] That ministry was set up on 21 May 2012 to deal with issues related to the Far East and, according to its website, it is 'a federal executive body that coordinates, in the Far Eastern Federal District, the implementation of state programmes and federal targeted programmes, including long-term ones, from the list approved by the Government of the Russian Federation.'[27]

From the available data, it can be deduced that it would not be possible to implement any of those 'state programmes' and achieve even a semblance of noteworthy development in the Far East without Chinese money playing a dominant role. Therefore, the current form of Chinese-driven development in the Russian Far East will inevitably lead to the loss of economic independence—and, following the disastrous attempt by Russia to invade Ukraine, this applies not only to the Far East.

Asia Times quoted in its 25 March 2023 issue a 'Jiangsu-based columnist' as saying that 'as Russia–Europe relations broke down, Russia has no choice but to allow Chinese capital to enter its key industries … It is necessary for Russia to strategically shift to the East as no European and US capital will invest in Russia.'[28] Somewhat alarmingly, the same report quoted another Chinese columnist focusing on the Russian Far East as saying that, 'this undeveloped land belonged to China … Is it possible that Russia sells it back to China at this time? … It is alright for China to help Russia develop its Far East region but we must get enough benefits, not just small profits … Who is begging for help? Who is the real owner of the Far East region? If Russia is sincere, it should at least return the Outer Manchuria and Kuyedao (Sakhalin) to China.'[29] It could be argued that those 'columnists' expressed only their own opinions, but such freedom of speech does not exist in Xi's China. Rather, those op-ed pieces should be seen as attempts by the Chinese authorities to 'test the waters' and see what the Russian reaction would be to statements of such a provocative nature.

There is also a much darker side to Chinese migration and investment in the Russian Far East that some Russian academics have highlighted in papers and articles. The climate in the Russian Far East may be harsh and, in the north, not suitable for human habitation, but in the south, business opportunities abound, especially in the booming underground economy, where thousands of ordinary Chinese migrants—not investors in major industries—work and have settled more or less permanently. However, they have never been especially welcome because they work harder than the Russians and the money they earn is not spent locally but sent back to their families in China.

Facing racial prejudice and, if they are in Russia illegally, the threat of deportation, many migrants choose—or are forced—to work for ethnic

Chinese gangs that are linked to the Triads, China's equivalent of the Mafia. And the influence of the Triads began as soon as it became easier to cross the border in the 1990s. Russian academic Viktor Larin noted in a chapter in a book published in Russia in 2004: 'In the second half of the 1990s, criminal offences were widely associated with the Chinese presence in the Far East. Extortion, robbery, murder and other criminal acts were committed both by Chinese and against Chinese and accounted for 2/3 of all crimes officially recorded in the Primorskyi Krai and Khabarovskyi Krai ... Consequently, it did not contribute to a positive image of the Chinese community in Russia.'[30]

On a more organized level in the turbulent 1990s, Chinese gangs became involved in the many casinos that were established in the Far East, in prostitution involving Russian as well as Chinese women, the smuggling of Japanese cars into the region and gunrunning to the Russian Far East as well as to Japan across the Japan Sea (or the East Sea, as it is called in Korea). Even Siberian tigers, an endangered species, and mammoth ivory found in the region's wilderness were smuggled across the border and sold in China. In 1996, the English-language *Vladivostok News* reported that ephedrine, known as mulka among addicts, was the most widespread drug in the Far East. A homemade adaptation of methamphetamine, it had begun to arrive 'in huge quantities from China.'[31]

The gangs also facilitated the movement of illegal migrants and extorted 'protection money' from local Chinese as well as Russian business people. The networks of the Chinese underground banking system—which handles more money transactions in China and in overseas Chinese communities than are sent through official banks—also reached the Russian Far East. This flow of black money cost the Russian government millions of roubles every year in lost revenue.[32] The traditional Russian criminals and the early Chinese crime bosses seemed to have some kind of symbiotic relationship, but the Chinese were far better organized and, therefore, had the upper hand in the fields where they operated. Many small-time Russian gangsters even worked for Chinese syndicates, either as contacts for local business deals or as security guards at the casinos as well as at Chinese-owned hotels and eateries.[33]

The Far East has long been a stronghold for Russian organized crime, but many of the leaders of local gangs that previously dominated the region were killed in bloody turf wars in the 1990s, while others went out of business or died in mysterious circumstances. Chinese gangs partly filled the vacuum, but there is one activity that remains in the hands of Russian gangs: the immensely lucrative trade in seafood. In the late 1990s and early 2000s, 15,000–17,000 tonnes of seafood worth at least US$83 million were exported every year to Japan, South Korea and China, an estimated 70 per cent of it illegally.[34] The fishing boats were registered in Russia and fly Russian flags so, strictly legally speaking, they were entitled to fish in the Sea of Okhotsk. But those fishing boats hardly docked at Russian ports. The seafood was sold in Japan, South Korea and China and the profits were deposited in banks in those countries, depriving local Russian authorities of taxes and other revenues from the trade.[35] The once famous king crab has become almost extinct as the fishing fleets scooped up whatever they could find in the waters off the Russian Far East.

That was how it was well into the early 2000s, and although the law-and-order situation has improved somewhat since Putin took over and managed to tame Russian organized crime—many would argue that he made alliances with the gangs and thus brought much of the random violence to a halt—the Chinese gangs are still active and operate independently of any Russian institutions. As the domestic economic situation in China has improved, fewer Chinese are going to Russia to find employment and seek business opportunities, and the gangs may not be as active as they used to be. But there is every indication that they will remain engaged in traditional pursuits such as gambling, prostitution, loan-sharking, extortion, gunrunning and, increasingly, timber exports. *The Diplomat* reported on 21 April 2011 that the logging industry in the Russian Far East is 'now beyond federal control, and overrun by criminal gangs.'[36]

A decade later, Russia felt compelled to announce that it would be banning the export of unprocessed logs 'as of 2022'.[37] But given rampant corruption in the Russian administration and the next-to-non-existent efficient law enforcement, nothing has changed on the ground. Putin's only decisive drive in the Far East against what was deemed 'organized crime' happened in February 2023 when Sergei Furgal, a former governor of the Khabarovsk region, was sentenced to twenty-two years in prison after a jury convicted him of attempted murder and ordering two killings in 2004 and 2005. Furgal, a member of the ultranationalist Liberal Democratic Party of Russia, was elected in 2018 in a runoff that he won against the region's longtime governor from Putin's ruling United Russia party. Furgal and his supporters insisted that the case against him was politically motivated and his arrest in July 2020 sparked mass protests in Khabarovsk and other towns and cities in the Far East. Radio Free Europe reported: 'The protests were held almost daily for many months, highlighting growing discontent in Russia's Far East over what demonstrators see as Moscow-dominated policies that often neglect their views and interests.'[38]

Apart from outright gangsterism, there are also concerns about food security in the Russian Far East. As thousands of hard-working Chinese settled in the border areas, many began to grow vegetables and other crops. Local Russians usually say that their land is not suitable for farming. The weather is too cold most of the year even in the south of the Far East, they argue. But Chinese farmers have nevertheless managed to cultivate the land—and sell their produce to local Russians. In the past, food was brought in from other parts of Russia, but when the Soviet Union collapsed, domestic distribution networks broke down as well. Besides, food produced by Chinese settlers is cheaper than anything cultivated by Russians.

Officially, foreigners cannot own land in Russia and a major problem is that Russia, despite the end of socialism, still has no law that regulates private ownership of land. As in the old days, all land belongs to the state, and individual farmers can only get the right to use it. But Chinese entrepreneurs have bribed local officials in order to acquire land from Russian farmers, and then they have hired agricultural workers from China. While quite a few products are grown locally by those Chinese cultivators, vast quantities of pork, fruit and even eggs, are also brought in from China. According to Lyudmila Erokhina, a researcher at Far

Eastern Federal University in Vladivostok, the Chinese now dominate the agricultural sector and food supply: 'We're totally dependent on them.'[39]

Not only electronic equipment and consumer goods but also agricultural produce come from across the Chinese border. It is almost impossible to find any Russian-made provisions in local shops and markets—apart from vodka, of which every supermarket has a generous supply. But it would not be fair to blame the Chinese migrants and merchants for not abiding by Russian laws. According to Alexei Maslov, a Russian China specialist: 'What has formed the background to the Chinese pursuit of economic opportunities, often described as illegal, has been the interpenetration of crime, government and business in Russia itself. The arbitrary power of bureaucrats and the burden of federal and local taxes, no less than the plethora of permits and bribes needed to do anything, have made it almost impossible to run a business entirely legally even if one wanted to, and even if one could find law-abiding government officials with whom to cooperate.'[40]

It is hard to imagine what a genuine Sino-Russian partnership would look like, let alone 'a new world order', which was the concept for an extended alliance of anti-Western nations that Xi and Putin envisaged when they met in Moscow in March 2023. According to a statement released by China after the meeting: 'They [the leaders] shared the view that this relationship has gone far beyond the bilateral scope and acquired critical importance for the global landscape and the future of humanity.'[41] Putin said on his website: 'We are working in solidarity on the formation of a more just and democratic multipolar world order, which should be based on the central role of the UN, its Security Council, international law, the purposes and principles of the UN Charter.'[42] That Russia had just violated the UN Charter by invading a neighbouring country was conveniently not mentioned, nor was the fact that the UN's General Assembly had overwhelmingly condemned the invasion in a resolution passed only weeks before the Xi–Putin summit in Moscow.[43]

But, surprisingly, many, especially in Asia, Africa and Latin America, are buying what Xi and Putin are selling. China and Russia's autocrats have propagated and won support for what Pankaj Mishra, an associate professor in the department of political science at the University of Chicago, calls 'a still-rich vein of anti-Westernism around the world.' Mishra argues that, 'in their [nations in Asia, Africa and Latin America] eyes, the "vaccine apartheid" practiced by rich Western nations during the Covid-19 pandemic confirmed yet again that the West will always protect its own interests, regardless of its rhetoric about human rights. They can see, too, the great contrast between the West's generous hospitality to Ukrainian refugees and the walls and fences it builds to keep out darker-skinned victims of its policies.'[44]

Also according to Mishra: 'The signs of resurgent anti-Westernism are everywhere: a viral video of Namibia's President educating a visiting German politician in the facts of European racism, Brazilian President Luiz Inácio Lula da Sailva blaming the US and NATO [the North Atlantic Treaty Organization] for the war in Ukraine and seeing China as an impartial mediator, Putin's popularity rising in Indonesia, and Indians in an opinion poll identifying the US as a bigger military threat than Pakistan (although still less of one than China).'[45]

The US-led invasion of Iraq in 2003 and the waves of chaos and violence that it unleashed throughout the region and even beyond has also done irreparable damage to the international reputation Washington wants to have as standing for 'liberty and justice for all', as it says in the pledge of allegiance to the American flag. It is not surprising that many people, especially in Asia, Africa and Latin America, want to challenge America's global hegemony and the hypocrisy that comes with it. But the despotic order represented by Xi and Putin is hardly an alternative.

Xi and Putin have nevertheless managed to successfully capitalize on Western insensitivities and policy failures and, when it comes to abstaining from criticizing Beijing's views on world politics, there is also another factor. China is rich and many poorer nations do not want to antagonize it unnecessarily because any criticism could jeopardize the possibility of getting Chinese investments, loans and grants. Lula may have been sincere when he said, during a visit to Beijing in April 2023, that Brazil and China 'can change world governance together' in a united front opposing the global power of the US.[46] But whether he wants to admit it or not, China's interest in Brazil—as in other resource-rich parts of the world—is mainly economic. It came as a surprise to nobody that Lula during his visit made it clear that he is counting on China to help reinvigorate Brazil's ailing industrial sector.[47]

Pro-Russian writers have also been busy peddling misrepresentations of reality through various international media outlets in order to convince their readers that it is the West, not China or Russia, that is the enemy of world peace. On the Asia Times website on 10 April 2023, M.K. Bhadrakumar, a former Indian diplomat, stated when it was announced that Finland had been accepted as a member of NATO: 'It signifies for Finland a historic abandonment of its policy of neutrality. Not even propagandistically can anyone say Finland has encountered a security threat from Russia.'[48]

Bhadrakumar is either feigning ignorance or unaware of Finland's modern history. Finland, originally a Swedish domain, came under Russian rule in 1809 and remained so until the Bolshevik revolution in 1917. The following year, Finland became a fully independent republic, but the threat from its eastern neighbour never ceased. Finland fought two wars against the Soviet Union in the 1940s: the so-called 'Winter War' in 1939–40 and 'the Continuation War' from 1941 to 1944. The Finns fought bravely against the vastly superior forces of the Soviet Union, but, in the end, they lost and had to cede 12 per cent of their territory to the Soviet Union. The Soviet Union took over East Karelia, including Finland's second largest city Viborg or Viipuri, the Salla area to the north and the Petsamo corridor, which had given the Finns access to the Arctic Ocean. The Soviets were also permitted to have naval bases in Finland: Hanko 1940–41 and Porkkala 1944–56.

Finland could easily have become another Estonia and been incorporated as one of the republics of the Soviet Union, or a Soviet satellite state like Poland, but it survived as an independent country through skilled diplomacy and by making concessions. Its foreign policy, though, had to take the Soviet Union's interests into account and the Finns were forced to do nothing in the international arena that could antagonize the power holders in Moscow. The collapse of the Soviet

Union brought an end to that dependence and paved the way for a more pro-Western stance, which better suited a developed, democratic nation like Finland than being a reluctant protégé of the Soviets.

Finland became a member of the European Union in 1995, and was one of the first to join the Eurozone in 1999. Finland's NATO membership is only a logical consequence of a shift to a more independent foreign policy, and this is important as the Russian threat continues to loom over the country. Andrej Illarionov, Putin's chief economic adviser from 2000 to 2005, stated in 2014 that after occupying Crimea that year, the Russian President will not stop trying to expand Russia until he has taken over Belarus, the Baltic states and Finland. According to Illarionov, Putin seeks to create 'historical justice' with 'a return to the days of the last tsar, Nicholas II, and the Soviet Union under Stalin.'[49] Illarionov also warned that Putin believes that the granting of independence to Finland after the revolution in 1917 was 'an act of treason against national interests.'[50] As a result, the *Independent* reported on 31 March 2014, 'Finland has increased border surveillance in recent weeks as Mr Putin moves to "protect what belongs to him and his successors".'[51]

Bhadrakumar may have pretended to be surprised when Finland joined NATO, but on the other hand, he is a prominent member of the Valdai Discussion Group, which was founded by the Russian International Affairs Council, a think-tank under the foreign ministry in Moscow.[52] Kremlin apologists peddling propaganda of the kind Bhadrakumar did in Asia Times serve China's interests as well because it divides international opinion and prompts many Asian, African and Latin American countries to declare their 'neutrality' in Russia's war against Ukraine, or even to go as far as believing it was NATO that somehow provoked Russia into sending tens of thousands of troops and thousands of tanks into Ukraine and unleashing brutal bombing campaigns against civilian neighbourhoods, schools and hospitals.

Putin has three role models: Peter the Great, tsar from 1682 to 1721 and the ruler who conquered land from Sweden at the Baltic Sea and there built a city named after himself, St. Petersburg; Catherine the Great, who reigned from 1762 to 1796 and whose forces conquered parts of Poland and extended Russian power to the Black Sea by occupying Crimea; and Soviet dictator Stalin, who led the country to victory in what the Russians refer to as the 'Great Patriotic War' against Nazi Germany in the 1940s. Stalin, according to Putin, may have a record of 'totalitarian repression' but also created 'a tightly centralized and absolutely unitary state.'[53] Statues of Peter the Great and Catherine the Great stand in the room where Putin entertains foreign visitors. But when Putin, in June 2022, oversaw a grand celebration in Moscow marking the 350th anniversary of Peter the Great's birth, the Russian political analyst Andrei Kolesnikov commented: 'Putin [...] is confused about history again ... Peter the Great has opened a window to Europe, Putin is hammering it up with rotten planks from the time of Ivan the Terrible.'[54]

It is also worth noting what Mishra of the University of Chicago wrote: 'As an ideology, anti-Westernism has little substantive or positive content. For geopolitical opportunists, however, it can be devastatingly useful: It should not be forgotten how much Japan once profited from its anti-Western stance, and how many influential collaborators it enjoyed even when brutally invading and exploiting Asian countries in World War Two.'[55] Xi and Putin are no defenders of freedom, human rights or democratic values. Both are despots who would not hesitate to use lethal force against their neighbours, as Putin has done in Ukraine and Xi threatens to do against Taiwan.

And in Russia as well as China, anyone who dares to oppose the established order risks ending up behind bars or worse. China's genocidal treatment of the Uighurs in Xinjiang and the Tibetans, and the propensity for Russian dissidents to fall out of windows in high-rise buildings or be poisoned by secret agents, could not possibly be what a 'new world order' should look like, or what Lula and other elected leaders who profess support for democratic values could accept as normal governmental behaviour in their own countries. They should do better than acting as apologists for two brutal dictatorships, which maintain only a very shaky relationship. Behind the glossy façade and official, bloated rhetoric lies a long history of conflicts and mutual mistrust.

Lord Palmerston, two-time Prime Minister of the UK in the nineteenth century, once said when asked to identify his allies and enemies: 'Therefore I say that it is a narrow policy to suppose that this country or that is to be marked out as the eternal ally or the perpetual enemy of England. We have no eternal allies, and we have no perpetual enemies. Our interests are eternal and perpetual, and those interests it is our duty to follow.'[56] In the same vein, not only countries like Brazil and mineral-rich African nations but even Russia is not an 'enteral ally' of China or vice versa. Tatyana Zabortseva, a professor at the Siberian Institute of Geography in Irkutsk, was quoted in a February 2023 report from the Estonian International Centre for Defence and Security, as saying that 'Eastern Siberia has effectively been turned into a "raw material pantry" for China.'[57]

As an example, Zabortseva mentioned after a conference in which Putin participated in December 2022 to celebrate the commissioning of the Kovykta gas field in eastern Siberia: 'The field's recoverable reserves are estimated at 1.8 trillion cubic metres of natural gas, but they are almost entirely reserved for Chinese consumers. For these purposes, the Power of Siberia pipeline was built, through which it is planned to pump about 27 billion cubic metres of gas to China annually […] And the inhabitants of Irkutsk region itself, where the Kovykta gas field is located, have no opportunity to use this natural resource. Instead, they use primarily coal and firewood for heating, and the level of gasification of households stands at a mere 1 percent, though the Russian authorities promise to bring it up to 3.22 percent in the coming years ... In other words, Moscow appears to value its relations with Beijing much more than it cares about the well-being of its own citizens.'[58]

The author of the report, Vadim Shtepa, a Russian academic who has been living in Estonia since 2015 due to persecution in Russia for his political views, went on to state: 'By expanding its raw material exports to China, the Kremlin tries to compensate for the losses sustained from the cessation of trade with Europe, although Russia is forced to sell oil and gas to its eastern partner at a large discount of up to 30 per cent against the world price. However, doing so also allows the Kremlin to solve a political problem and ensure—if not support from Beijing—then at least its neutrality with regards to Russia's military adventure in Ukraine.'[59] And it is economic interests and security concerns for China, nobody else, that guide Beijing's foreign policies and endeavours. As Shtepa writes in his excellent and insightful analysis of Putin's policies vis-à-vis China: 'Politically, the Chinese "dragon" is strategic and unlikely to fully endorse Russia's aggression in Ukraine. China's economy dwells on the mass production of consumer goods and is wary of international sanctions that could impede its economic growth were Beijing to actively support Moscow.'[60]

He goes on to say: 'Therefore, the Kremlin's calculation of "friendship with China against the West" looks like wishful thinking on its part. Thus far, Chinese weapons deliveries to Russia remain out of the question.'[61] And why would the Chinese trust and give unconditional support to a nation that grabbed large parts of their country and, when China was weak and vulnerable, forced it to sign some 'unequal treaties'? What about the Blagoveshchensk massacre, the ethnic cleansing in the 1930s, and the conflicts, including a brief war, in the 1960s? To the Chinese, the Russians are still uncivilized barbarians whose culture and lifestyle are vastly different—and inferior—to their own assumed '5,000 years of history'.[62]

Putin and Xi also have incompatible dreams of re-establishing the glory of ancient empires. Swedish Sinologist Lars Ellström argues: 'It is extremely unlikely that the historical contradictions between the Russian and Chinese imperial dreams can be bridged by some recent, written or verbal agreements. Those dreams have, as I see it, very deep roots on both sides.'[63] Michael Sheridan, a journalist and author, expressed the same views in an April 2023 essay about Sino-Russian relations: 'Russia and China are not friends. The two Asian giants tangled for centuries over the vastness of resource-rich desert and mountain between them. They remain uneasy neighbours. Their leaders, Xi Jinping and Vladimir Putin, recently proclaimed partnership in a "new order". But they are trapped by geography, birth rates and strategy in a very old order; one that explains why the Chinese leadership distrusts the Kremlin, fears its own subjects and keeps an iron grip on the borderlands.'[64]

Meanwhile, China's plunder of Russia's natural resources continues unabated—and with the Chinese calling the shots. Besides exports of natural gas to China, logging has long been another source of dissatisfaction.[65] According to Shtepa, Chinese companies enjoy long-term lease agreements that allow them to access thousands of hectares of forests in Siberia and the Far East. There is not a single pulp mill in the region, so all the timber is shipped directly to China: 'The Far East has essentially been turned into a joint Moscow–Beijing colony for raw materials. The two authoritarian powers completely ignore the interests of the local population, as earlier exemplified by the distribution of natural gas produced at the Kovykta field in Irkutsk.'[66]

But ignoring the local population—and provoking resentment—is something the central authorities in Moscow cannot afford to do. Most of the machines and steel from the region's once-vibrant heavy industry may have ended up as scrap metal in China, but three important production sites of the military aviation industry are still there: the aircraft plants at Komsomolsk-on-Amur and Ulan-Ude, where different kinds of Sukhoi fighter aircraft are manufactured, and the Progress production site in Primorskyi Krai, manufacturer of helicopters for military and civilian use.[67] The Russian Eastern Military District in Khabarovsk and the Pacific Fleet headquarters at Vladivostok may not be as important as they were during the Soviet era, but they remain crucial for Russia's defence in the east.

Vladivostok may be far from Moscow, and seven time zones away while the easternmost zone; Kamchatka, is nine hours ahead of the capital, but this is an area where any widespread dissent could have disastrous consequences—and there have been sporadic outbursts of anti-government sentiment. Protests against the arrest and sentencing of Sergei Furgal in February 2023 reflected resentment with the way Moscow interfered, unjustly, the demonstrators claimed, with the local administration. In December 2008, more than a thousand people protested in Vladivostok against the imposition of higher import-duties on non-Russian made cars, a decision that came from Moscow. Most people in the Far East drive Japanese cars—even the police—with the steering wheel on the right-hand side, as is the case in countries like Japan where they drive on the left-hand side of the road. Most Japanese cars are smuggled in from Niigata across the Japan Sea (the East Sea in Korea), often with no duties paid other than bribes to the police.

The protesters blocked roads and lit bonfires in the centre of Vladivostok, and for a brief period also blockaded the city's airport. The local police were reluctant to take any action against the rioters because they were sympathetic to their demands—and that prompted the Russian authorities to airlift extra, and more loyal, police units from Moscow. They detained some protesters who were shouting: 'Putin, resign!' According to a survey that was made public in 2018, the incidence of poverty in the Far East is almost 40 per cent higher than the Russian average, while mortality rates and what is termed 'quality of life indicator' are among the worst in Russia, and crime rates one-third higher than in the rest of the country—and that, despite the region's abundant natural resources and immense mineral wealth. The region east of the Urals produces almost 70 per cent of the total value of Russia's exports and has 85 per cent of its natural resources.[68]

It is impossible to say how much local people in the Far East resent the power and policies of the central authorities today—and to what extent they are opposed to China's domination of the local economy. But if local polls are to be believed, attitudes towards the Chinese have actually changed for the better. In 1998, 43 per cent of the Chinese in Vladivostok and 35 per cent in Khabarovsk stated that the attitude of local Russian people to them was either bad or not very friendly, while 47 per cent of the Russians in Primorskyi Krai were convinced that China posed a threat and that their land might even be annexed by China.[69]

A local opinion poll taken in 2016 reportedly showed that 80 per cent of what was termed 'Eastern Siberians' viewed their southern neighbour as an ally and development partner.[70] At the same time, and somewhat paradoxically, 59 per cent considered China's ascent as a potential threat to Russian interests and 55 per cent opposed a visa waiver programme involving both countries.[71]

It is always hard to judge the reliability of Russian opinion polls, but these results could be interpreted as, yes, they see China as a development partner, but the Chinese have to be kept at arm's length and not engage in any unsavoury activities while in Russia. There is also a common enemy, the US, the hatred for which serves to combine the interests of local Russians, or Russians anywhere, and the Chinese.[72]

But whether the Russians like it or not, the Chinese are in the Far East to stay—and the resource-rich region forms a vital part of Xi's BRI and, especially, the curiously named 'Polar Silk Road'. A major obstacle for implementing this grand scheme is that China and Russia have fundamentally different interpretations of what it actually means. Russia is looking for Chinese capital investment in the Far East to build plants where the area's natural resources can be processed and, in that way, re-establish and even expand the area's industrial base that fell apart after the collapse of the Soviet Union. The Chinese, on the other hand, are focused on infrastructural projects useful for importing the same natural resources.[73]

According to Gaye Christoffersen at Johns Hopkins University: 'Later, China insisted, as a Near-Arctic state, on equal partnership in developing the Northern Sea Route, while Russia demanded respect for its sovereignty and rejected China's Arctic claims.'[74] China's interest is solely in securing transportation routes and access to natural resources wherever those can be found, and that, not development aid, was the thought behind the Chinese vision of a trade route connecting China with Europe through the Arctic Ocean.

Ports and other facilities along that route would be high on the list of priorities, not, as Putin envisaged, investment in the construction of processing plants in the Russian Far East that would help develop the region and provide jobs for the local population. When Putin and Xi issued a joint declaration in Moscow on 21 March 2023, Putin's interpretation of the agreement was that China would invest in metallurgical, machinery and pipeline projects in the Far East.[75]

According to Jeff Pao, an independent writer for the Asia Times: 'While state media highlighted China's interests in the Far East plan, many Chinese commentators poured cold water on the agreement, both by warning of the regulatory and investment risks in Russia and calling for the resolution of sovereignty disputes before committing capital to the region.'[76]

It is also unclear how accurate the official figures on Chinese investment in the Far East actually are. Do they represent actual investment or only commitments that may or may not be fulfilled? Or are they little more than wishful thinking on the part of the Russians? Russian Prime Minister Mikhail Mishustin has long been promoting a plan to have the Chinese invest US$165 billion in seventy-nine identified projects in energy, mining and agriculture in the Far East. He proudly announced that all those projects had been confirmed in an online meeting with his Chinese counterpart Li Keqiang on 5 December 2022. But the official statement issued by the Chinese on 7th December did not mention anything of that sort.[77] In December 2022, the Russian media outlet Ng.ru reported that Moscow has plans to set up 'a special economic region in the Far East covering an area of 6.96 million square kilometres exclusively for Chinese investments.'[78] If that were really true, the entire Far Eastern Federal District with its 6,952, 600 square kilometres would become what the website called a 'special economic region' for the Chinese.

Russia's war against Ukraine has also complicated matters. *The Diplomat* reported only a few months after Putin sent his troops into Ukraine that any plans to develop the so-called 'Polar Silk Road' have been downgraded and that is because 'Beijing has been trying, under complex circumstances, to maintain a "Goldilocks" policy toward Moscow since the start of the conflict. Beijing has refused to condemn the Ukraine invasion or to join in sanctions against the Putin regime,' but even if it has exported drones and possibly other military equipment to Russia, it has also cautiously sought to avoid being seen as too close to Moscow. The main concern is that extensive military sales to Russia 'would irreparably damage Sino-European relations and leave Chinese firms open to the same Western economic punishments currently being inflicted on the Russian economy.'[79]

That balancing act, *The Diplomat* concluded, 'has manifested itself in the Arctic in the form [of] a considerable slowdown of Sino-Russian activities in the region.'[80] This cooperation had already been affected by the pandemic, but since the Ukraine conflict, China has continued to purchase Russian oil at a steady rate, while backing away from other areas of bilateral cooperation: 'Work by Chinese firms on the Arctic LNG 2 project in Siberia has been affected by concerns about European Union sanctions, including the shipping of modules to Russia in relation to the project, which have also been delayed due to concerns about violation of EU sanction rules. The Chinese shipping firm COSCO, which previously had been an enthusiastic supporter of the opening of the [Polar Silk Road] for increased Arctic sea trade, has shown no signs of wanting its vessels to use the route this year.'[81]

So what remains of the 'Polar Silk Road'? Surprisingly, little. The war in Ukraine has also had a devastating impact on some of the indigenous communities east of the Urals. When Putin, on 21 September 2022, announced his 'partial mobilization order', a disproportionally high number of recruits were drawn from impoverished regions and ethnic minorities. Many came from Buryatia, a Russian republic north of Mongolia where the population is Mongol and Buddhist, and Tuva, another Mongol-Buddhist republic in the east. Al Jazeera interviewed Victoria Maladaeva, vice president of the Free Buryatia Foundation, who said: 'The chances of a Buryat dying in the war in Ukraine is 7.8 times higher than [an ethnic] Russian; a Tuvan is 10.4 times more likely.'[82] Dagestan, a predominantly Muslim republic near Georgia, has also seen many of its young men be sent to war and returned in coffins.

Websites have appeared calling for Buryatia to break away from the Russian Federation and become independent. That may never happen, but the Ukraine war has caused the Russian Federation—or the proposed rebirth of the Russian empire Putin wants to see—to shake in its foundations. The Far East may still be overwhelmingly ethnic Russian, but even that is nothing that can be taken for granted. The Russians there are often called 'flowers without roots' because all of them have an ancestral hometown or village in European Russia.[83] The Russians came to the Far East voluntarily as settlers or forcibly as convicts—and now many of their descendants are moving back to the west.

The early, wild days of the Huaqiao may be more or less over as local and cross-border trade has become more regulated. Business opportunities still abound, but not quite so much as they did a few decades ago. Now, the 'Polar Silk Road' may also have lost its appeal and got stuck in the ice of the Arctic Ocean. The grand plans of the 2010s are likely to be replaced by a diminished, localized BRI. The Chinese will concentrate on resource extraction and some infrastructural programmes in the immediate border areas, which, in their view, are in any case lands that were lost to a Western imperial power in the nineteenth century.

Optimists and Putin-supporters may dismiss the fears of a 'Chinese takeover' as a myth, but the reality is that the Chinese are already well-entrenched in the Russian Far East and no economic activity, let alone development, can happen there without them taking on a leading role. Beijing, not Moscow, has become the de facto 'Ruler of the East'. In the not-too-distant future, Vladivostok may be known as Haishenwai even outside China. Or maybe not. But that is what many Russians fear and, perhaps, what many Chinese would like to happen.

3

THE GREAT GOLDEN PENINSULA

DURING THE INDOCHINA WARS IN THE 1960s AND 1970s, Washington's security planners talked about what they termed 'the domino theory'; if communism was not stopped in south Vietnam, it would spread from the Soviet Union through China and north Vietnam to Southeast Asia and even as far as Australia and the Pacific. The countries would fall, one after another, like domino bricks on a gaming table.

But that thinking did not take into account the rivalry between the two Communist giants, the Soviet Union and China. Centuries of mutual animosity between the Vietnamese and the Chinese was also overlooked. The West only came to realize what should have been obvious when Soviet-allied Vietnam, now reunified, invaded Cambodia and overthrew the Chinese-allied Khmer Rouge regime in Phnom Penh in January 1979. Mao Zedong's chief strategist, Kang Sheng, argued that the north Vietnamese leadership and the National Liberation Front in the south were too close to Moscow to be trusted.[1]

Kang's plan was to spread revolution to the region through the Communist Party of Burma (CPB), and then down the areas of operation of the Communist Party of Thailand (CPT), the Communist Party of Malaya (CPM), the Communist Party of North Kalimantan in Sarawak and Sabah (the communists did not recognize Malaysia, which they considered a colonial creation), and PKI, the powerful Partai Komunis Indonesia. Unlike the Vietnamese communists, the leaders of those communist parties were loyal to Beijing. The plan, absurd as it may seem, also included the Communist Party of Australia (Marxist-Leninist), a tiny group of Australian Maoists.

It was hardly surprising that, given the weakness of all those Maoist parties, the plan did not materialize, and Kang himself died of bladder cancer in December 1975. Considered one of the most radical—and evil—of China's early communist leaders, he fell into disgrace when Deng Xiaoping and his reform-minded faction in the communist party rose to power in the late 1970s. According to authors John Byron and Robert Pack: 'In the course of a secret 1978 speech condemning Kang Sheng, Hu Yaobang [then head of the party's organizational department] had compared Kang to Feliks Dzerzhinsky [first head of Lenin's ruthless secret police] and to the callous murderer who followed in Dzerzhinski's footsteps, Lavrentiy Beria. It was an assessment shared by a majority of informed Chinese.'[2]

But all that does not mean that Myanmar has lost its importance for China as a conduit to the rest of southern and southeastern Asia. The difference is that, in the past, China exported revolution. Now it exports consumer goods, and in order to do that and expand, China needs access to Indian Ocean ports in order to avoid the established routes through the contested South China Sea and the congested and potentially vulnerable Strait of Malacca, which could easily be blocked in case of a regional conflict.

Darshana M. Baruah from the Carnegie Endowment for International Peace argued in an 18 April 2023 testimony for the US House of Representatives Foreign Affairs Committee on the Indo-Pacific: 'Nine of China's top ten crude oil suppliers transit the Indian Ocean. The Indian Ocean is also the primary theater of transit for China for engagements with Africa, Middle East, island nations, and littorals across the vast ocean. Going beyond, it is also the main trading route between China and Europe.'[3]

There are only three countries that border China that could serve as such an outlet for China's exports—and, at the same time, as an inlet for oil from the Middle East and minerals from Africa: Myanmar, India and

Pakistan. The Chinese have already built a highway down to Nathu La on the border with the Indian state of Sikkim, but it is highly unlikely that India would allow its northern neighbour—a regional rival and in many ways a bitter enemy—to extend lines of communications through Sikkim and West Bengal down to the port of Kolkata.

Pakistan is a possibility as a country that has had a military and political relationship with China for decades. As early as 1959, the two countries began building a highway over the Karakoram mountains, connecting Xinjiang in westernmost China with the Pakistani lowlands. It was completed and opened for traffic in 1979 and, strategically and economically, it is an important route as the establishment of the China–Pakistan Economic Corridor (CPEC) shows. This bilateral project was launched on 20 April 2015, when Xi Jinping and Pakistan's then Prime Minister Nawaz Sharif signed no less than fifty-one agreements and memorandums of understanding valued at US$46 billion.[4] The infrastructural project includes road and rail networks down to the Indian Ocean ports of Gwadar and Karachi.

But there are problems as well. Xinjiang is far from China's industrial centres and the Karakoram Highway climbs up to 4,714 metres above sea level and is, in winter, often blocked by snow and ice. It is considered one of the most dangerous highways in the world; Pakistan's chronic political instability is another factor making the CPEC a hazardous route for trade of any substantial volume.

Impoverished and conflict-stricken Myanmar is, after all, the best of the three options that China has. Myanmar may be even more unstable than Pakistan, but the weaknesses of these two nations are widely different. Pakistan is unstable at the centre, governments come and go and there is always the possibility of yet another coup launched by the country's powerful military. Myanmar, on the other hand, has always been remarkably stable at the centre where the military or military-controlled governments have been in power since 1962. The unrest has been in the frontier areas where China maintains links with several ethnic rebel armies and, therefore, can exercise considerable influence over the activities, violent and otherwise, of those groups.

Wholly in line with Deng Xiaoping's market-oriented reforms in the post-Mao Zedong era, the thought of replacing the old revolutionary highway south with new, commercial trade routes was first presented by Pan Qi, a former vice minister of communications, in an article for the 2 September 1985 issue of the official weekly *Beijing Review*.[5] He argued several decades before the China–Myanmar Economic Corridor (CMEC) was established in 2018 that China would have to find an outlet for trade for the landlocked south-western provinces of Yunnan, Sichuan and Guizhou, with a combined population of 160 million people. Myanmar was the obvious answer, and the article mentioned, as possible routes for Chinese exports, railways from Lashio and Myitkyina close to the Chinese border in north-eastern and northern Myanmar respectively, and the Irrawaddy river, which runs from the north to the south of Myanmar and into the Indian Ocean.

Pan Qi did not, however, mention that various rebel groups at that time controlled almost the entire length of the 2,129-kilometre border between China and Myanmar: the Kachin Independence Army (KIA) in the north and the CPB in the northeast. But all that changed in the late 1980s and early 1990s. The Myanmar communists went underground and resorted to armed struggle against the government shortly after Myanmar's independence from Britain in 1948—and for a while overran large areas of central, southern and north-western parts of the country.

At the same time, ethnic Karen, Mon, Karenni, Muslim and Arakanese rebels rose up to fight for independence from the new Union, which, at least in theory, was federal in order to satisfy the demands and interests of the country's many ethnic minorities. Between 60 and 70 per cent of Myanmar's fifty-three million inhabitants are Bamars, or Burmans, and 30 to 40 per cent belong to various other ethnic groups. When the then military government changed the official name of the country from 'Burma' to 'Myanmar' the argument was that 'Burma' was a colonial name, while 'Myanmar' was a more indigenous one that included all 135 'national races' of the country, the Bamars being one of them.

But it was not the British who named Myanmar Burma. The once British colony has always been called Burma in English and 'bama' or 'myanma' in Burmese. The best explanation of the difference between bama and myanma is to be found in the old Hobson-Jobson dictionary, which, despite its rather unorthodox name, remains a very useful source of information: 'The name (Burma) is taken from Mranma, the national name of the Burmese people, which they themselves generally pronounce Bamma, unless speaking formally and empathically.'[6]

Both names have been used interchangeably throughout history, with Burma being the more colloquial name and Myanmar a more formal designation. If 'Burma' meant only the central plains and Myanmar the Bamars and 134 other nationalities, how could there be, according to the Myanmar Language Commission, a 'Myanmar language'? Clearly, Burma and Myanmar (and Burmese and Myanmar) mean exactly the same thing, and it cannot be argued that the term 'Myanmar' includes any more people within the present union than the name 'Burma' does, or that 'Burma' is a colonial one.

So the confusion is an old one and when the independence movement was established in the 1930s, there was a debate among the young nationalists as to what name should be used for the country: bama or myanma. The nationalists decided to call their movement the 'Dohbama Asiayone' (Our Burma Association), instead of the Dohmyanma Asiayone, and this was the reason: 'Since the *dohbama* was set up, the nationalists always paid attention to the unity of all the nationalities of the country ... and the *thakins* [the nationalists] noted that *myanma naingngan* [the *myanma* state] meant only the part of the country where the Burmans lived. This was the name given by the Burmese kings to their country. But this is not correct usage. *Bamanaingngan* is not the country where only the *myanma* people live. Many different nationalities live in this country, such as the Kachins, Karens, Kayahs, Chins, Pa-Os, Palaungs, Mons, Myamars, Rakhines and Shans. Therefore, the nationalists did not use the term *myanmanaingngan* but *bama naingngan*. That would be the correct term. There is no other term than *bama naingngan* or *bamapyi*. All nationalities who live in *Bamanaingngan* are called *bama*.'[7]

Thus, the movement became the Dohbama Asiayone and not the Dohmyanma Asiayone. Likewise, the Burmese edition of *The Guardian*

Monthly, another official publication, concluded in February 1971: 'The word *myanma* signifies only the *myanmars* whereas *bama* embraces all indigenous nationalities.'[8] In 1989, the ruling military decided that the opposite was correct, but the truth is that there is no term in any language which covers both the *bama/myanma* and the ethnic minorities since no such entity existed before the arrival of the British.[9]

And this is not merely a question of semantics. The country, with its present boundaries, is a creation of the British, and successive post-independence governments have inherited a chaotic entity that is still struggling to find a common identity—and where civil wars have been raging for more than seventy years. And China has all along been the only outside power that has managed to take full advantage of the armed rebellions, political as well as ethnic.

By the late 1950s, the central government had managed to reassert control over most of the country. The CPB had been pushed back into small pockets across central Myanmar with its headquarters in the Pegu Yoma mountains north of Yangon. The rebellion in Arakan, now Rakhine State, was more or less over, and the Karen and other ethnic insurgents in the east had lost most of the territory they had wrested control over after independence. But then, in 1958, the Shans rose in rebellion, followed by the Kachins in 1961. The wars were far from over, and they intensified in 1968, when heavily armed CPB fighters poured across the border with China at Mong Ko, a small town in nort-eastern Shan State—and that was part of Kang Sheng's plan.

When the CPB had been forced into defensive positions in the early 1950s, 143 Myanmar communists had trekked to China to look for help. They were well received by the Chinese and allowed to remain in Chengdu in Sichuan Province, where they were given political training. But no military aid was forthcoming at this time; the government in Beijing was not willing to antagonize the neutralist Myanmar government led by U Nu for the sake of a then relatively small group of Myanmar communists.

All that changed after Ne Win, an ambitious and unpredictable general seized power in Myanmar in March 1962. The CPB exiles in

Chengdu were introduced to a group of ethnic Kachin fighters, who were not communists but had retreated into China in 1950 to escape the onslaught of the Myanmar Army. Unlike the Myanmar communists, the Kachins had military experience, and they formed the nucleus of the group of fighters who crossed the border in 1968. But most soldiers in the new CPB army were actually Red Guard volunteers from China, and it was not until it had taken over Kokang and the Wa Hills along the Chinese border that the party was able to recruit indigenous fighters. Kokang is an area inside Myanmar's Shan State populated by ethnic Chinese and Wa hill tribesmen, who were headhunters well into the 1970s.

By 1973, the CPB had wrested control over a 20,000-square-kilometre large area along the Myanmar–China frontier, from Panghsai in the north, near Ruili in Yunnan and down to the Mekong river, which forms the border with Laos.

China provided the CPB with assault rifles, machine guns, rocket launchers, anti-aircraft guns, radio equipment, jeeps, trucks and petrol. Even rice, other food supplies, cooking oil and kitchen utensils were sent across the frontier into the new revolutionary base area that the CPB had established. The Chinese also built hydroelectric power stations inside this area and provided the CPB with a clandestine radio station, *The People's Voice of Burma*. Thai and Indonesian communists were also present at the headquarters of the 'new' CPB established at Panghsang, a town in the Wa area right on the Chinese border.

However, the plan was not to stay in the border mountains. The new base areas there were seen only as springboards from where the China-supported CPB would push down to the Pegu Yoma and other footholds in central Myanmar, where the 'old' communist forces were still holding out, and the future of the party, if any, would be. The Myanmar military, though, soon realized what was happening—and that it would not be possible to defeat the well-equipped CPB forces in the northeast. The government's strategy was to hold on to its positions along the front in the north-east—and to wipe out the old CPB stronghold in the centre. Those communist forces had never benefited from Chinese aid, and were armed mainly with guns left over from World War II and assorted weapons they had managed to capture from Myanmar's army and police.

In early 1975, the Myanmar Army launched a major offensive in the Pegu Yoma, which was captured and, by 1979, all remaining CPB camps and base areas in central Myanmar had been overrun. The Myanmar Army had managed to contain the CPB in Kokang, the Wa Hills and other remote mountain areas along the Chinese border, where the CPB did not belong and had never intended to stay. Kang Sheng's plan to spread revolution to Myanmar and beyond had failed.

But this also meant unforeseen complications for the diehard Maoist, mainly Burman, leadership of the party. To them, the Wa and other hill tribe recruits, who made up the bulk of the CPB's army, were only disposable cannon fodder—and they were treated as such. The fighting had taken its toll on the hill tribe communities. Thousands of young men and even boys had died in the war, and the survivors were tired of fighting for an ideology of which they had little or no understanding. Discontent was growing among the rank-and-file and their families.

There were also problems with the CPB's backers in China. Inspired by the Cultural Revolution, the CPB had had its own purge of 'revisionists' in the Pegu Yoma. Two leading members of the party, yebaw (comrade) Htay and Hemendranath Ghoshal, were called 'Myanmar's Deng Xiaoping' and 'Myanmar's Liu Shaoqi' respectively—and brutally beaten to death. This was remembered when Deng reasserted power in Beijing in the late 1970s. Then came the economic reforms in China, and an entirely new brand of foreign policy. Chinese support to the CPB was significantly reduced. It was not completely cut off, but it was curtailed enough for the Wa people in Kokang and elsewhere in the CPB's north-eastern base area to notice that something had changed.[10]

On the night between 16 and 17 April 1989, Wa mutineers stormed the quarters at the Panghsang where the top leadership was staying. The CPB's ageing, staunchly Maoist leaders, nearly all of them Burmans, fled across the nearby Nam Hka river, which forms the border with China. There, Chinese trucks were waiting for them, and they were sent off into retirement in Kunming and other cities in Yunnan. They were provided with new housing and pensions, but told that they could no longer engage in any political activity.

For the first time in history, a communist insurgency had been defeated from within its own ranks. Although it has never been acknowledged officially by any of the leaders of the mutiny or former CPB cadres, it is widely assumed that China had a hand in the events of April 1989.[11] Over the years since the death of Mao in 1976, the CPB had become increasingly anachronistic and the Chinese needed new partners in the rebel-held areas of Myanmar.

The former CPB army split up into four different forces based along ethnic lines. The United Wa State Army (UWSA) became by far the largest in terms of the number of soldiers and the size of the area under its control. Mutineers in Kokang north of the Wa Hills formed the Myanmar National Democratic Alliance Army (MNDAA) and a group with a similar same, National Democratic Alliance Army (NDAA), was set up along the Chinese border east of the UWSA-controlled area. In the small area that the CPB had controlled adjacent to the Chinese border in Kachin State, local forces formed the New Democratic Army-Kachin (NDA-K).

Although all four of them had distanced themselves from communist ideology, they did not ally themselves with Myanmar's other, many ethnic resistance armies. Instead, they entered into ceasefire agreements with Myanmar's military. In exchange for not fighting the central government, they were allowed to retain their armies and control of their respective areas—and to engage in any kind of trade to sustain themselves.

The only valuable commodity in those former CPB areas at that time was opium. In the late 1980s, Myanmar's opium production more than doubled as a result of the ceasefire agreements with the former CPB forces. According to the US government, the 1987 opium harvest of Myanmar yielded 836 tonnes of raw opium; by 1993, production had increased to 2,575 tonnes.[12] Furthermore, the ceasefire agreements with the Myanmar military enabled the former CPB forces to bring in chemicals, mainly acetic anhydride—which is needed to convert raw opium into heroin—by truck from India and China. Within a few years after the CPB mutiny, intelligence sources were able to locate twenty-five new heroin laboratories in the areas controlled by the MNDAA, UWSA and NDAA. In the NDA-K area, the forests were cut down and sold as timber to China.

Entirely new organizational structures and boom towns rose from the ashes of the CPB. In Mong La—the first such economic metropolis and the site for the headquarters of the NDAA—the proceeds from the trade were invested in casinos, hotels, karaoke bars, brothels and even a venue that sported shows with transvestites brought in from Thailand. There was also, incredibly, a 'drug eradication museum'. Officially, the NDAA was in charge of an anti-drug campaign in this area, and began receiving delegations from various United Nations agencies, including personnel in charge of its drug control programme. Post-mutiny, the town also received thousands of tourists from China, who came across the border in chartered buses.

Before long, the old communist headquarters Panghsang was also transformed into a bustling town of some 25,000 residents, with modern buildings and paved roads. And, of course, karaoke bars, discos and shady establishments where commercial sex was available. Panghsang has its own Wa-run bank, administrative offices, schools, hospitals, courts and prisons. No doubt the ousted Burman communist ideologues who once ruled Panghsang would turn in their graves if they could see what had become of their old headquarters, from where they tried to launch a proletarian revolution in Myanmar.

The UWSA and the other groups had enough money to finance this remarkable transformation of the former CPB area, but not the vocational skills that were needed to build houses in the new cities and towns that sprung up in the 1990s or the roads between them. Construction material was needed too, and someone had to provide electricity in an area where there had been none. All this was done by Chinese contractors who also employed Chinese labourers and craftsmen. Without Chinese participation, it would not have been possible to bring modern development to the hills of north-eastern Myanmar. Not surprisingly, the Chinese yuan became the preferred currency in those areas, and mobile phones are connected to Chinese networks, as is the internet.

The UWSA has also become stronger and better equipped than the CPB ever was—and its guns and other supplies have been obtained from China. These include the latest models of Chinese-manufactured automatic assault rifles, man-portable air defence systems (MANPADS), rocket-propelled grenade launchers, truck-mounted heavy machine guns, 122mm howitzers, 107mm surface-to-surface free-flight missiles, Xinxing ('New Star') wheeled armoured personnel carriers and even weaponized drones.[13] It is uncertain how much of the UWSA's arsenal are gifts rather than purchases, but the volume and the kind of weaponry that has been supplied clearly shows that the decision to arm the Wa was taken by security planners in Beijing, not some local arms dealers in Yunnan.

At the same time, the UWSA's ceasefire agreement with the Myanmar military seems to be holding, which seems to indicate that the Chinese—whose decisions matter in this context—do not want the Wa to fight, but to be strong enough to deter the government's forces from launching any attacks on the Wa-controlled area on the border. Such a war would create instability and, most likely, an undesirable flow of refugees into Chinese territory.

The UWSA has also established a new base area on the Thai border after defeating the Möng Tai Army of Khun Sa, a notorious drug lord who eventually surrendered to the Myanmar authorities. The Shan people, who had lived there before the Wa arrived, fled to Thailand, where most of them still reside. The exact strength of the UWSA is a well-kept secret, but it is believed to be at least 30,000 plus local militia forces, which could be mobilized in case of an emergency.

A strong and well-equipped UWSA gives the Chinese leverage when they have to negotiate deals with the Myanmar government. This became evident when Aung Min, then minister of the Myanmar President's office, visited Monywa, a town north-west of Mandalay, in November 2012. He was there to meet local people protesting a controversial Chinese-backed copper mining project in the area, and openly declared: 'We are afraid of China ... We don't dare to have a row with [them]. If they feel annoyed with the shutdown of their projects and resume support to the communists, the economy in the border areas would backslide. So you'd better think seriously.'[14]

By 'the communists' he clearly meant the UWSA and its allies. And the UWSA's allies include a number of ethnic armies that comprise not only former CPB forces like the MNDAA, the NDAA and the NDA-K (before it fell apart due to infighting in the early 2000s) but also the old Shan State Army (SSA; formed in 1964) and newly established armies such as the Ta'ang National Liberation Army (TNLA), an ethnic Palaung force in northern Shan State and the Arakan Army (AA) in Rakhine State. And, unlike the UWSA, the SSA, the TNLA, the AA, and in recent years the MNDAA as well, have been and are still engaging in heavy fighting with the Myanmar Army. And that gives China another role in Myanmar's civil wars: that of a peacemaker, as no other outside player has the kind of influence China exercises over Myanmar's ethnic armies and can negotiate with them.

It should not be forgotten that China at the same time maintains close relations with Myanmar's military as well as governmental central authorities. Support for the UWSA and its allies serves as a 'stick' in Beijing's relationship with Myanmar, while diplomacy, peacemaking and promises of aid and investment are the 'carrot'. China is also a major supplier of arms to the Myanmar military. After the Myanmar military had crushed a nationwide uprising for democracy in August–September 1988, the US, the European Union, Australia and even Japan had imposed sanctions and boycotts on Myanmar, but China blocked any attempt to have the United Nations Security Council take action against the junta that seized power on 18 September 1988. When Western nations stopped trading with Myanmar, the Chinese border remained wide open. From the late 1980s to the mid-1990s, China exported an estimated US$1.2 billion worth of armaments to Myanmar, ranging from battle tanks, heavy artillery and surface-to-air missiles to defence radars, jet fighters, transport aircraft, frigates and patrol boats.[15] Without all that assistance, combined with the China trade, the Myanmar junta would probably not have survived.

China's long-term goal is, of course, to yield influence over the Myanmar government and exercise enough control of the ethnic resistance in order to enable China to maintain and strengthen its economic corridor from Yunnan down to the Bay of Bengal. The Chinese are not interested in a final, peaceful solution to Myanmar's internal problems, and they do not want chaos either; only a certain degree of instability, which they can manipulate to their advantage.

A problem for the Chinese, though, was the UWSA's involvement in the narcotics trade, first opium and heroin and then synthetic drugs like methamphetamine. Those drugs found a ready market not only in Thailand, Laos, Vietnam, Cambodia and Northeast India but also in China. In 2010, China had 1,545,000 registered drug users with 1,065,000 of those addicted to heroin from Myanmar. The number of known drug addicts in China in 2016 was more than 2.5 million, of whom as many as 1.5 million were using synthetic drugs, not heroin. Wa leaders as well as MNDAA and NDAA officials were summoned to Kunming and read the riot act.

The US has also highlighted the UWSA's involvement in the drug trade. On January 2005, Rosalynn R. Mauskopf, US attorney for the eastern district of New York, and Anthony P. Placido, the special-agent-in-charge for the New York field division of the Drug Enforcement Administration (DEA), announced the unsealing of an indictment against eight high-ranking UWSA leaders on drug-trafficking-related charges. On the list were five Wa: UWSA commander Bao Youxiang and his brothers Bao Youri, Bao Youliang and Bao Youhua, and Bao Huachiang, an unrelated Wa officer—and three ethnic Chinese Wei brothers: Wei Xuegang, Wei Xuelong and Wei Xueyin.[16] Wei Xuegang was a notorious drug lord who had established a close relationship with the UWSA. There was also an additional sealed list with names of thirteen people with UWSA connections who had also been indicted, twelve of whom were Sino-Bamar and Sino-Thais who were new on the scene. The thirteenth name was Li Ziru, one of the Red Guard volunteers from China who had joined the CPB in the late 1960s.[17] He, however, died in late 2005.

Thus, the DEA lists revealed an important feature in drug production under the aegis of the UWSA. Although the four Bao brothers and Bao Huachiang were on the unsealed list, the trade was, in fact, run by well-connected ethnic Chinese drug lords. The UWSA provided them with protection and a safe area where they could run their heroin laboratories in exchange for taxes and other revenues. The Wa did not have the necessary connections to run a worldwide drug network stretching to the streets of New York, Sydney or Vancouver, where heroin manufactured in the UWSA area was available for sale.

The initial capital for the economic development of the Wa Hills undoubtedly consisted of revenues from the drug trade, but, over the past decade, the Wa economy has become diversified and includes income from tin mining and investments in commercial enterprises in Myanmar, China and Thailand, such as construction companies, import-export businesses and real estate dealings. Poppy fields have given way to rubber plantations and tea gardens. But it is a capitalism with many distinctly Chinese characteristics, as researcher Hans Steinmüller points out in a study: 'The kind of authoritarian capitalism that has developed in the Wa State has similar affects as in China. Even though relative inequality has risen exponentially, living standards are higher and absolute poverty is lower than in the past.'[18]

Tin exports became the first major alternative to drugs. As researcher Seamus Martov wrote in The Irrawaddy in 2016, a new tin mining operation located in the UWSA-controlled area 'appears to be responsible for elevating Burma [Myanmar] in just a few years from being a bit player in the global tin industry "to the status of the World's third largest tin producing country."'[19] Quoting a report published by the UK-based International Tin Research Institute, Martov writes that there was a 4,900 per cent increase in Myanmar's tin production over a five-year period, from 2009 to 2014, which is 'a development completely unforeseen by commodity analysts and one that has had significant ramifications for the tin industry worldwide.' Needless to say, the tin was exported solely to China and, as Martov states, thanks to tin concentrate imports from

UWSA-held territory, 'China for the first time in six years also became a net exporter of refined tin in 2014.'[20]

In more recent years, rare earth mining has become big business in areas which are not controlled by the Myanmar government. A huge mine at Pangwa in an area controlled by the former NDA-K has attracted media attention, and, as Radio Free Asia reported in August 2023: 'An increase in the illegal mining of rare earth metals in northern Myanmar is being driven by demand from neighboring China for terbium and dysprosium—elements that are used in the production of electric vehicles … In the first six months of 2023, the value of rare earth minerals exported from Myanmar to China reached nearly US$773 million, according to Chinese customs data.'[21] Reports also suggests that there is extensive rare earth mining in the area controlled by the UWSA as well, but, when asked, the Wa leadership would neither confirm nor deny that this is happening.[22]

China's involvement with the former CPB forces in the north and north-east is, of course, not officially part of the BRI. But seen in the broader perspective, it plays a vital role in Beijing's 'carrot-and-stick' policy. In 2018, Myanmar signed a memorandum of understanding on the BRI and the CMEC became the flagship project under that framework.[23] The most important BRI projects in Myanmar are a deep-sea port with a special economic zone at Kyaukphyu on the coast in Rakhine State, gas and oil pipelines from there to Yunnan—and a planned network of highways and high-speed railways connecting Kyaukphyu with China's own infrastructure. Other special economic zones were also set up, and Chinese companies became involved in building what is called New Yangon City, an entirely new locality opposite the old capital Yangon, which still serves as the country's commercial centre. In other words: projects from which China, rather than the general population, would benefit.

And those projects are not gifts; Myanmar has become heavily in debt to China. In 2020, Myanmar's auditor general, Maw Than, said in news conference in the capital Naypyitaw that the country's debt at the time stood at about US$10 billion, of which US$4 billion was owed to China. 'The truth is the loans from China come at higher interest rates compared to loans from financial institutions like the World Bank or the IMF [International Monetary Fund],' Maw Than said. 'So, I would like to remind the government ministries to be more restrained in using Chinese loans.'[24] The danger is real and could push Myanmar into a debt trap like that of Sri Lanka, Pakistan and several African nations.

It is worth noting that the memorandum of understanding was signed when pro-democracy leader Aung San Suu Kyi was state counsellor, or de facto Prime Minister, which goes to show that the Chinese would be willing to deal with whoever is in power in Myanmar. They may prefer an authoritarian, military-dominated regime to a democratic one, but a popularly elected government can also be a partner as long as it does not endanger China's long-term plans. The Aung San Suu Kyi government assumed office in April 2016, after an election had been held in November 2015. Her largely civilian government lasted until the military stepped in and arrested her and her cabinet on 1 February 2021. A junta called the State Administration Council (SAC) took over and Myanmar was once again ruled by a military dictatorship. Thousands of opponents to the new regime were thrown in jail, where many of them were tortured. And, on 25 July 2022, four pro-democracy activists were executed by hanging for their anti-coup activities. Many more, no one knows exactly how many, died in jail or were extrajudicially executed after they had been apprehended by the military.

Atrocities committed by the SAC have also been tied to BRI projects. In order to 'clear' the border areas for trade, the Myanmar military has forcibly evicted villagers from their homes while those living close to, or in, rebel-held areas have been subjected to attacks from the air. A Kachin women's NGO in a report titled 'Bloodstained Gateways' urged China to stop pushing ahead with its BRI projects in Myanmar 'as they are fuelling conflict and abuses. These projects should be cancelled, and no new investments considered until the military regime is removed and elections held under a new federal democratic constitution, guaranteeing free, prior and informed consent of local communities to any new projects.'[25]

But it is unlikely that there will be any such suspension. Myanmar remains the strategically most important part of BRI in Southeast Asia, perhaps in all of Asia, because it connects China with the Indian Ocean. However, China has also extended its reach to other Southeast Asian countries. One of them is Laos, which shares a 505-kilometre border with China. Laos was a supposedly neutral kingdom during the Indochina wars in the 1950s, 1960s and 1970s. But that neutrality was violated by north Vietnam, which sent guns and other military hardware down the so-called Ho Chi Minh Trail, which went through Laos down to south Vietnam, where resistance forces were fighting the government in Saigon and the US forces.

The Americans, who had pledged to respect Laos' neutrality, bombed the trail and fought a proxy war, using a hill tribe army to combat the north Vietnamese as well as the communist *Pathet Lao* ('the Lao Nation'), which had bases in the mountains in the north-east. The war ended on 2 December 1975, when the Pathet Lao seized power in the capital Vientiane, abolished the monarchy and proclaimed a communist state, the Lao People's Democratic Republic.

The takeover was peaceful and a far cry from when the Khmer Rouge marched into the capital Phnom Penh on 17 April 1975, executed 'traitors' and emptied the entire population of the city. Or when communists took over Saigon on 30th April. No shots were fired in Saigon that day, but the takeover was, to say the least, dramatic—with helicopters evacuating the Americans, who were there along with the south Vietnamese, who feared the communists, followed by north Vietnamese tanks rolling into the city and taking up positions around the presidential palace and other government buildings. In Vientiane, there were no such scenes. But even if the change of governments was entirely peaceful, the new order led to the introduction of a totalitarian one-party state under the Lao People's Revolutionary Party (LPRP).

The new communist government in Vientiane had close relations with Vietnam as well as China, but during the Sino-Soviet conflict it tended to side with Moscow and Hanoi. When that conflict was over in the 1990s, and China as well as Vietnam had abandoned their former, austere socialist systems in favour of capitalism, even Laos started to embrace free-market reforms. The LPRP remained in power, but it was now free to establish closer relations with its northern neighbour.

Chinese businessmen began to flock to the country, which became flooded with consumer goods from China. But those goods were meant not only for the relatively limited market in Laos, a poor country with 7.4 million people, most of whom are farmers. Instead, Laos became China's gateway to Thailand and beyond, and that was why the most important BRI project in Laos was the construction of a high-speed railway from Yunnan to Vientiane. The railway, opened in December 2021, is only the beginning of a massive infrastructure drive that aims to transform all of Southeast Asia. If all goes to plan, the railway will continue from Vientiane across a new bridge on the Mekong river to Nong Khai in Thailand and then, eventually, all the way down to Singapore.

As the Czech-based European Values Center for Security Policy reported in October 2023, Laos had 'hoped that the "Iron River"—a Lao monicker for the railroad—would transform the country from "landlocked" to "land-linked", attracting foreign investment and enhancing tourism, logistics, and people-to-people exchanges. For Laos, the railway is undoubtedly an essential step towards its people's economic development and welfare.'[26]

But that has come at a heavy price. Around US$3.6 billion of the railway's total cost of US$5.97 billion has been financed by a loan from the Export-Import Bank of China and the remainder by the Lao-China Railway Company, which comprises three Chinese state-owned firms holding 70 per cent and a Lao state enterprise holding the remaining 30 per cent. But even the Lao share of the project expense is covered in part by loans from China—and that as Laos' US$20 billion economy is weighed down by an estimated US$12.6 billion in foreign debt, including the US$5.97 billion owed to China for the construction of the railway and related projects.[27]

It is uncertain how Laos will get out of its predicament, but an indication of what can be expected came as early as March 2021. The government in Vientiane signed a twenty-five-year concession agreement with a majority-owned Chinese company, Électricité du Laos

Transmission Company Limited (EDLT), that allows it to build and manage large parts of the country's power grid for a period of twenty-five years, after which the operation will be ceded to the Lao authorities.[28]

EDLT was created in 2020 as a joint venture between the Lao state power company, Électricité du Laos, and the China Southern Power Grid Company, in which the latter holds the most shares. EDLT was formed after the Lao government found itself swamped by rising debt levels amid the economic downturn of the Covid-19 pandemic. Now it will be even worse—and Laos has lost control of its electric power grids.

As Brad Parks of AidData, a research entity at William & Mary, which tracks China's lending, told *The Washington Post* in October 2023: 'There is no country in the world with a higher amount of debt exposure to China than Laos. It is a very, very extreme example. Laos went on a borrowing spree and got in over its head.'[29] Moreover, as *The Washington Post* reported, a Chinese company provides security for the high-speed railway, and, apart from being caught in a debt trap, 'Laos has had to make compromises, including on its own sovereignty, to appease Beijing and seek some financial forbearance, allowing Chinese security agents and police to operate in the country …'[30]

Cambodia, downstream the Mekong river from Laos, has also become what can be aptly described as a Chinese client state—and that is a remarkable transformation for a country whose then Prime Minister Hun Sen, in a 1988 essay, referred to China as 'the root of everything that is evil in Cambodia.'[31] China has emerged as a major donor to the country, and unlike aid from the West, Chinese assistance comes here, as elsewhere, with strings attached. China is also a major investor in Cambodia, mainly in the garment industry, but also in agriculture, mining, oil refining, metals production, hotels and tourism. Gone are the days when China supported Hun Sen's sworn enemy, the dreaded Maoist Khmer Rouge.

China was the main supporter of the Khmer Rouge when it was in power from 1975 to 1979 and then, until the mid-1990s, waged a guerrilla war against the regime that Vietnam had installed when the latter had invaded Cambodia in December 1978 and January 1979. The Khmer Rouge then fought a democratically elected coalition government, which assumed office following a United Nations-brokered peace treaty in the early 1990s. Hun Sen was seen as a puppet of Vietnam, and he missed no opportunity to lash out against China.

The situation began to change when Hun Sen ousted his then coalition partner, royalist leader Prince Norodom Ranariddh, in a June 1997 coup. Cambodia's Western donors were not amused: the US and Germany suspended non-humanitarian aid until free and fair elections were held. Japan, Cambodia's largest donor then said it would halt new projects.

But China came to the rescue. China was the first country to recognize the regime after the coup—and Hun Sen won praise from Beijing for shutting down and expelling Taiwan's liaison office in Phnom Penh. Hun Sen claimed that Taiwan had been covertly supporting Prince Ranariddh's political party, FUNCINPEC (the French acronym for the National United Front for an Independent, Neutral, Peaceful and Cooperative Cambodia). According to long-term Cambodia watcher Julio Jeldres: 'Hun Sen's actions opened the door for Chinese influence in Cambodia ... In December [1997] China delivered 116 military cargo trucks and seventy jeeps valued at US$2.8 million.'[32]

In February 1999, Hun Sen paid an official visit to China and obtained US$200 million in interest-free loans and US$18.3 million in foreign-assistance guarantees. And then Chinese investors, businessmen and other migrants arrived. Imports of Chinese-made consumer goods soared as roads were built linking Cambodia with China through Laos. As journalist David Hutt put it in a 2016 article for *The Diplomat*: 'Cambodia went from denouncing China to being Beijing's most faithful client state.'[33]

Over the decades since the early days of the newly established friendship between Beijing and Phnom Penh, China's political and economic influence has become even stronger—and the rulers of Cambodia more authoritarian. After suffering through war, Cambodia was meant to become a democracy, but the United Nations' plan for a bright future for the country was scuttled by Hun Sen. His Cambodian People's Party (CPP) was originally known as the Khmer People's Revolutionary

Party, and was a Soviet- and Vietnam-allied communist party. But when the peace deal was being brokered by the United Nations, it abandoned Marxism-Leninism and assumed its new name.

However, the CPP never gave up its authoritarian roots. After the 1997 coup, Cambodia was on the path towards a one-party state. Ranariddh and most of his men in FUNCINPEC went into exile, and Sam Rainsy, an activist and economist who became the next opponent to Hun Sen's regime, was forced to leave the country in 2005 and was sentenced in absentia to ten years in jail in 2010. In July 2013, King Norodom Sihamoni granted Sam Rainsy amnesty, and he returned to Cambodia where hundreds of thousands of his supporters waited along the roads.[34] In 2016, he was forced the leave the country again after being accused of defaming the Hun Sen government. He had accused it of having orchestrated the murder of Kem Ley, a political commentator and critic of Hun Sen.[35] Kem Sokha, an Opposition leader who remained in the country, was arrested in September 2017 and accused of committing treason against the nation. A year later, Kem Sokha was released on bail, but, in March 2023, he was convicted and sentenced to twenty-seven years of house arrest.[36]

The many NGOs that were formed during the United Nations intervention have been silenced and elections have become a farce there. The CPP won all 125 seats in the July 2018 election, and 120 in July 2023. In that most recent election, FUNCINPEC candidates managed to secure five seats, but their ability to manoeuvre is extremely limited. After that election, Hun Sen stepped down after thirty-eight years in power and his son Hun Manet, a general in the army, became the new Prime Minister.

Hun Manet was born in Khmer Rouge-ruled Cambodia in 1977 and grew up in Phnom Penh. He joined the resurrected Royal Cambodian Armed Forces in 1995 and, in the same year, entered the US Military Academy at West Point. Later, he received an MA in economics from the University of New York and a PhD in economics from the University of Bristol in the UK. In the military, he rose quickly through the ranks and became a lieutenant-general in 2013. In April 2023, three months before the election, he was promoted to a four-star general in what was seen as a final step before taking over as Prime Minister in August.

Despite his Western education, Hun Manet is not likely to stray away from the pro-Chinese policies laid down by his father. In October 2023, Hun Manet met Xi Jinping in Beijing for a BRI forum. He also met representatives of the China Machinery Engineering Corporation, China National Energy Engineering & Construction, the China Datang Corporation, Genertec International and the China Railway Construction Corporation, underscoring the importance that the Chinese placed on the visit.[37]

Cambodia has received billions of dollars in infrastructure funding from China, including a new airport at Siem Reap, the town closest to the Angkor Wat temples, the country's main tourist attraction. Roads, bridges, expressways, hydropower plants, seaports, airports and special economic zones have also been built. Hun Manet and his Chinese hosts have also discussed how to modernize Cambodia's old and rundown rail network and connecting it to Bavet on the border with Vietnam and with Siem Reap.[38] The stated aim of the BRI projects in Cambodia is to turn the country into a key hub for trade and connectivity in Southeast Asia.[39]

There is a darker side to Cambodia's seemingly blossoming relationship with China. Sihanoukville on the coast was until about a few decades ago a sleepy beach town catering mainly to Western backpackers. Now, high-rise buildings dominate Sihanoukville's skyline, and, as Matthias Alffram, a political science student at the University of Montreal, wrote in May 2022, the city has become 'the focus of Chinese foreign direct and private investment, led by real estate development and casino resort construction.'[40] The massive influx of Chinese capital has been 'accompanied by a wave of Chinese tourists, businessmen and workers. In 2017, Sihanoukville added 1,20,000 tourists and 78,000 permanent residents from China—unsettling numbers, given that the province's total population is only 1,50,000. This massive migration of Chinese nationals upended the economic and social fabric of the local communities, leading to negative impacts.'[41] The casino business especially has attracted a criminal clientele, which, in turn, has made corruption endemic in the city.

But more troubling from a geopolitical point of view, China has funded and actively participated in the modernization and upgrade of Cambodia's naval base at Ream on the Gulf of Thailand. In July 2019, *The Wall Street Journal* published a report saying that 'US officials'—presumably intelligence officers—had been shown a secret agreement that allowed access for Chinese troops, weapons and ships for thirty years and automatic renewal every ten years thereafter.[42] The hosting of any foreign armed forces would be against the Constitution of Cambodia as well as the 1991 Paris Peace Agreements, which paved the way for the United Nations to intervene.

The Cambodian government vehemently denied that there was such an agreement, but in 2021, Defence Minister Tea Banh admitted that China was helping build infrastructure at Ream—and continued to maintain that there were 'no strings attached.'[43] Be that as it may, suspicions remain and it is hardly any secret that China is seeking access, temporarily or permanently, to naval facilities in the Indian and Pacific oceans. In 2017, China established its so far only military base abroad—in Djibouti, on the Horn of Africa—and is currently looking for ports where its ships could, at least, dock and refuel.

The Vietnamese, with their long history of resistance against attempts by any Chinese empire to control them, have never been particularly enthusiastic about Xi's BRI. According to Murray Hiebert, an author and senior associate at the Washington-based Centre for Strategic and International Studies: 'Vietnam's praise for the BRI is primarily diplomatic posture to soothe China. Hanoi has no real interest in the BRI for infrastructure, although it accepts real estate and manufacturing investment from Chinese companies.'[44]

A historic visit by Xi to Vietnam in December 2023 was meant to improve relations between the two communist-ruled neighbours. The visit coincided with the fifteenth anniversary of the establishment of the Vietnam–China Comprehensive Strategic Partnership in 2008. Thirty-six documents on political exchanges, foreign policy, national defence and maritime cooperation were signed, and Nguyen Phu Trong, the secretary general of the Communist Party of Vietnam, assured China that its 'efforts to foster ties with other countries' reflect Hanoi's 'omnidirectional foreign policy.'[45]

What he was referring to was, of course, Vietnam's newfound friendship with its old adversary on the battlefield, the US. As long as the Soviet Union existed, Vietnam could rely on Moscow for support. China was the enemy, and, in March 1979, after Vietnam had intervened in Cambodia and forced the Khmer Rouge from power, Chinese troops launched an attack across the common border 'to teach Vietnam a lesson.'[46] In the end, it was Vietnam that taught China a lesson. Even though many of Vietnam's elite regiments were deployed in Cambodia, the Chinese troops did not manage to get very far into Vietnam. The Soviet Union did not come directly to Vietnam's defence, but instead deployed naval ships in the waters in the area and supplied the Vietnamese with material and intelligence.

The collapse of the Soviet Union in 1991 threw Vietnam into a crisis and the government in Hanoi had to look elsewhere for allies. After Vietnam had withdrawn its troops from Cambodia, it decided to make peace with its former enemies in Southeast Asia, who had backed the anti-Vietnamese resistance. In 1995, Vietnam, surprisingly—considering the history and political direction of the bloc—became the seventh member of the Association of Southeast Asian Nations (ASEAN). And, in the same year, Vietnam and the US established diplomatic relations.

In November 2000, US President Bill Clinton visited Vietnam, and George W. Bush followed in 2006. Barack Obama received a near-rock-star welcome when he arrived in Hanoi in May 2016, had noodles and drank beer in a local restaurant and held talks with government officials. Obama stated that 'as Vietnam has transformed, so has the relationship between our two nations. We learned a lesson taught by the venerable [Buddhist monk and teacher] Thich Nhat Hanh, who said, "In true dialogue, both sides are willing to change".'[47]

Putting aside the agreements Xi managed to sign during his visit to Hanoi, it was clear even then that the two countries do not see eye-to-eye on all issues. Xi wrote a commentary for Vietnam's *Nhan Dan* newspaper suggesting that China and Vietnam should build 'a community of common destiny'. The Vietnamese, on their part, mentioned 'a community of shared destiny'.[48]

Vietnam is also embroiled in two territorial disputes with China: the Spratly Islands and the Paracel Islands in the South China Sea. The Paracels, which are known as Hoang Sa in Vietnamese and Xisha in Chinese, were under French rule when they controlled the whole of Indochina, and were transferred to the non-communist government of south Vietnam when it was established in 1954. China occupied the islands in 1974 and built a military installation on Woody Island, one of the main islands in the Paracels, complete with an airfield and a harbour.[49] The south Vietnamese sent warships to the Paracels to expel the Chinese navy, but failed.

After the reunification of Vietnam in 1976, the government in Hanoi publicly renewed its claims to the Paracels—and praised the non-communist south Vietnamese forces, which took part in the battle in 1974.[50] Today, about a thousand Chinese settlers from the mainland live on the Paracels, the airport and the seaport have been upgraded, and a city hall, a post office, a hospital and a school have been built on Woody Island to solidify China's claim to the islands.

The Spratlys—known as Truong Sa in Vietnamese and Nansha in Chinese—are an entirely different story, because, historically, they were never inhabited nor actually controlled by any country. Japan had a presence on Taiping Island, which is also known as Itu Aba, until the end of World War II when it was taken over by the Republic of China. Taiping is the only one of the Spratlys that can actually be called an island, and Taiwan still controls it. The island has an airport, big enough to receive C-130 Hercules planes. The airport and other installations are protected by about 600 men from Taiwan's coast guard defence forces.

China and Taiwan claim the entirety of the Spratlys, as does Vietnam, while the Philippines, Malaysia and Brunei claim some of them.[51] The Chinese have mentioned the voyages of the fifteenth-century explorer Zheng He to justify their claims to the Spratly Islands.[52] He was supposed to have sailed past those islands and, therefore, the Chinese argument goes, they should belong to China. But that is a highly dubious claim to sovereignty. The detailed accounts and maps, which were compiled by Zheng He's aide Ma Huan, list more than 700 places in Southeast Asia and the Indian Ocean, including remote islands in the Andamans, the Nicobars, Maldives and Lakshadweep.[53]

Chinese cartographers were no doubt aware of the existence and location of the Spratlys and Ma Huan mentioned them as well, but not in such great detail as other places in his logbooks. The reason is quite simple: the Spratlys are not actually islands, but treacherous shoals and underwater reefs, which the ancient navies—including Zheng He's fleet of wooden junks—sailed around to avoid being shipwrecked. But that has not prevented China from making its revisionist assertions and, in recent years, literally cementing those claims by turning shoals and reefs into man-made islands.

Any opposing views, meanwhile, are branded by Beijing as interference in China's internal affairs. Even when the Permanent Court of Arbitration in The Hague in July 2016 ruled in favour of a complaint brought to it by the Philippines, concluding that China has no 'historical right' to the territory it claims in the South China Sea, including most of the Spratlys, China was infuriated and rejected the ruling. Xinhua hit out at what it described as an 'ill-founded' ruling that was 'naturally null and void', while *The People's Daily* said in an editorial that the tribunal had ignored 'basic truths' and 'trampled' on international laws and norms.[54]

China has been equally hardline when it comes to where the maritime boundary should be between its claims and Indonesia's Natuna Islands. Although not part of the dispute over the Spratlys, China's so-called 'nine-dash-line', a set of line segments on various maps delineating the southern stretch of the Chinese claim, overlaps with Indonesia's exclusive economic zone around the islands. And Beijing has refused to budge an inch on the issue. Indonesia has fortified its defences on the Natuna Islands and the government in Jakarta has on a number of occasions sent warships to the area to deter China from crossing what Indonesia considers its maritime boundary.

Vital oil supplies from the Middle East to East Asia's booming economies pass through the South China Sea, and the US, the UK, Australia, France and India have sent ships through the disputed maritime area to secure those shipping lanes and prevent them from being totally controlled and dominated by China. Confrontations involving ships from the claimant nations are not uncommon and, in 1988, Chinese and Vietnamese naval vessels clashed over who would control a speck of land called Johnson South Reef. Outgunned by the Chinese navy, Vietnam was forced to withdraw and the deadly incident ended with China occupying six reefs it had previously not controlled.[55]

That clash, and the 1979 war, have not been forgotten in Hanoi. It is unlikely that it will ever be a truly close relationship between China and Vietnam. The cultural and historical ties between Vietnam and China have been lucidly explained by Le Hong Hiep, a lecturer at the Faculty of International Relations, Vietnam National University, in Ho Chi Minh City (formerly Saigon): 'The Chinese "charm offensive" is likely to expand globally, but may encounter major setbacks in Vietnam. While voluntary borrowings from China have formed a substantial layer of the country's culture, Vietnam is also a country where memories of a millennium of forceful Chinese cultural assimilation are still alive today.'[56] Consequently, Le Hong Hiep continues, 'Chinese attempts to spread its soft power into Vietnam are likely to be limited by the country's over-familiarity with Chinese culture. Vietnam's traditional resistance to unwarranted Chinese cultural influence now stands as yet another obvious challenge that China must overcome if its "charm offensive" is to ever succeed in this particular southern neighbour.'[57] No amount of Chinese pressure will change the fact that BRI is and will remain a non-starter in Vietnam.

Thailand, the other main economic power in mainland Southeast Asia, did not appear on most BRI maps for several years after Xi's initial announcement in Kazakhstan in 2013. According to Benjamin Zawacki, a political analyst with the Asia Foundation: 'A list from inside China in early 2019 contained seven BRI projects in Thailand, although most had not been notably publicized as part of the initiative, and several hardly publicized at all.'[58] The BRI flagship in Thailand is supposed to be the continuation of the high-speed railway in Laos, but that was being discussed as early as 2010, three years before Xi's announcement. And the future of that project is uncertain. Then Prime Minister Prayuth Chan-o-cha even cancelled it in 2016. The Thais are more interested in a high-speed railway from Bangkok to Chiang Mai, which would be far from the border-crossing with Laos, and they seem to prefer to cooperate with Japanese partners rather than Chinese companies.[59]

On 27 May 2015, the Thai government and Japanese agencies signed an agreement for the project's first phase, a 380-kilometre-long line from Bangkok to Phitsanulok. The second phase would cover the remaining 288 kilometres to Chiang Mai, and the Japanese side has proposed Shinkansen-style trains, which can reach a maximum speed of 300 kph—faster and certainly safer than those made in China.[60]

The plan to build a new railway from Bangkok to the border town of Nong Khai, where it would connect with the new line through Laos, has not been completely abandoned. In Thailand, the existing rail network has a track gauge of a metre; the high-speed trains require standard 1,435-millimetre tracks. But these planned railways are years behind schedule and, judging from what has been said so far, will go only as far as Nakhon Ratchasima in Thailand's north-east, 330 kilometres from Nong Khai. And even the Bangkok–Nakhon Ratchasima portion of the proposed railway is far from being completed. According to Thai sources, 'The contract governing the Thai-Chinese high-speed railway construction may need to be renegotiated.'[61] It smacks of delaying tactics on the Thai side to avoid having to scrap the project altogether, which would antagonize the Chinese at a time when relations between Thailand and China are closer than ever before in history.

A major obstacle is what the Chinese want from the project: China will be in charge in the first three years and, between the third and the seventh years, both countries will have close shares and later Thailand will take the responsibility with China being its adviser.[62] That, many Thais would argue, would be an infringement on the country's sovereignty. Questions have also been raised about how the project will be financed. Thailand is supposed to borrow from local financial institutions, while

China will arrange a loan from the Export-Import Bank of China or its Asian Infrastructure Investment Bank. But the Thai condition is that the interest rate would not exceed what is available through local financing.[63] Thailand is not interested in getting stuck in a debt trap situation and, unlike Laos, it has the power and the means to resist Chinese pressure.

A possible BRI project, although never mentioned as such, would be a canal across Thailand's southern isthmus, which would shorten shipping routes from the Indian Ocean to the South China Sea and beyond. If it ever materialized, it could cut out the Malacca Strait and Singapore, which inevitably would cause problems between Thailand and its partners in ASEAN. Singapore is the largest transhipment port connecting the two oceans, and Malaysia also has major transhipment terminals in Tanjung Pelepas and Port Klang.[64]

The plan, called the Kra Canal after the name of the isthmus, is not new, but has never been more than that, a lofty proposition that few took seriously. But the plan was revived in late 2023, when Thai Prime Minister Srettha Thavisin mentioned it—but now as a 'land bridge' connecting the ports of Ranong and Chumphon in southern Thailand.[65] Rather than digging a canal, it would be an overland connection consisting of roads and possibly railways. According to news reports, Srettha 'has already sought interest in the project from China, welcoming investors from the country.'[66]

Thailand has a long and troubled relationship with China. A large portion of the population, and especially the commercial elite, is of Chinese origin. The majority of those partially or fully of Sino-Thai descent can trace their origin to migrants from the Shantou area in the southern Guangdong Province who arrived in waves in the nineteenth century, and some even before that. In Pinyin, or standardized Mandarin Chinese, they are called Chaozhou, while they are known as Chiu Chow in Hong Kong and the US. In Thailand, they are called Teochew and call Shantou 'Swatow'.

The Sino-Thai community went through the usual transition that overseas Chinese go through, from being labourers and coolies to becoming merchants, business tycoons and bankers. But the republican ideas that they brought with them from China—in the movement against the emperor before the 1911 revolution, which had its strongholds in southern China, and after that when the Chinese republic was established the following year—were seen as subversive in the Kingdom of Siam, as Thailand was then called. All Chinese schools in Bangkok and elsewhere were closed and the migrants had to adopt Thai names and were required to pass Thai-language tests. The outcome has been a marriage of convenience between the Sino-Thai plutocracy and the Thai monarchy and military, which can be seen as a major factor contributing to the economic success of Thailand.

For decades, and especially during the Cold War, Western-allied Thailand had close relations with Taiwan. But in 1975, diplomatic relations were established with Beijing and, gradually, ties between the two countries improved. The Chinese community in Thailand has always sent money back to relatives in Shantou, but did so clandestinely. After 1975, Sino-Thais no longer had to hide their Chinese ancestry and many even began to learn Mandarin, which is distinct from their native Teochew dialect.

But some degree of distrust remains, and the Thai military has never completely forgotten that China for years supported the outlawed CPT with weapons and other equipment. That aid ceased only when China wanted to send military supplies through Thailand to the Khmer Rouge, which, after 1979, was resisting the Vietnamese and their allies in Cambodia. Thailand responded by demanding that China end all support for the CPT. China agreed, and the CPT began to crumble. A general amnesty was declared in 1980, and thousands of CPT activists returned home. Many of them, like the well-known student activists Thirayuth Boonmee and Seksan Prasertkul, later became prominent academics. Others, among them Chaturon Chaiseng, went on to serve as government ministers.[67]

Today's Thailand may be very different from what it was during the Cold War. China has become Thailand's largest trading partner with the bilateral trade amounting to US$78.92 billion, and millions of Chinese tourists visit Thailand every year. But Thailand's security planners still prefer to keep China at arm's length. The reluctance to link up with the Lao railway is one example of that. When the Thai government in November 2023 proposed that Chinese law enforcement officials should operate in Thailand in a joint effort to crack down on organized crime, it was first approved—and then scrapped after public backlash, drawing criticism that it compromised national sovereignty, and a rebuke even from Thailand's police chief.[68]

There are also other reasons for Thailand's lukewarm response to the BRI. Thailand has its own development programmes and is unlikely to agree to be subordinate to Chinese-initiated projects funded by loans from Chinese banks and being carried out at least in part by Chinese contractors.

Thailand, though, may be a brilliant example of how overseas Chinese can be successfully integrated in host countries. The situation is entirely different in Malaysia. Thanks to the British colonial policy of importing labour from abroad, Malaysia has three distinct ethnic groups: the indigenous Muslim Malays, the Indians who are mostly Hindu but some also Muslim (then referred to as 'Pakistani', although their ancestors came mostly from northern India) and the Chinese, who are either Buddhists or Christians or they practice Confucianism, Taoism and other traditional beliefs. Their respective cultures are different and intermarriages between the three communities are rare.

The Malays and local tribes, who are referred as bumiputera, or 'sons of the land', made up 70.1 per cent of the population in 2023, while the Chinese accounted for 22.6 per cent and the Indians 6.6 per cent.[69] For many years, the Chinese, and to some extent the Indians, dominated trade and commerce, while the Malays were economically disadvantaged. The ethnic tensions exploded into riots in May 1969. Malays, armed with parangs and kris—daggers and swords—burned cars and shops, killed and looted in the Chinese areas, while the Chinese organized resistance and fought back. The army was brought in, and once peace was restored, the official figure of deaths was 196, but the actual figure could have been as many as 600, perhaps more.[70]

The Bumiputera policy was introduced after the 1969 riots in order to help the Malays get into business. They were granted a privileged status over the ethnic Chinese, and the policy has, therefore, been described as racially discriminatory. And it did not work as envisaged in 1969. Many Chinese-owned enterprises hired Malays as frontmen, giving rise to what became known as 'Ali Baba businesses'; the Chinese ('Baba') would pay a Malay ('Ali') to become a silent director of his company—and that caused more problems than it actually solved.[71] And it has led to Chinese migration out of Malaysia. Since the bumiputera policies were introduced, more than a million Malaysian Chinese have left for Australia, New Zealand, Canada, the US, France and the UK, and even nearby Singapore, where they can enjoy the same rights as other residents and citizens.[72]

In a historical context, the Malay–Chinese divide became obvious also during the Japanese occupation in World War II. The Malays, glad to see the British colonial power leave, were inclined to side with the Japanese, while the Chinese, who made up the bulk of the fighting force of the CPM, resisted the occupation—and were supported by the British. For his services during the war, the CPM leader Chin Peng was awarded an Order of the British Empire by Louis Mountbatten during a ceremony in Singapore in 1945. That decoration was withdrawn when Chin Peng led the CPM into rebellion against the British in 1948. A bitter civil war ensued, which lasted well into the 1960s. Chin Peng and other leading cadres of the party then moved to China, where they stayed until their comrades back home finally laid down their arms. Peace talks were held in Hat Yai in southern Thailand in late 1989, and Chin Peng came to Thailand to lead the CPM delegation. The talks were brokered by the Thais, and Chin Peng eventually died there in 2013. He was never allowed to return to Malaysia.[73]

If Chinese media are to be believed, the Malaysian government is very enthusiastic about the BRI. An October 2023 report on the official news site, China Daily, stated that Prime Minister Anwar Ibrahim 'has highlighted the significance of the China-proposed Belt and Road Initiative in enhancing the growth of his country, lauding the BRI for creating job opportunities and building infrastructure, especially in the rural heartland.'[74] Anthony Loke, Malaysia's transport minister, praised the BRI during a trip to China in November 2023, calling it a 'development model' that will 'change the destiny of developing countries across the world.'[75]

But apart from railways connecting shipping ports on Malaysia's east and west coasts, nothing much else seems to have been achieved. And an entirely different picture of the impact of the BRI was painted by Mahathir Mohamad, the grand old man of Malaysian politics, in 2018. Standing beside Li Keqiang, China's Premier, at a press conference in Beijing, shocked the audience by saying, 'We should always remember that the level of development of countries are not all the same. We do not want a situation where there is a new version of colonialism happening because poor countries are unable to compete with rich countries, therefore we need fair trade.'[76]

As *Nikkei Asia* reported at the time: 'There is a crowning irony in Mahathir's evocation of neo-colonialism, as this was precisely the charge that he used to lay against the West and Western investment when he was at the height of his powers in his first period in office in the 1980s and 1990s.'[77] After visiting Beijing, Mahathir, then Prime Minister, cancelled a number of Chinese-initiated infrastructure projects saying that his debt-ridden country could not afford them.[78] Relations with China appear to be smoother after Anwar Ibrahim became Prime Minister in November 2022, but China cannot count on Malaysia becoming a strategic development partner in the same way as Myanmar and Laos, or even Thailand. And then there is, of course, the South China Sea where China's territorial claims overlap with those of Malaysia.

Singapore, where 74.1 per cent are of Chinese descent, 13.4 per cent of Malay, 9.2 per cent of Indian and 3.4 per cent of Eurasian, Armenian and other ethnicities, was part of the original Malaysia when it was founded in 1963. The new state consisted of the Malayan Federation, which had become independent in 1957, the protectorates British North Borneo (which became Sabah) and Sarawak, and the old crown colony of Singapore. After the merger, the central government in Kuala Lumpur and the local authorities in Singapore, led by veteran politician Lee Kuan

Yew, disagreed on a number of issues. On the surface, it was about trade restrictions between Singapore and the other states of the federation, but the main problem for the Malay policymakers in Kuala Lumpur was the fact that Singapore was overwhelmingly Chinese. The Malay and Chinese communities in Singapore clashed in 1964 and, in 1965, Singapore was expelled from Malaysia and became an independent republic.

The island state of Singapore became a success story. Benefitting from its strategic location as a transhipment point for regional trade, oil refining and banking, Singapore's living standard is fully on par with that of the most advanced economies in the West. Therefore, the BRI is not what Singapore needs. As the Singapore *Law Gazette* stated in 2021: 'Arguably, being an advanced developing economy, Singapore does not require external financing to develop its public infrastructure unlike many other Asian developing economies that have much to gain from Chinese investments.'[79]

Indonesia, Southeast Asia's largest and most populous country, had close relations with China as long as the nationalist, fiercely anti-Western leader Sukarno was in power. Indonesia also had the largest and most influential communist party, Partai Komunis Indonesia (PKI), in a country not ruled by one. During the first years of the 1960s, the US State Department estimated that the PKI had about two million members, which corresponded to 3.8 per cent of the entire working-age population.[80] The figure could also have been as high as three million. Sukarno was not a communist himself, but favoured the PKI over the other, centrist and rightist, political groupings.

Military nationalists, who saw Sukarno and his PKI allies as a threat to Islam and Muslim values, stepped in and unleashed a bloody crackdown on communists as well as ethnic Chinese, who were also perceived as enemies of the state. No official investigation into the killings has ever been done, but it is believed that somewhere between 500,000 and two million people died as a result of the carnage the military, in conjunction with militant Muslim groups, unleashed throughout the archipelago.[81]

The new government under Lieutenant-General Suharto suspended diplomatic relations with China in 1967. In the same year, orders were issued banning Chinese literature, culture and characters, and encouraging the abandonment of Chinese names. But he maintained close relations with some wealthy tycoons like Mochtar Riady (born as Lie Mo Tie) of the Lippo Group, and Sudono Salim (born as Lim Sioe Liong), once the richest man in Indonesia and the founder of the conglomerate Salim Group. Suharto, like the Thai generals, realized that he needed support from the ethnic Chinese business community in order to survive in power and make the country prosper.

Diplomatic relations between Jakarta and Beijing were restored in 1990 and, after the fall of Suharto in 1998, his successor Bacharuddin Jusuf Habibie began to rebuild confidence with the Sino-Indonesians. Many, among them prominent businessmen, had fled the country during the Asian economic crisis and the upheavals of 1997–1998. He wanted them to come back, and help rebuild the Indonesian economy, which was on the verge of collapse. In May 1998, anti-Chinese riots had also swept through Jakarta as many ordinary people thought the Chinese were responsible for the crisis. In 2000, Habibie's successor President Abdurrahman Wahid, better known as Gus Dur, lifted the ban on celebrating Chinese New Year, and other Chinese traditions could again be celebrated freely. The post-Suharto era has also seen many Sino-Indonesians entering politics, including Mari Elka Pangestu, who served as minister of trade from 2004 to 2011 and minister of tourism and creative economy from 2011 to 2014.

Life has become easier for the Sino-Indonesians, and the Indonesian economy did not collapse. The country has seen a remarkable recovery—and development—since the dark years of the late 1990s. But Indonesia is far from being a close ally of China. The Jakarta–Bandung railway should have become a showcase project of the BRI, but it has turned into a brilliant example of how development schemes should not be implemented. It is not only the length, only 143 kilometres, but also the fact that it takes up to an hour of heavy traffic just to get to the boarding point at each end that has made the project an embarassment.[82]

A plan to extend the railway to Surabaya, which would make sense for a high-speed railway connection, has not seen the train leave the station in Bandung. According to initial budgeting, the cost would be US$6.07 billion, but that has been increased to US$7.27 billion and the government has had to go back on its promise not to use the state budget to cover the gap.[83] Now, Indonesia has to ask for a US$560 million loan from the China Development Bank to cover part of the extra cost of US$1.2 billion. Compounding the problem are calculations by economists saying that the railway is not expected to turn a profit for more than forty years.[84] And the dispute over the maritime border around the Natuna Islands is far from solved and continues to cause frictions in Indonesia's relations with China.

For centuries, Southeast Asia has been known to the Chinese as 'the Great Golden Peninsula', a land of milk and honey, which was abundant with business opportunities and easy lifestyles. Now, it has become a diplomatic and political minefield. Yes, China has had some success with Myanmar, Laos and Cambodia. But the much-hyped high-speed train is likely to screech to a halt at Vientiane's station, and Cambodia, squeezed between Thailand and Vietnam, is unlikely to become a hub of connectivity in the region. In Myanmar though, Xi may succeed where Kang Sheng failed. It will, and to some extent already is, China's gateway to the Indian Ocean and beyond.

4

COLLISION COURSE ON THE ROOF OF THE WORLD

THE OUTBREAK OF A MAOIST INSURGENCY TWENTY YEARS AFTER the death of the Chairman, and the emergence of an entirely new political and economic direction in China, may seem like a historic abnormality. But that is exactly what happened in Nepal on 13 November 1996. In February of that year, groups of mostly young men armed with daggers, hunting rifles and home-made bombs raided police stations in Rolpa and Rukum in the remote, impoverished western part of Nepal. At the same time, fifty attackers and two soldiers died in a clash in Jarayotar of Sindhuli District, south-east of the capital Kathmandu. Those incidents marked the beginning of a bloody, ten-year conflict between Nepalese government forces and the Communist Party of Nepal (Maoist) {CPN(M)}.

Led by Pushpa Kamal Dahal, alias Prachanda ('the fierce one'), the party's revolutionary rhetoric seemed as though copied from bulletins issued during the 1966–1976 Cultural Revolution in China. Although Prachanda and his deputy, Baburam Bhattarai, were well-educated, middle-class intellectuals, their party found an appeal among the downtrodden—mainly Mongol peoples, the Magars, Tharus and others—who had long been treated as second-class citizens by the Bahuns (the local term for Brahmins) and Chhetris (Kshatriyas) of the lowlands.

The CPN (M) grew into a formidable threat to the rulers of the Himalayan kingdom. Lower-caste and tribal people from the highlands made up the bulk of the CPN (M)'s fighting force, which, at its peak in the early 2000s, numbered as many as 36,000 men and women in arms.[1] The Nepalese Maoists never received any outside support and were armed with guns smuggled in from India, some made in clandestine weapon factories in Bihar across the border, and whatever they could capture from the Nepalese military and police.

Over 17,000 people, including rebels, civilians, policemen and government soldiers, were dead and several hundred thousand people had been displaced by the time a peace treaty was signed on 21 November 2006 between the government of Nepal and the CPN (M). The deal allowed the Maoists to take part in mainstream politics, while they placed their weapons in storage monitored by observers from the United Nations. The CPN (M)'s troops were also supposed to be integrated into the regular Nepali Army.

Before that could happen, in April 2006, demonstrators in Kathmandu and elsewhere had begun agitating against the hugely unpopular King Gyanendra. His powers were severely curtailed and, as part of the peace deal with the CPN (M), the monarchy was abolished on 28 May 2008. CPN(M) was by then the largest party in the Constituent Assembly, having won 220 out of 575 contested seats in a general election in April. On 18th August, Prachanda was sworn in as the new Prime Minister of the Federal Democratic Republic of Nepal.

Throughout the civil war, the Chinese had been watching the turbulent developments in Nepal with unease. They were not pleased to see a communist party in a neighbouring country having 'Maoist' in its name and espousing an orthodox version of communism that had been discarded in China. Prachanda had once even referred to 'the Chinese counter-revolution after the death of Comrade Mao Zedong' and called the Cultural Revolution 'the highest expression of conscious class struggle.'[2]

China's relationship with Nepal has always been motivated by geostrategic considerations rather than ideology, with the aim of building a strategic corridor in the Himalayas to counter India's traditional dominance over these frontier areas. Diplomatic relations between Beijing and Kathmandu were established in 1955 when Nepalese dignitaries visited China and, in 1957, Chinese Premier Zhou Enlai visited Nepal. A boundary agreement was settled upon on 21 March 1960 and that was followed by the Sino-Nepalese Treaty of Peace and Friendship on 28th April.

After the introduction in 1961 of what was called the panchayat system, which established Nepal as an absolute monarchy, King Mahendra Bikram Shah Dev and Queen Ratna Rajya Lakshmi Devi paid an official state visit to Beijing. During that visit, China signed an agreement with Nepal for the construction of a highway from Tibet to Kathmandu. China even pledged to provide Kathmandu with a generous grant to build the highway on the Nepalese side of the border. A formal boundary agreement was finally signed on 5th October. The final delimitation on the entire border between Nepal and China would be made on 'the basis of the traditional customary boundary line and in accordance with the principles of equality, mutual benefit, friendship and mutual accommodation.'[3]

The highway was officially opened in 1967 and became the first road of its kind across the Himalayas. Although never officially acknowledged at the time, the Nepalese side was keen to lessen its traditional dependence on India and open an alternative route for trade and other exchanges—and China saw Nepal as a weak link in India's northern lines of defence that could be exploited to extend Beijing's influence over the Himalayas.

The Maoist insurgency, and political upheavals in Nepal in the 1990s, forced the Chinese to re-evaluate their relationship with the Nepalese monarchy. Prachanda was invited to China shortly after he had been sworn in as Prime Minister. The old revolutionary firebrand met Chinese President Hu Jintao and Premier Wen Jiabao and was impressed with China's economic progress. To the surprise of many of his hardline followers, Prachanda declaimed: 'The friendship between China and Nepal endured the test of time ... The Nepali government and people [are] striving for national stability and development, and [hope] to get support and cooperation from China.'4 Dengism rather than Maoism became Prachanda's new ideology when he entered mainstream politics. He began to emphasize the importance of economic growth through capitalism instead of copying what China did when it was ruled by Mao.

Prachanda's first government lasted less than a year, only till May 2017. Nepal's internal turmoil was far from over, and a number of short-lived governments came to dominate the country's political scene. The CPN (M) split into different factions, and Bhattarai, who also served as Prime Minister for a while, decided to embrace democratic socialism instead of Maoism.

Not everyone in the CPN (M) was pleased to see their old leaders changing their policies in such an abrupt and, in their view, extreme way. In November 2012, Padam Kunwar, a twenty-five-year-old Maoist activist slapped Prachanda across the face, smashing his glasses at a reception in Kathmandu.5 Kunwar was arrested by the police and taken away drenched in blood after Prachanda's supporters hit his head and face. In May that year, a Kathmandu tea shop owner hit another CPN (M) lawmaker across the face, saying he and other party leaders had 'betrayed the people'.6

Resentment was also strong among the party's former fighters from the non-Bahun peoples in the mountains. But Prachanda and other 'reformed' Maoist leaders had made their choice. They probably felt more at home in the corridors of power in Kathmandu than among the Magars or the Tharus. But they left behind a political tinderbox that can ignite any time the downtrodden feel they have to stand up for their rights. The peace accord may have ended the civil war, but Nepal remains socially divided and politically unstable.

Prachanda led a new government from August 2016 to June 2017, and he has, for a third time, been Prime Minister since December 2022. Meanwhile, the trade between China and Nepal increased fivefold during 2009–2012 and a Confucius Institute was opened at Kathmandu University 'for [the] promotion of Chinese culture and language.'7 Free Chinese language classes were offered not only at the Confucius Institute but also in colleges, primary and secondary schools, and even for government officials and soldiers in the Nepali Army.8

The new Chinese charm offensive culminated in a visit by Xi Jinping to Nepal in October 2019, the first by a Chinese President since Jiang Zemin travelled to Kathmandu in 1996. Xi and then Nepalese Prime Minister, K.P. Sharma Oli from the Communist Party of Nepal (Unified Marxist-Leninists), reportedly signed twenty bilateral agreements, spanning roads, inland waterways, energy and agricultural development. The construction of a railway linking Kerung in Tibet with Kathmandu was also discussed.[9] Nepal was going to benefit from China's BRI, which it had signed on to in 2017, and prosper. That was, at least, the idea behind the new, strengthened partnership between China and Nepal.

During his visit to Kathmandu, Xi seized the opportunity to issue a stern warning to unspecified enemies: 'Anyone attempting to split China in any part of the country will end in crushed bodies and shattered bones.'[10] The stern message was without doubt directed at Tibetans, whose families fled after an uprising against the Chinese invasion of their homeland had been brutally crushed in 1959. Approximately 20,000 Tibetan refugees live in twelve designated camps in Nepal's Kathmandu and Pokhara, 200 kilometres west of the capital.[11] But unlike the 150,000 Tibetans who sought refuge in India, who are free to be politically active when Chinese leaders are not there on a visit, those in Nepal face growing curbs on expression, including bans on publicly criticizing Chinese policies and showing support for the Dalai Lama.

Even so, the Chinese are well aware of the fact that between 3,000 and 5,000 Tibetans fleeing Chinese repression reach India every year via Nepal. Xi had brought with him an extradition treaty aimed at deporting all Tibetan refugees from Nepal back to China.[12] The Nepalese did not sign it, well aware of the international outcry that would have caused. Xi had to be content with a pact on mutual legal assistance in criminal matters, which covers criminal offenses and not political cases.[13] China and Nepal also signed a joint statement saying: 'The Nepali side reiterated its firm commitment to the one-China policy with Tibet and Taiwan affairs as being China's internal affairs, and the determination on not allowing any anti-China activities on its soil.'[14]

Even though Xi did not get all that he wanted, Nepal's move away from having India as its closest economic and strategic ally to drifting into China's orbit is obvious. But that relationship has also been wrought with problems. The big issue is not the danger of coming under China's hegemony—but money. In September 2023, Prachanda paid an eight-day visit to China but the note to the press that was released after his return to Kathmandu did not mention the BRI. There had, as a matter of fact, been very little to show what could be described as substantial progress. *The Kathmandu Post* reported on 29 October 2023: 'Two mini projects of Nepal have been listed in the outcome document of the third Belt and Road Forum for International Cooperation, which concluded on October 18 in Beijing ... The Chinese side ... mentioned the Panda Pack project and Amity Living Water Project as part of the Belt and Road Initiative. However, rather than being new ventures, the projects are already in operation in Nepal.'[15]

The Panda Pack project, which aims to improve the basic learning conditions of primary school students and was launched in 2019, is a joint initiative between the China Foundation for Poverty, which was registered in Lalitpur in 2015 as an NGO, and Alibaba Philanthropy.[16] The Amity Living Water Project was launched by the Amity Foundation, a faith-based, independent social organization founded in 1985 on the initiative of Chinese Christians led by Bishop K.H. Ting.[17] The money for those projects may come from Chinese sources, but it was never before claimed that those projects were BRI schemes.

Controversy also surrounds the new international airport at Pokhara. Although never officially listed as a BRI project, Chen Song, the Chinese ambassador to Nepal, claimed in a post on Twitter (now known as X) a day before its inauguration on 1 January 2023 that, 'this [Pokhara airport] is the flagship project of the China–Nepal BRI cooperation.'[18] This forced the Nepali Foreign Minister N.P. Saud to clarify that, 'the project implementation plan of the BRI is at a stage of discussion between Nepal and China. Not a single project in Nepal under the BRI has been executed. The project implementation plan of the BRI is still under consideration.'[19]

The foundation stone for the airport was laid by then Prime Minister Oli in April 2016, but the project was delayed several times because of protests by locals who lost land, and later on by the Covid-19 pandemic. When work on the airport eventually got started, a Chinese contractor was assigned to build it, and the Nepali government signed a US$215 million soft-loan agreement with China to cover the cost. According to an investigation by *The New York Times*, the construction cost had been deliberately inflated and it lacked items that normally would be required in building a new airport, such as taking into account local rainfall and soil conditions that could leave it vulnerable to flooding.[20]

Furthermore, the airport has failed to attract any international flights, which means that it will not generate the revenue that would be needed to cover what has been spent on building it. But Nepal is still obliged to repay the loan it took out from China, and *The New York Times* noted that the airport may become one of the many debt traps that have followed in the wake of the launch of Xi's BRI. In November 2023, Nepal's anti-corruption agency, the Commission for the Investigation of Abuse and Authority, announced that it had opened an investigation into the construction of the airport, and how it was constructed.[21]

A much bigger project is the proposed railway from Tibet to Kathmandu. The Chinese had promised to cover the cost for the construction of the railway on their side of the border, and it has already been built most of the way to Kerung from the railhead at Shigatse, 250 kilometres south of the Tibetan capital Lhasa, which since 1984 has had a rail connection with Qinghai and the rest of China. From Kerung, on the border, it is only 75 kilometres to Kathmandu, but because of the difficult terrain and other complexities, the estimated cost for that section of the proposed railway is over US$3 billion, with some estimates being as high as US$5.5 billion.[22] The project includes a plan to blast a 30-kilometre-long tunnel under Nepal's Langtang National Park, Nepal's first national park in the Himalayas.

But an agreement has yet to be signed about the funding, and, needless to say, Nepal would be unable to bear the cost. Only yet another loan from China would make it possible for Nepal to agree to build such an expensive railway. Prachanda did not raise the railway issue during his September 2023 visit to China, and writer Sajira Shrestha explained the reason in an article for *My República*: 'Nepal is apprehensive because it is already grappling with the financial burden of repaying the loan for the Pokhara Regional International Airport and was hesitant to shoulder yet another financial obligation with China.'[23]

The Nepalese leaders have consistently asked for grants instead of loans, which China has always proposed. And that is precisely the reason for the BRI's overall failure in Nepal, not only when it comes to the railway, but other projects as well. As *The Kathmandu Post* pointed out in a commentary on the BRI on 11 September 2023, the memorandum of understanding that Nepal signed in 2017 lacks any clarity regarding funding modality: 'The BRI has a loan component, and projects are carried out with loans, not grants. According to AidData, a research lab at the College of William & Mary, Chinese loans for BRI projects typically have an interest rate of 4.2 percent with a grace period of fewer than two years and a maturity of fewer than ten years.'[24]

In contrast, according to *The Kathmandu Post*, 'soft loans from multilateral donors, such as the World Bank and the Asian Development Bank, have a maximum interest rate of 1.3 percent and a longer repayment period. Nepal simply can't undertake large-scale infrastructure projects with such commercial loans without a guarantee of return on investment.'[25]

The railway, if ever built, would have a profound impact on the geopolitics of the region. Nepal would then definitely be closer to China than India. There have even been talks about extending the line all the way to the pilgrimage site Lumbini on the Indian border, the birth place of the Buddha.[26] But the Indians doubt that only pilgrims would benefit from such a railway, and it would be even more challenging from a security point of view than the yet-to-be-built line from Tibet to Kathmandu.

India has countered by suggesting that a cross-border railway be built from Raxaul, on the India–Nepal border, in Bihar to Kathmandu.[27] The 136-kilometre line would be broad gauge, or 1,676 millimetres, as opposed to the railways in Tibet, which are standard gauge, or 1,435 millimetres.

In that way, no Chinese trains would be able to use the proposed Indian-built railway even if there was a line from Tibet to Kathmandu.

The defence of India's northern border means, in effect, defence against China.[28] India's frontier with China starts at Kashmir and the border with Pakistan in the west and runs along the crest of the Himalayas to the northernmost tip of Myanmar in the east. In effect, that means that Nepal and Bhutan, two independent countries, fall within the area south of the Himalayan watershed that India deems necessary to yield considerable sway over, in order to safeguard its geostrategic security.

If China succeeded in extending its sphere of influence over the Himalayas, its shadow would loom over the entire subcontinent, and that is why India finds it necessary to play a role in the domestic politics of the Himalayan states. This has not always been popular with the Nepalese, who often see it as gross interference in their domestic affairs. Nepalese politicians have a long history of distancing themselves from India—and India has always reacted strongly when they have done exactly that.

In 1989, India closed nineteen of its twenty-one border crossings because Nepal had purchased anti-aircraft guns and other weapons from China. And in September 2015, the border was closed down for imports and exports for four-and-a-half months. Although India claimed that the blockade had been imposed by Madheshi, natives of the southern plains, who felt a new Constitution had marginalized them, it was seen by others as an Indian reaction to Nepal's increasing cooperation with China. The border closure caused an extreme shortage of cooking oil and transportation fuel in a country that was ailing from the April 2015 earthquake.[29]

Such actions have, not surprisingly, fuelled even more anti-Indian sentiment in Nepal. But, in spite of such feelings among the population at large, relations with India remain strong and two out of the nine proposed BRI projects have been awarded to Indian instead of Chinese companies: the Tamor Hydroelectricity Project and the Phukot Karnali Hydroelectric Project.[30] Those agreements were sealed when Prachanda visited India in June 2023. The Tamor project was initially awarded to the Power China Corporation, but has been handed over to Sutlej

Jalvidyut Nigam of India, while the one at Phukot Karnali will be built by an Indian public sector company, the National Hydroelectric Power Corporation.[31]

The much smaller Bhutan, east of Nepal, presents an entirely different, less complicated story. Bhutan is the last surviving Buddhist kingdom in the Himalayas with less than a million people and it is roughly the same size as Switzerland. The kings have committed themselves to building a nation based on Buddhist spiritual values rather than crass materialism. The former King Jigme Singye Wangchuk, who reigned from 1972 until his abdication in favour of his son, the present King Jigme Khesar Namgyel Wangchuk, coined the term Gross National Happiness as a model for Bhutan's development.

The country was an absolute monarchy until the king himself initiated democratic reforms in 2005. Bhutan is now a constitutional monarchy with political parties, an elected national assembly and a Prime Minister. The most recent elections were held in January 2024, the People's Democratic Party won a majority of seats and its leader, Tshering Tobgay, became Prime Minister for a second time (he was Prime Minister from July 2013 to August 2018 as well). His main job will be to turn around the economy, which has been sluggish in recent years, and to tackle youth unemployment, which has doubled over the past five years and, in January 2024, stood at 28.6 per cent.[32] Many have gone to Australia to seek employment opportunities there.

With Tobgay as Prime Minister, ties with India are expected to grow even stronger. His father was one of the young men recruited in the 1950s to build the country's first official standing army, an effort that was initiated and supported by India, and his mother was one of the workers on the first modern road linking Bhutan to India which was built after the 1962 border war between India and China.[33] Before that road was built, the only way to get to the capital, Thimphu, and other towns in the highlands was by yak or mule caravans along treacherous, winding mountain trails. That road broke Bhutan's isolation, but it was not until 1999 that the country got television and internet and became truly connected with the outside world.

Today, a modern road network covers Bhutan and it is the only South Asian country that has education and healthcare systems that cover all its citizens. The economy is still based mainly on agriculture and forestry, while substantial revenues come from hydropower exports to India and high-end tourism. On 13 December 2023, Bhutan officially graduated from the United Nations' list of least developed countries, making it only the seventh country to do so.[34]

Relations between Bhutan and its southern neighbour were first formalized in 1910, when the then British colonial government in India signed an agreement with the Bhutanese. They agreed to 'be guided by the advice of the British Government in regard to its external relations', while the British pledged to exercise no interference in the internal administration of Bhutan.[35] On 8 August 1949, Bhutan and the government of independent India entered into a similar agreement, which reconfirmed Bhutan's status as a nation dependent on India but with a high degree of autonomy.[36]

Bhutan gradually managed to strengthen its independence and, in 1971, it became a member of the United Nations. In 2007, a revised treaty was signed with India, according to which 'the Government of the Kingdom of Bhutan and the Government of the Republic of India shall cooperate closely with each other on issues relating to national interests. Neither government shall allow the use of its territory for activities harmful to the national security and interests of the other.'[37]

Bhutan is the only neighbouring country with which China does not yet have diplomatic relations, which India appreciates. In the early 1990s, when more than 100,000 Nepalese-speaking people living mainly in southern Bhutan were forcefully driven out, India sent all of them on to Nepal. Bhutan does not share a border with Nepal, so India was the first country to which the Lhotshampas, as they are called, arrived. India did not want to house them as that would cause serious problems with its strategic relationship with Bhutan. The Bhutanese government alleged that some of the Lhotshampas had been involved in anti-monarchy activities, and also claimed that the number of Nepalese-speaking people in the country had increased dramatically because of illegal migration from Nepal and Nepalese-inhabited areas of northern West Bengal in India.

The Lhotshampas were housed in camps in southern Nepal run by the United Nations High Commissioner for Refugees and the Nepalese authorities. But despite efforts to repatriate those who could prove that they had Bhutanese citizenship, Bhutan did not want them back. Nor would Nepal give them citizenship or even permanent resident status. In the end, nearly all of them were resettled in third countries, more than half of them in the US, while others went to Australia, Canada, Norway, the Netherlands and Denmark.[38]

Given the fact that Bhutan is squeezed between two regional superpowers—the old partner, India, and China, with which it has no official relations— the King and the government in Thimphu have always been careful in their handling of relations with its northern neighbour as well. Bhutan remains one of the few Buddhist countries in the world that the Dalai Lama has not visited. That is partly because Bhutan and Tibet practice different schools of Vajrayana Buddhism, but the main reason is that the Bhutanese do not want to provoke or even offend the Chinese. Around 6,000 Tibetan refugees fled to Bhutan after the 1959 uprising, and they were allowed to stay as long as they did not engage in any political activity. In 1981, the Tibetan refugees were told to accept Bhutanese citizenship or leave the country. Most of them left for India.

China has tried to woo Bhutan into being part of the BRI, but with no success. Bhutan has welcomed the initiative as such and praised China's contributions to 'world peace and prosperity'.[39] But Bhutan declined to participate in the second BRI Forum for International Cooperation in Beijing in April 2019. However, China's strategic interests in South Asia go beyond the stated 'peaceful' goals of the BRI. In South Asia, the BRI is merely part of a larger vision of expanding influence across the Himalayas to secure China's position as Asia's leading superpower at the expense of India. That vision, which has guided China's diplomatic, economic and political forays into Nepal, has in recent years also come to include Bhutan.

Chinese circus artistes and acrobats have performed in Bhutan, footballers have come to play 'friendship games', and a limited number of Bhutanese students have received Chinese scholarships to study at universities in China. Tourism has also expanded. In the early 2000s, only nineteen Chinese tourists visited Bhutan. In 2015, Chinese visitors numbered 9,399 of a total of 155,121 visitors, fourth after India, Bangladesh and the US.[40] The number declined during the Covid-19 pandemic, but has since been picking up again. In January 2024, Bhutan Live reported that, 'Bhutan has secured its place as an outstanding destination in the Chinese market.'[41]

However, most exchanges between Bhutan and China take place when the two sides meet for talks about the common border, which runs for 477 kilometres through the Himalayas. China and Bhutan have held twenty-five rounds of talks between 1984 and 2023 to settle the border issues. When the talks began, China laid claim to three areas of Bhutan, a 269-square kilometre large area called Doklam (and Donglang by the Chinese) in the west and the two northern areas of Jakarlung and Pasamlung measuring 495 square kilometres.[42]

In June 2017, Chinese road construction crews, protected by Chinese troops, started to build a road through the disputed area in the west, which led to a formal protest from Bhutan and a seventy-two-day stand-off between Indian and Chinese forces. The Doklam area, as it is called, is of strategic importance to Beijing, as its inclusion would widen the corridor China controls between western Bhutan and the Indian state of Sikkim. That corridor, the Chumbi Valley, is an old route over the Himalayas that China wants to keep firmly under its control in case of a conflict with India. The area south of Sikkim is equally sensitive from a security point of view: the Siliguri Corridor, also known as the Chicken's Neck, a narrow strip of land that connects India's seven Northeast states with the rest of the country.

India's response to the roadworks made it appear as the belligerent party while at the same time raising concern in Bhutan, where India's military presence is politically sensitive. Although Bhutan relies on India for its national defence, Bhutanese politicians are keen to demonstrate that they are leaders of an independent country and are capable of managing their own military affairs. The stand-off ended inconclusively when both India and China agreed to withdraw from the area in August 2017.

Chinese troops returned to the area in September 2018 and, a few months later, the road was not only completed but the Chinese had also constructed a village called Pangda about 2 kilometres within Bhutanese territory. By then, the Chinese had added another disputed area to their list: the Sakteng Wildlife Sanctuary in eastern Bhutan, bringing the number of areas they claim to four. Some would argue seven if some smaller areas where the border is not clear are included.[43]

It is not in China's interest to wait for the border to be clearly demarcated. As long as the issue is alive, the Chinese can continue its seemingly never-ending border talks with the Bhutanese, but that has not prevented them from treating the contested areas as if they were theirs—and posturing as though there is actually nothing to talk about. The new Pangda village with 124 settlers is only one example of that. More new villages have been identified at Dramana and Shakhatoe, north of Doklam. Recent satellite photos taken in November 2021, obtained by the Chatham House think-tank in London, show a collection of new buildings and other structures in those areas.[44] In the north, the Chinese have already seized the Jakarlung Valley and the nearby Menchuma Valley. Chinese-constructed road networks and several areas that appear to be developed can be seen in the same collection of satellite photos.[45]

China's BRI may have become irrelevant in the context of the Himalayan states. Not one BRI project in Nepal can be described as a success story, and Bhutan is not even part of it. But it is here the two giants of Asia are standing eyeball-to-eyeball—and where Xi's dream of expanding his influence over and across the Himalayas is being challenged.

It began with the Chinese invasion of Tibet in 1950. Tibet, which until then had had closer ties with India than China, ceased to be a de facto independent country and, for the first time in history, India had a common border with China. One of the few in the Indian government who understood that this meant the geopolitics of the region had changed dramatically was the home minister, Vallabhbhai Patel, who only a month before his death in December 1950 wrote to Prime Minister Nehru: 'We have to consider what the new situation faces us as a result of the disappearance of Tibet, as we know it, and the expansion of China up to our gates. Throughout history, we have seldom been worried about our north-east frontier. The Himalayas has been regarded as an impenetrable barrier against threats from the north. We had a friendly Tibet which gave us no trouble. The Chinese were divided. They had their domestic problems and never bothered us about our frontiers.'[46]

Throughout the 1950s, India believed that China was a friend, and relations seemed to blossom under the Hindi slogan *Hindi Chini Bhai Bhai* or 'Indians and Chinese are brothers'. India officially recognized that Tibet is part of China in 1954, when the two countries signed the Agreement between the Republic of India and the People's Republic of China on Trade and Intercourse Between India and Tibet Region of China and India.[47] India made sure China's Premier Zhou Enlai could attend the April 1955 conference in the Indonesian city of Bandung, which was attended by twenty-nine mostly newly independent countries in Asia and Africa and led to the founding of the Non-Aligned Movement.[48]

Zhou almost did not make it. The Kashmir Princess, the Air India plane that Nehru had sent to Hong Kong to fly him to Jakarta, crashed into the South China Sea on 11 April 1955. A bomb had been planted on the plane by the Nationalist Chinese, Kuomintang agents from Taiwan, and Zhou was obviously the target. The plane, a Lockheed L-749A Constellation, had been chartered by the Indian government; and sixteen of those on board were killed, while three survived.[49] Among the dead were Chinese and east European journalists.

But Zhou had been delayed and he was not on that flight. He left China three days after the crash because he wanted to fly to Yangon and meet Nehru and Myanmar Prime Minister U Nu before continuing to Indonesia to attend the Bandung conference.[50] After returning to China from the conference, Zhou sent Xiong Xianghui, a high-ranking intelligence officer, to Hong Kong for talks with the British authorities there. In June 1956, forty-four Kuomintang intelligence agents were expelled from Hong Kong. But no one was ever charged with the crime.[51]

Between June 1954 and January 1957, Zhou paid four visits to India and, in October 1954, Nehru went to Beijing, where he met not only Zhou but also the supreme leader, Mao. *Hindi Chini Bhai Bhai* seemed to be holding and the Non-Aligned Movement, with India as its strongest voice, became a powerful force on the international arena.

The first overt sign of friction in Sino-Indian relations was when disturbing news was coming out of Tibet in the mid- and late-1950s. The Chinese occupation had been brutal. Local Tibetans who were suspected of being opposed to China were arrested and publicly executed, Buddhist monasteries were destroyed and monks were imprisoned or executed without apparent reason.[52] This led to an uprising among the Khampas, nomads of eastern Tibet, who had a long tradition of safeguarding their independence. Their resistance attracted the attention of the US Central Intelligence Agency (CIA), which decided to intervene.

The Americans airdropped arms, ammunition and other supplies from planes that took off from air bases in Okinawa and Thailand. They flew to Kurmitola air base in East Pakistan, then a US ally, and from there north and through the narrow stretch of Indian airspace between Nepal and Bhutan. No modern radar facilities existed at that time, and the planes could fly undetected to and from the skies over Tibet. Some Khampas managed to get out and were trained on the US-held island of Saipan, now part of the Commonwealth of the Northern Mariana Islands and still an American possession, and in the Rocky Mountains in Colorado.[53] Nehru may not have been aware of the CIA's clandestine operations, but he certainly must have taken at least some of the reports from inside Tibet seriously. The Chinese oppression was real and well-documented.

Then came the uprising in Lhasa. In March 1959, thousands of Tibetans took to the streets of the Tibetan capital to protest against the occupation. It was brutally crushed by the Chinese army, which, ironically, is officially called the People's Liberation Army. Hundreds of civilians and monks were killed, and tens of thousands fled over the Himalayas to safety on the other side. Among them was the Dalai Lama, who arrived in India on 31st March after an arduous journey on horseback from Lhasa. He had been escorted by Khampa warriors, who took care of his security—and kept in touch with the CIA in Okinawa via radio transmitters.

The Dalai Lama was granted asylum by the Indian government and set up a Tibetan government in exile, first in the hill station of Mussoorie in present-day Uttarakhand, and then, more permanently, in McLeodganj in the hills above Dharamshala in what is now Himachal Pradesh—and that was the beginning of China's open hostility towards India. On 25 August 1959, Chinese troops crossed the de facto border at Longju in the north-east, killing two Indian soldiers and, on 31st October, Chinese troops attacked an Indian position at Kongka La in Ladakh in the north-west and killed seventeen Indian soldiers.

Zhou believed that there was a connection between the Lhasa uprising and the Indian government. At a meeting with the politburo of the Communist Party of China (CPC) shortly after the uprising had been crushed, he went on to speculate that both the British and the Americans had provided support for the protesters in collusion with India, and alleged that 'a commanding centre of the rebellion has been established in Kalimpong [in northern West Bengal].'[54] Zhou was correct in saying that the Tibetan resistance has representatives in Kalimpong and that some CIA liaison officers were there as well, but that was not an Indian government operation. Gyalo Thondup, an elder brother of the Dalai Lama was there and had contacts with several American and other agents, among them an anthropologist, Prince Peter of Denmark and Greece, who was expelled by the Indian government in 1957, accused of 'undesirable activities'.[55]

George Patterson, a now deceased British Tibetologist, who was fluent in several local dialects and wrote extensively about Tibet and its relations with India and China, said in 1963: 'There is another side to Chou [Zhou], which is not as well-known as the charming, brilliant, and even "moderate", exterior which he uses to win friends and influence people.'[56] Patterson mentions as an example when Zhou himself murdered a whole family, including servants and babies, by strangulation. Their 'crime' was that they had broken with the communist party and, allegedly, passed on sensitive information to the nationalist police.⁵⁷ Zhou was as much a hardliner as the dreaded security chief, Kang Sheng.

Some contemporary Indian writers, among them Avtar Singh Bhasin, have suggested that the border dispute with China, and even the 1962 war, probably could have been avoided if Nehru had been more willing to listen to China's version of the dispute. Bhasin writes in *Nehru, Tibet and China* that Zhou showed some degree of flexibility in his letters to Nehru, while the latter remained steadfast in his belief of where the boundary should be. Nehru's 'rigidity', Bhasin argues, 'stood in the way of finding a solution through negotiations and discussions by sitting around a table.'⁵⁸

Bhasin's book is meticulously researched and brilliantly written, but fails to take into account that Zhou's diplomatic niceties stood in sharp contrast to what had been written about Nehru in communist, Chinese-language publications. In an editorial on 2 September 1949, the communist publication *Hsin Hwa Pao* stated after the Tibetan authorities in July of that year had decided to expel Chinese citizens from the country: 'The affair ... was a plot undertaken by the local Tibetan authorities through the instigation of the British imperialists and their lackey Nehru administration in India. The purpose of this anti-Chinese affair is to prevent the people of Tibet from being liberated by the Chinese People's Liberation Army.'⁵⁹ In September 1949, *Shijie Zhishi*, a Shanghai-based fortnightly published by the CPC's Culture Committee, denounced Nehru as a 'running dog of imperialism' and a Chiang Kai-shek-like 'loyal slave' of the enemies of the revolution.⁶⁰

According to a declassified CIA report, former Myanmar Prime Minister Ba Swe wrote a letter to Nehru in 1958, warning him to be 'cautious' in dealing with Zhou and the Chinese on the Sino-Indian border issue.⁶¹ At the time, Myanmar was involved in border talks with the Chinese and had some experience of Chinese doublespeak. Nehru reportedly replied by declaring Zhou to be 'an honourable man' who could be trusted.⁶² If India at that time had had more policymakers and security officials who could read what was written about Nehru and his government in the Chinese communist media, New Delhi's China policy in the 1950s could have been more enlightened and not confined to platitudes like *Hindi Chini Bhai Bhai*.

The border between then British India and Tibet was discussed and agreed upon at meetings that were held in Shimla, the summer capital of British India in the foothills of the Himalayas, in 1913 and 1914. British India's chief negotiator, Henry McMahon, a Shimla-born colonial officer, also served as chairman of the conference. He was assisted by Archibald Rose, a British diplomat, explorer and businessman, and Charles Bell, the then British political representative to Sikkim on issues concerning Tibet. Negotiating for the British was also Sonam Wangfel Laden La, or Laden La for short, an ethnic Bhutia from Sikkim who served as a high-ranking police officer in the colonial administration.

Tibet sent its Prime Minister Lama Lönchan Shatra as a representative of the 13th Dalai Lama, the predecessor to the current 14th Dalai Lama. Lama Lönchan Shatra was accompanied by two other high-ranking Tibetan officials, Trimon Norbu Wangyal and Khenchung Tenpa Dhargyal. The Tibetans were there mainly to get international support for their 4 April 1912 declaration of full independence.[63] China's main delegate was Chen Yifan, or Ivan Chen, a diplomat who was fluent in English, who was assisted by Deputy Commissioner Wang Haiping, but the power behind Chen and Wang was Lu Hsing-chi (Lu Xingqi in Pinyin), a more influential officer who had played a crucial role in fostering divisions between the Dalai Lama and the second-most important lama in Tibet, the Panchen Lama.[64]

The main point of contention during the nine months of negotiations was where the border should actually be. The Chinese side objected to the presence and status of the Tibetans at the conference as they insisted that Tibet was an integral part of China, so they refused to sign the treaty that was concluded on 3 July 1914. But the British and the Tibetans agreed that the border should be based on the watershed principle and follow the crest of the Himalayas. That line became known as the McMahon Line and is the one that independent India has always considered to be its north-eastern border.

The Chinese have never recognized that border; instead, they place it somewhere in the foothills of the Himalayas. Why is hard to say, because China has never controlled that area, now part of Arunachal Pradesh. Even if one accepts the argument that Tibet was part of China, no Tibetan government has controlled it either. Lhasa collected taxes in some areas close to Tibet, Tawang in the west, Walong and the east and Upper Subansiri and Siang in the middle. But there was never any Tibetan administration there.

It may be correct that some British maps did not show the McMahon Line until much later, but that was not, as some foreign academics have claimed, because the British did not want to provoke the Chinese, who did not recognize that border.[65] The reason has been explained by Pradip Phanjoubam, a journalist and a researcher from Manipur: 'British policy at the time was determined not by any fear of the Chinese, but of the Russians, in what was referred to as the Great Game.'[66] China was weak and not really a factor to be reckoned with, but making deals with Tibet, a signatory to the Shimla Agreement, could be seen as a violation of the 1907 Anglo-Russian Convention, under the terms of which Britain and Russia had pledged not to enter into any agreements with Tibet unless done through Chinese mediation.

The British did send some officials into the mountains north of the Assam plains during the colonial era, but it was not until after India's independence that the area was gradually placed under central governmental control. It became known as the Northeast Frontier Agency (NEFA) in 1954, a part of Assam, and later, in 1972, as the separate union territory of Arunachal Pradesh, which achieved full statehood on 20 February 1987.

Somewhat contradictorily, China has never disputed the watershed principle when it comes to defining its borders with Nepal and Bhutan. It is only in India's north-east region, the Chinese argue, that an entirely different concept should be applied. In an official Chinese publication from 1989, Sikkim is treated as an independent country, and even there the watershed principle must have been accepted because Beijing does not seem to have any territorial claims to that state or question its borders with China: 'The foreign ministry issued a statement, condemning India for its annexation of the Kingdom of Sikkim ... the Chinese government solemnly states once again that it absolutely does not recognize India's annexation of Sikkim [in 1975] and firmly supports the people of Sikkim in their just struggle for national independence and in defence of state sovereignty against Indian expansionism.'[67] Sikkim was a semi-independent kingdom, and an Indian protectorate, until a referendum was held in April 1975. The monarchy was abolished and Sikkim became India's twenty-second state.

There are many theories as to why the Chinese attacked in October 1962, and for years Neville Maxwell's *India's China War*, which was first published in 1970, dominated the narrative.[68] According to Maxwell, India was to blame, and he referred to a classified Indian intelligence document compiled by Lieutenant-General T.B. Henderson Brooks and Brigadier Premindra Singh Bhagat to back up his claim. The war was provoked by Nehru's Forward Policy, which was decided upon at a meeting in New Delhi on 2 November 1961, as well as, Maxwell claimed, the construction of Indian defence installations not only on but even beyond the line that separates NEFA and Chinese-held Tibet. But the Brooks–Bhagat report does not say that. It merely states that Nehru's government did not give the armed forces the necessary tools to implement the Forward Policy, and that there was a lack of cooperation between the government in New Delhi and the military in the field.[69]

Furthermore, it falls on its absurdity that such a massive attack could have been prompted by Nehru's Forward Policy, which was laid down less than a year before the war and aimed at securing India's existing borders, not any expansion into some other territory. If Maxwell is to be believed, China would have been able to build new roads and military camps in the area during that short period of time, and move at least 80,000 troops and tonnes of supplies, including heavy military equipment over some of the most difficult terrain in the world. Those troops would also have to be acclimatized to high-altitude warfare and the supply lines established and secured to the rear bases inside Tibet.

Furthermore, Brig. John Dalvi, who was captured by the Chinese and remained in their custody inside Tibet until May 1963, discovered that the Chinese had erected prisoner-of-war camps to hold up to 3,000 men. Chinese interpreters who knew all the major Indian languages were present in those camps.[70] It is obvious that Chinese preparations for a war with India began years before the attacks took place, not sometime after the November 1961 announcement in New Delhi.

So why did the Chinese attack, and when was the decision to launch a war against India taken? Basically, there were three reasons behind the decision. The first was that India had granted the Dalai Lama asylum and allowed him to set up a government in exile in India. At a meeting at the Jinjiang Hotel in Shanghai on 25 March 1959, after the Lhasa uprising and as the Dalai Lama was still on his way to India, Deng as well as Mao declared that 'when the time comes, we certainly will settle accounts with them [the Indians].'[71] That was when the Chinese decided to 'teach India a lesson'—not in 1961 or 1962. Bruce Riedel, one of America's leading experts on US security as well as South Asian issues, concurs: 'Probably as early as 1959, Mao decided that it would have to take firm action against Nehru.'[72]

The attack must also be understood in the context of internal problems in China at the time. In 1958, Mao initiated the disastrous Great Leap Forward to modernize China. By 1961, anywhere between seventeen and forty-five million people had died as a result of his policies, which caused a famine rather than, as intended, any rapid industrialization. Mao was discredited and, very likely, on his way out. He must have felt that he had to regain power—and the best way to do that would be to unify the nation and especially the armed forces against an outside enemy. India was a 'soft' target because it had granted the Dalai Lama asylum and then there was the issue of the border that China did not recognize.

The third reason was that until the outbreak of the 1962 war, India and especially Nehru had been the main voice of the newly independent countries of Asia and Africa, which was clearly demonstrated at the 1955 Bandung conference and the birth of the Non-Aligned Movement. Although Zhou was present at the meeting, he and Beijing had other plans and ideas. China wanted to be the 'revolutionary bulwark' of what later became known as the Third World, and India had to be dethroned from the position it had held throughout the 1950s. In that respect, the 1962 war worked to China's advantage. Nehru died a broken man in 1964 and Mao became the icon of many Asian and African liberation movements.

The capitalist China of 2024 may not be the same as it was under Mao's dogmatic rule and there may not be another all-out war in the Himalayas. But Chinese maps still show most of Arunachal Pradesh as Chinese territory. The Chinese call it Zangnan, or southern Tibet, and have on three occasions—April 2017, December 2021 and April 2023—announced that they have 'standardized' the spelling of villages, mountains and rivers in Arunachal Pradesh, basically giving them new, Chinese-sounding names.[73] Six places were given new names in 2017, fifteen in 2021 and eleven in 2023, and Chinese state media quoted Zhang Yongpan from the Institute of Chinese Borderland Studies, Chinese Academy of Social Sciences, as saying China's move to standardize the names 'falls within China's sovereignty.'[74]

The June–August 2017 stand-off between Indian and Chinese forces at Doklam was followed by clashes in the Galwan River Valley in Ladakh in May and June 2020, and a clash at Yangtse in Arunachal Pradesh in December 2022—all of which serve as reminders that the conflict is far from over.

But it is important not to fall into the trap of believing that the conflicts in the Himalayas are about border demarcation. For China, it is about hegemony. Now, as was the case during the 1962 war, China is flexing its muscles to show India and the world that it has become a new superpower, a role it has not held since the last Ming emperor was overthrown in the seventeenth century and replaced by a Manchu-led dynasty, and, in 1912, a shaky republic, which Mao's communists crushed in 1949, establishing the People's Republic of China.

India's long history of conflicts, violent and non-violent, with China makes it impossible for New Delhi to even consider joining the BRI. Xi has had much better luck with India's archenemy Pakistan—a long-time ally of China. Pakistan and China signed a memorandum of understanding aimed at establishing what has become known as the China–Pakistan Economic Corridor (CPEC), a major undertaking under the aegis of the BRI, on 20 April 2015. The precise content of the plan was not officially disclosed until 2017. On 14 May of that year, the daily newspaper *Dawn* revealed that it had acquired documentation that outlined what 'Chinese intentions and priorities are in Pakistan for the next decade and a half, details that have not been discussed in public thus far.'[75]

According to the agreement, thousands of acres of agricultural land would be leased out to Chinese enterprises to set up 'demonstration projects', and the Chinese agreed to help Pakistan establish a system of monitoring and surveillance 'in cities from Peshawar to Karachi' and build 'a national fibreoptic backbone [...] not only for internet traffic but also terrestrial distribution of broadcast TV, which will cooperate with Chinese media in the "dissemination of Chinese culture."'[76] A major component of CPEC is also to build a 3,000-kilometre network of roads, railways and pipelines to transport oil and gas from the Pakistani port of Gwadar on the shores of the Arabian Sea to Kashgar in Xinjiang.[77]

Like the China-Myanmar Economic Corridor (CMEC), the essence of CPEC is to get outlets to the various seas of the Indian Ocean. It, as part of such strategic thinking, also predates the BRI by several decades. The construction of the Karakoram Highway in the 1960s and 1970s was China's first attempt to gain such access and establish a close economic as well as security-related relationship with a neighbouring country. But the CPEC may be even harder to implement than the CMEC. Pakistani journalist F.M. Shakil pointed out in 2020 that 'Partisan politics, massive corruption and raging insurgency have stalled progress' on the CPEC, the total value of which is estimated at a whopping US$60 billion.[78]

Security, or the lack of it, is a major issue, internally in Pakistan as well as in neighbouring Afghanistan. This can be observed at Gwadar, the strategically most important project under the CPEC and the BRI in Pakistan. The port's strategic location was recognized centuries ago by Arab and Portuguese seafarers and traders. In 1783, the ruler of

Balochistan, once an independent khanat, granted sovereignty over Gwadar to the sultan of Muscat on the Arabian Peninsula. Muscat, later known as Muscat and Oman before finally becoming only Oman, ruled Gwadar as well as Zanzibar on Africa's eastern coast. Gwadar became an important entrepot for the slave trade and, as a reminder of those days, there are still small communities of descendants of African slaves living in the south of today's Pakistan.

When Muscat and Oman became a British protectorate in 1891, Gwadar remained under the official rule of its sultan and was never part of British India. But the Omani sultan's interest in the enclave began to decline in the 1950s and, because of his close relationship with the then independent India, he offered to sell Gwadar to India, not Pakistan. India, however, was not interested in acquiring Gwadar, and only then did the sultan turn to Pakistan, which bought it for US$3 million. It was in December 1958 that Gwadar became part of Pakistan.[79]

In 1954, when Gwadar was still under Omani rule, the United States Geological Survey, on Pakistani government's request, identified it as a suitable place for a deepwater port. But its potential as a major hub for the region's sea traffic remained undeveloped until the Chinese moved in with their construction crews in the early 2000s. Most of the workers on the port project, and the 2,292-acre special economic zone that surrounds it, were brought in from China rather than being recruited locally.

Gwadar is part of Balochistan, a Pakistani province which has long been wracked by insurgency. The rebels are demanding self-determination, and are protesting against what they see as the province's exploitation by the government in Islamabad and, more recently, by Chinese economic interests. On 23 November 2018, heavily armed militants attacked the Chinese consulate in Karachi, killing seven people—two policemen, two civilians and the three attackers. No Chinese was killed in that attack, but Balochi rebels claimed responsibility for the attack and issued a statement saying, 'We have been seeing the Chinese as an oppressor along with Pakistani forces', which are 'destroying the future of Balochistan.'[80] But immediately after the attack, a foreign ministry spokesman in Beijing stated that it would not affect relations between China and Pakistan, including the CPEC, because the two countries are 'all-weather strategic cooperative partners.'[81]

Then came an attack on the five-star Pearl Continental Hotel in Gwadar on 11 May 2019, which was built by a Chinese contractor and where Chinese nationals often stay. The Balochistan Liberation Army said it carried out the attack in which five people were killed and six wounded.[82] Yet another attack was carried out on 21 June 2021, this time against the Chinese-run Karachi Stock Exchange. Four people were killed when militants stormed the compound, but the attackers never managed to get into the actual stock exchange building.[83] Less than a month later, on 16 July, a bomb attack on a bus killed nine Chinese citizens, including engineers working on a CPEC-related hydropower dam project.[84] That attack does not seem to have been carried out by Balochi militants though. Pakistani officials indicated that it was the work of the East Turkestan Islamic Movement, a group that seeks independence for Xinjiang, which the local Muslim Uighurs call East Turkestan.[85]

Pakistan's fragility as a country is rooted in its not particularly long history. While Myanmar with its current borders is a colonial creation—and that poses a problem for the BRI there—Pakistan was built on even less solid grounds, hence the ethnic unrest in many parts of that country. The name 'Pakistan' was coined by Choudhry Rahmat Ali, a student at Cambridge University in Britain, in a pamphlet titled *Now or Never: Are We to Live or Perish Forever?*, which was published under a pseudonym in January 1933.

Rahmat Ali was actually born in Balachaur in the part of Punjab that now belongs to India. But as a Muslim activist, he advocated the establishment of a separate nation consisting of the Muslim-majority parts of British India. 'Pakistan' was an acronym where P stood for Punjab, A for Afghan (the Pashtun-inhabited Northwest Frontier Province of British India), K for Kashmir, I for Indus or Sindh and STAN for the last part of the name Balochistan. 'Pak' means pure in Persian and Pashto, and 'stan' is country, so Pakistan then stands for 'the land of the pure'.[86]

The problem with that acronym was that it did not include the most populous Muslim-majority province of British India: East Bengal. That province became the eastern part of Pakistan upon independence in 1947 and separated from the western, main Pakistan by more than 2,000 kilometres of Indian territory. In 1971, East Pakistan managed to break away after a bloody war that claimed several million lives. Religion was not the main issue behind that war as Muslims were fighting against Muslims, rather it was the effort by the leaders in the west to impose their official language, Urdu, on the Bengali-speaking east.

When India was partitioned in 1947, the rulers of the princely states had the right to decide which country they wanted to belong to. The Hindu maharaja of the Muslim-majority Jammu and Kashmir, Hari Singh, declared that he wanted his state to join India—and that marked the beginning of a conflict between Pakistan and India, which continues to this day.

The deep-rooted hostility between India and Pakistan is the reason why Pakistan, officially the Islamic Republic of Pakistan, has become a close ally of communist-ruled China. In the early years after independence, when India established close relations with the Soviet Union, Pakistan allied itself with the West and, in 1954, became a member of the Southeast Treaty Organization (SEATO), which also encompassed the US, France, Great Britain, New Zealand, Australia, the Philippines and Thailand. In 1955, Pakistan joined Iran, Iraq, Turkey and Great Britain to form the Central Treaty Organization (CENTO).

Both those pacts were dissolved in the late 1970s, and by then Pakistan and China had already moved closer to each other. The turning point was the 1962 war between India and China, which made the value of strategic cooperation apparent to Pakistan as well as China.[87] Then came the war between India and Pakistan in 1965. According to researcher Andrew Small, that war saw 'the real prospect of Chinese intervention on Pakistan's behalf' and 'formed the basis of China's status as the "all-weather friend" in the Pakistani public imagination.'[88]

Also according to Small: 'The 1971 Indo-Pakistani war [that led to the creation of Bangladesh]—in which Beijing failed to come to Islamabad's aid—ostensibly showed the limits of the relationship. Yet in many ways it set in motion security cooperation of an even more significant nature.'[89]

After the devastating failure to keep Pakistan together in 1971, China helped the country develop a set of military capabilities to ensure that it would never face 'the same fate again'.[90] And now exist the CPEC and the BRI, which are part and parcel of the cooperation between Pakistan and China and go way beyond economic exchanges and the building of roads and railways. For China, it is still part of the policy to be able to exercise enough influence over Pakistan in order to secure access to the Indian Ocean, and for Pakistan, the essence of the relationship is to have a close ally who can stand on its side in the conflict with India.

How much Pakistan values its friendship with China is evident in its stance on the Xinjiang/East Turkestan issue. Pakistan has never hesitated to show solidarity with the Palestinians in their conflict with Israel, but the then Prime Minister Imran Khan expressed in July 2021 his country's support for the Chinese government's policies and actions in Xinjiang, which the United Nations High Commissioner for Human Rights has described as 'crimes against humanity'.[91] Although the United Nations report does not label China's suppression of the Uighurs as 'genocide', which the US government does, it did find widespread and systemic abuse of human rights, including 'arbitrary and discriminatory detention' of perhaps more than a million people.[92]

Likewise, it may seem paradoxical that the Chinese authorities would be eager to forge an alliance with the Taliban in Afghanistan. But long-term geopolitical interest, not necessarily ideology and certainly not religion, have always been the main driving force behind Chinese foreign policy. The departure of the last Western troops from Kabul on 31 August 2021 meant that a potentially unpredictable, Islamic regime took over a strategically important—and extremely volatile—country in Central Asia.

The West responded with boycotts, sanctions and vague promises of a 'carrot' in the form of humanitarian aid funnelled through the United Nations. China, on the other hand, decided to engage in a dialogue with the Taliban, and was able to do that through its trusted allies in Islamabad.[93] A week before the final fall of Kabul, Moeed Yusuf, Pakistan's then national security adviser, had a long discussion with Zhao Kezhi, state councillor and party committee secretary of China's Ministry of Public

Security, the country's main intelligence agency. Yusuf later tweeted after the discussion: 'Pleasure to speak to my Chinese counterpart, excellency Zhao Kezhi, on ways to further strengthen our bilateral relationship. We discussed the situation in Afghanistan and agreed to maintain close coordination, including countering spoilers. We are moving forward with a vision.'[94]

China's interest in maintaining a relationship with the Taliban is obvious. The Chinese must first and foremost make sure that Islamic-run Afghanistan does not become a sanctuary for the separatist movement in Xinjiang. Hu Xijin, the editor of the official Chinese mouthpiece, *The Global Times*, emphasized that point in a commentary that was published on 23 August 2021, and went on to say that he expected the incoming Taliban government to 'keep distance from the US and other forces that turn out to be hostile to China. They should refuse to act as a pawn for those forces to jeopardize China's strategic interests.'[95]

Apart from such concerns, China has also shown interest in mining in Afghanistan. In 2006, US researchers conducted an aerial survey of Afghanistan and claimed that the country could possess mineral deposits worth US$1 trillion.[96] According to a Brookings Institute report, Afghanistan sits on some 2.3 billion metric tonnes of iron ore and 1.4 million metric tonnes of rare earth minerals.[97]

Relying on such reports and some Soviet-era data, the new Taliban government has tried to utilize the country's largely untapped mineral deposits to attract foreign direct investment. However, apart from illicit mining, often conducted by corrupt Kabul officials and their associates, as well as some investment contracts such as the copper mine at Mes Aynak, there has been no substantial foreign investment flowing into Afghanistan's mining industry.[98]

China signed an agreement with the former Afghan government in 2007 to extract copper from Mes Aynak. Two Chinese companies, Metallurgical Corporation of China (MCC) and the Jiangxi Copper Corporation, were awarded the contract, but the work never started because of security issues and the discovery of some old, pre-Islamic Buddhist artifacts at the mining site.[99] But China is still there in some capacity. During a recent visit to Afghanistan by an MCC official, the Afghan minister for mines and petroleum, Shahabuddin Delawar, described the project as 'important and vital', and said the extraction of copper from Mes Aynak is 'one of the top priorities' for his government.[100]

Chinese companies could possibly overcome issues related to corruption, but Western sanctions against the Taliban regime makes it difficult even for them to engage in mining in Afghanistan, both in Mes Aynak and elsewhere, because they could then also be subjected to international sanctions. But, even so, some small-scale Chinese investors are known to be operating in Afghanistan and the ores they mine can always be brought to China and refined there to disguise the origin of the raw material.

In October 2023, Afghanistan's acting commerce minister, Haji Nooruddin Azizi, told Reuters that the Taliban administration wants to formally join the BRI and will send a technical team to China for talks.[101] It is plausible that those talks will be not only about copper and other minerals, but also that the Chinese side will get assurances from the Taliban that they will not, in any way, support or provide sanctuary for Uighur groups from Xinjiang. The cash-strapped and boycotted Afghan government may well agree to that, and China would then score an important victory in its campaign against the Uighurs. China could provide the Afghan government with loans it cannot repay, and then be able to dictate its conditions on security-related issues.

As for Pakistan, it is already heavily in debt to China. According to the IMF, as of February 2022, Pakistan owes China US$18.4 billion, or 20 per cent of its total external debt liabilities of US$92.3 billion. Islamabad has asked China for a bailout package of US$9 billion, but it is uncertain if Beijing will agree to that, or use the debt to make sure Pakistan does not deviate from its 'all-weather' relationship with China, or extract other kinds of concessions.[102] In 2018, the debt crisis forced Pakistan to turn to the IMF for a bailout as its foreign exchange reserves had dropped to US$8 billion, or barely enough to cover two months' worth of imports.[103] That may happen again.

Apart from concerns over the debt burden, there is also growing resentment against China, and not only among the Balochis, but in other fields. According to F.M. Shakil, the Pakistani journalist, there are now officially 2,000 registered Chinese business entities in the country, which, government adviser Ishrat Husain says, benefit Chinese interests more than Pakistani.[104] But many others are not registered, and the actual number could be as high as 5,000, and those that are not registered with Pakistani tax authorities do not pay taxes. Shakil quotes analysts saying that non-CPEC enterprises, which nevertheless have established themselves in the wake of the BRI, are increasingly driven by cheap labour and securing access to raw materials that are shipped back to factories in China.[105]

Pakistan is even less likely to distance itself from the BRI than Nepal. For security reasons—and economic development, controversial as it may be— Islamabad needs to stay close to China because there is no other country that can play the role of a close ally. But Pakistan has to pay a high price for its 'all-weather' relationship with China. Economically, it is completely under the sway of Chinese companies and Beijing's fiscal policies. And, as the Uighur issue shows, Pakistan has had to give up even the pretence of having an independent, enlightened foreign policy. The only bulwark against China's push across the heights of the Himalayas is India. But India also has a troubled relationship not only with Nepal but even more so with the island nations of the Indian Ocean, whose influence over trade routes between East Asia, the Middle East, Africa and Europe is far greater than the size of those small countries would suggest.

5

THE INDIAN OCEAN

OCEAN-GOING SHIPS HAVE ALWAYS BEEN A LARGER AND MORE important mode of transport for sending goods from China and the Far East to the rest of the world than by camel caravans trudging along some imaginary 'Silk Roads' through the deserts and over the mountains of Central Asia. And, in this regard, it is of crucial importance to China to have unhindered access to shipping lanes across the Indian Ocean.

In April 2023, Darshana M. Baruah of the Washington-based Carnegie Endowment for International Peace testified before the US House of Representatives Foreign Affairs Committee on the Indo-Pacific saying: 'Nine of China's top ten crude oil suppliers transit the Indian Ocean. The Indian Ocean is also the primary theatre of transit for China for engagements with Africa, [the] Middle East, island nations, and littorals across the vast ocean. Going beyond, it is also the main trading route between China and Europe.'[1]

China's interest in the Indian Ocean is therefore clear, Baruah said, 'at least on the economic side,' adding that 'as history will tell us, the flag follows trade. There is little doubt in the strategic importance of the Indian Ocean for China and this interest will only continue to grow.'[2] Such important trade routes need protection, and that is why the Chinese for the first time in history are busy building a blue water navy—and now have a naval base in Djibouti. It is an ideal place from which shipping lines from the Indian Ocean and on to the Red Sea and the Suez Canal can be supervised and, if necessary, defended.

There was also another reason why China chose to establish its first overseas military base in Djibouti. It is easier to set up a military base in Djibouti than anywhere else in the world. Small countries with few natural resources often become financial centres and tax havens in order to raise revenue and sustain their status as independent nations. Djibouti decided to take advantage of its strategic location and lease out plots of land to foreign countries where they can build military bases. France, the formal colonial power from the days when Djibouti was French Somaliland, has the oldest base in the country, now housing 1,450 men from the army, air force and navy.[3]

After the terrorist attacks in New York and Washington on 11 September 2001, the US military took over Camp Lemonnier, an old French Foreign Legion base, and turned it into a modern facility. Some 4,000 Americans are stationed there along with aircraft, drones and naval vessels. Japan's only overseas military base is also in Djibouti with 600 men from the Japanese navy and air force. The Italians have a military support base there as well, while troops from Germany and Spain are hosted by the French.[4] In June 2023, Saudi Arabia announced its intention to build a military base in Djibouti.[5]

The Chinese reached an agreement with the government of Djibouti to build a base there in 2015, and, two years later, it was officially opened when ships from China's South Sea Fleet docked at the facility.[6] Today, about 2,000 naval personnel are based there and the Chinese have built a pier long enough to accommodate aircraft carriers as well as a 400-metre runway with an air traffic control tower.[7] While all the other foreign bases are located south of Djibouti City, the Chinese base is located close to the Port of Doraleh, 5 kilometres west of the capital.

It could be argued that one Chinese base in a foreign country is nothing compared to the hundreds of military bases the US maintains across eighty countries in all continents. But it is a new development, which should be seen in the context of Beijing's long-term vision of gradually becoming the most powerful force in the Indian Ocean.

The Djibouti facility may be China's only permanent naval base so far, but Chinese contractors are involved in upgrading existing ports and building new ones across the region: Kyaukpyu in Myanmar, Chittagong (now Chattogram) in Bangladesh, Hambantota in Sri Lanka, Gwadar in Pakistan and Ream in Cambodia, which is purely a military facility.

The BRI in the Indian Ocean region is an important component in that strategy, and Djibouti was one of the first countries to show interest in the BRI, joining it officially on 1 September 2018. The construction of the US$590 million Doraleh Port began before that, in 2015, and it was inaugurated two years later—the same year as the Chinese military base was opened. The port was built by a Chinese contractor and initially partially owned and operated by DP World and China Merchants Holdings. Although the Djibouti government took over its container facility in 2018, Chinese companies remain its main users.[8]

Apart from the port, the Chinese have also invested in infrastructure projects, including the 752-kilometre-long Djibouti–Addis Ababa railway that was built to provide Ethiopia with a new outlet to the sea after the loss of Eritrea, which became independent in 1993. Djibouti's share of the cost of the railway includes a US$492-million loan from China, and it is doubtful whether Djibouti will ever be able to repay it. Other loans have funded a pipeline to transport natural gas from Ethiopia to Djibouti for export to China, and a free-trade zone and business centre near Doraleh.[9] The outcome could be that Djibouti, like several other countries that have accepted Chinese loans, ends up in a debt trap with a possible loss of strategic assets.[10]

Involvement in such massive development projects sets the Chinese apart from the operators of the other foreign bases in Djibouti. They are only paying rent or, like the US, support in education, health, governance and democracy programmes.[11] Or France, which has an ordinary defence agreement with Djibouti and finances a project aimed at improving the livelihood of farmers. Since French is the official language of Djibouti, the government in Paris also provides students with scholarships to institutions of higher learning in France.[12] In Djibouti, as elsewhere, the BRI is tied to China's geostrategic interests.

Sri Lanka is the only of the Indian Ocean countries so far that had to hand over an important asset because it was unable to repay Chinese loans. According to Cissy Zhou, a staff writer for *Nikkei Asia*, Sri Lanka has been a supporter of the BRI from the very beginning in 2013 and 'has frequently been depicted by China critics as falling into an alleged "debt trap", enticed into accepting unsustainable loans for infrastructure projects and allowing Beijing to gain strategic or military influence by seizing assets in times of financial distress.'[13] And the critics are right. That was exactly what happened in 2017.

The Chinese government financed the first phase of the construction of a new port at Hambantota on the southern coast of Sri Lanka. It was supposed to benefit from its location along the shipping route from the Malacca Strait to the Suez Canal and was a showcase project, which the then President Mahinda Rajapaksa launched shortly after the Sri Lankan government in 2009 had won a twenty-seven-year-long war against the separatist Liberation Tigers of Tamil Eelam (LTTE), or the Tamil Tigers.

The Exim Bank of China lent an estimated US$306 million to the project, while the Sri Lanka Ports Authority's share was around US$46 million. The interest rate was set at an exorbitant 6.3 per cent and the loan had to be repaid in biannual instalments over a period of eleven years.[14] The China Harbour Engineering Company was contracted to build the port, and the second phase of the project became even costlier: US$800 million at the same interest rate.

The port was never a success and did not generate any substantial revenue. Sri Lanka defaulted on the loan and the then Prime Minister, Ranil Wickremesinghe, had to go to Beijing to try to solve the issue. The solution was that a new entity called the Hambantota International Port Group (HIPG) was created to take over the project. It became a joint venture after China Merchant Ports, a Hong Kong-based, Chinese-controlled company, bought an 85 per cent stake in HIPG and was awarded the sole right to operate and develop the port for ninety-nine years.[15] In effect, Chinese interests took over the port and it will remain in Chinese hands at least until the year 2116. Although the Sri Lankan government has repeatedly said that the port is purely for commercial use and no Chinese naval vessel will be permitted to use it as a base, the Australian defence expert David Brewster believes that such a scenario cannot be ruled out: 'New Delhi worries that China's influence will one day reach a point where the Sri Lankan government simply cannot say no.'[16]

The fate of a nearby, new international airport looks no better. A loan to cover US$190 million of the total cost of US$209 million was provided by the Exim Bank of China. But because it is located far from the capital, Colombo, and major tourist centres, the Mattala Rajapaksa International Airport—'Mattala' after the nearest town and 'Rajapaksa' after the President—became a financial burden as well. India stepped in and pledged to pay US$300 million for a joint venture that would get a forty-year lease to the facility. In effect, India would buy out Sri Lanka's debt to China and, in the process, hopefully get some goodwill in its island neighbour.[17] But that deal fell through and Sri Lanka is stuck with what has been described as the world's emptiest international airport. And yet another huge debt to China.

But Sri Lanka seems unfazed. Wickremesinghe went to China in October 2023 to participate in the celebrations of the tenth anniversary of the BRI, and assured Xi of Sri Lanka's continued active participation. Sri Lanka's total foreign debt amounts to US$46.9 billion, of which 52 per cent is owed to China, the largest lender.[18] Eager to minimize China's influence, India has provided Sri Lanka with US$4 billion in assistance to mitigate its worst economic woes. But that may not be enough for India to reassert the influence it had in Sri Lanka before the Chinese arrived in the early 2000s.

Today, China is also the main supplier of military hardware to Sri Lanka's armed forces, and Chinese weapons helped the government defeat the LTTE. China helps train Sri Lankan military personnel as well. Colombo has repaid China diplomatically by supporting its 'one China principle'—that Taiwan is part of China—and Sri Lanka was one of the fifty-three countries that supported China's crackdown on its pro-democracy movement in 2020 and the draconian security laws that were imposed on the former British colony Hong Kong.[19]

Before international tourism to the Maldives began in the 1970s, Sri Lanka—or Ceylon in the old days—was the main gateway to the islands, first by ship and, after an airport was built in 1960, by plane. There was also a weekly flight to and from Trivandrum (now Thiruvananthapuram) in southern India and irregular flights, but only for British military personnel, to a Royal Air Force base on Gan Island in the southern Addu Atoll. That base was established in 1941 and closed in 1970. Today, land has been reclaimed to enlarge Hulhule, the island on which the Maldives' airport was built, and a bridge links it with the capital Male, a separate island. The airport has direct flights to Europe, the Middle East, Japan, China, Singapore and Bangkok. The Maldives has successfully promoted its islands and coral atolls as a destination for luxury tourism, and the country has prospered as a result.

Before tourism took off, no buildings in Male were taller than two storeys and the roads were unpaved. It is now a modern city with high-rise buildings and shopping centres. But in order to shield the local Muslim population from the sight of scantily clad tourists, all resorts are located on outlying atolls to which foreign visitors are carried by speedboats directly from the airport. More than half of the people who work in those resorts come from India, Sri Lanka, Nepal, Indonesia, Bangladesh and the Philippines. Many managers are Westerners. The resorts are a world apart from the rest of the country.

China's interest in the Maldives—as expressed by President Xi Jinping when he visited the islands in September 2014 and told fairy tales about a 'Maritime Silk Road' and Zheng He's supposed exploits to his hosts—is not, needless to say, primarily in the booming and highly lucrative tourism industry. The Maldives may be a small country in terms of land area, 298 square kilometres, and with a population of only 515,000, but its exclusive economic zone covers about 859,000 square kilometres of ocean and its more than a thousand widely scattered islands offer strategic vantage points from which to monitor, even control, vital shipping lanes from East and Southeast Asia to the Middle East and Europe.

Not surprisingly, the Maldives has come to play a pivotal role in Xi's BRI. But it is also in and around the islands of the Maldives that China's forays into the Indian Ocean are clashing with India's immediate security interests.

The extension of the runway at the Maldives' international airport, which needed more land to be reclaimed, was developed by the Beijing Urban Construction Group, a project with a total cost of US$400 million, which the Maldives had to borrow from Chinese banks.[20] The 1.39-kilometre-long bridge between the airport island and Male was opened in 2018 and built by China Harbour Engineering and funded by a US$126 million Chinese government grant and a US$68 million loan from the Export-Import Bank of China.[21]

An entire new island, Hulhumale, has also been built to ease the pressure on overpopulated Male. Chinese state companies lent US$547.9 million for the construction of 11,000 apartments in high-rise blocks on Hulhumale, and a further US$180.9 million to extend the electrical grid to the new, articifial island.[22] The debts the Maldives owes to private Chinese companies are estimated at US$935 million, on top of the US$600 million directly owed to Beijing by the government in Male.[23] Some observers believe that the total amount the Maldives owes to Chinese banks could be in the order of US$3 billion, an unaffordable sum for a small country like the Maldives.[24] In other words, the BRI and affiliated projects have made the Maldives economically dependent on China for decades to come.

Perhaps the most controversial Chinese construction project in the Maldives is a plan to build a Joint Observation Station on Makunudhoo, an island in the north-western part of the country. It will be operated by the State Oceanic Administration of China and the Ministry of Environment and Energy of the Maldives.[25] An agreement to this effect was signed in Beijing by the Maldives Minister of Economic Development Mohamed Saeed and China's Foreign Minister Wang Yi on 7 December 2017 along with a memorandum of understanding 'between the government of the People's Republic of China and the government of the Republic of Maldives on cooperation within the framework of the

Silk Road Economic Belt and the twenty-first century Maritime Silk Road Initiative.'[26] Ten other agreements covered a construction at the airport, a free trade agreement, and loans from Chinese banks to finance all development projects in the Maldives that China had agreed to.[27]

China's increasingly close relations with the Maldives is a cause for serious concern in India. The proximity to India means that the Maldives with its huge exclusive economic zone—more than any other island nation in the Indian Ocean—is on the strategic red line that India does not want China to cross. That proximity also means that India's relations with the Maldives predate China's by several centuries. Culturally and linguistically, the Maldives are also much closer to India than China. The first settlers are likely to have been Buddhist and Hindu migrants from today's India and Sri Lanka. Islam was introduced by Arab traders; Dhovemi Kalaminja, the last Buddhist king of the islands, became a Muslim and adopted the name Sultan Muhammed-ul-Adil in 1153.[28] The Portuguese were the first Europeans to conquer the Maldives, which they did in 1558. But they were driven out after a revolt in 1573, and the Maldives remained an independent sultanate until 1887, when the British arrived and established a protectorate. The sultans were not deposed and the Maldives remained a British-dependent monarchy save for a brief period in 1953–1954 when it was declared a republic. The Sultanate of the Maldives became fully independent on 26 July 1965, but, on 11 November 1968, it was once again a republic.

Ibrahim Nasir, who had served as Prime Minister under the last Sultan Muhammed Fareed Didi, became the first President of the Maldives—and started the tourism industry. The first resort was opened in 1972, and became an instant success among wealthy Western tourists looking for a 'tropical paradise'. But tourism revenues were not enough to make up for the income that the British base on Gan used to generate before it was closed in 1970. An economic crisis ensued, and Ibrahim Nasir went into exile in Singapore in 1978, taking with him millions of dollars from the treasury.

Ibrahim Nasir was succeeded by Maumoon Abdul Gayoom, who was educated at the Al-Azhar University in Cairo and at the Royal College in Colombo. Gayoom remained president until November 2008, further developed the tourism industry and maintained close ties with India. A coup attempt in November 1988, which involved the arrival of Tamil Tiger mercenaries from Sri Lanka, was put down by Indian troops who were airlifted to Male to restore order. India also provided development aid and was the first country to assist the Maldives during the December 2004 tsunami.

But as Gayoom grew more authoritarian, the movement for democracy grew stronger. In 2008, the first contested presidential election was allowed to take place. Gayoom lost and Mohamed Nasheed, a former political prisoner, journalist and pro-democracy activist, won and became the country's first democratically elected President. And that was also when the India–China divide began to have a devastating impact on domestic politics, causing the flight of politicians to other countries and changes of government that amount to coups.

Nasheed was forced out of office during a political crisis in February 2012. He said at the time that his ouster amounted to a coup by his conservative opponents, a claim that was dismissed by an enquiry commission operating under the auspices of the Commonwealth. Nasheed ran unsuccessfully for re-election in 2013, and was then sentenced to thirteen years in jail under an obscure anti-terrorism law. The 2013 election was won by Abdulla Yameen, who paved the way for closer relations with China. The Maldives joined the BRI, Chinese capital began to flow into the country and Yameen personally inaugurated the 'China–Maldives Friendship Bridge' between Hulhule and Male in 2018 (the bridge has since been renamed the Sinamalé Bridge).

Nasheed was allowed to leave for Britain, where he was given political asylum. He then returned to the Maldives when his old friend and political companion Ibrahim Solih was elected President in 2018. Both Nasheed and Solih are seen as pro-India. The Indian Prime Minister Narendra Modi attended Solih's inauguration ceremony on 17 November 2018 as the only foreign head of government. Modi also held bilateral discussions with Solih just after his ceremony and conveyed India's desire to work closely with the Maldives in areas such as infrastructure development and healthcare.[29]

Solih pursued a policy he called 'India First' and it seemed that Chinese influence was on the wane. But then, in November 2023, a pro-Chinese politician, Mohamed Muizzu, was elected President. In January 2024, Muizzu paid a state visit to China, where he was received by Xi, who pledged to increase investment in the Maldives under what the Chinese President called 'a comprehensive strategic cooperative partnership'.[30]

Muizzu also visited Turkey and the United Arab Emirates—and ordered the withdrawal of Indian troops, which had been stationed in the Maldives since Nasheed signed a security agreement with India in 2009.[31] The Maldives is back in China's embrace, but apart from pro-Indian politicians, there are also other things the Chinese have to worry about. Nasheed, on a visit to London in September 2014, revealed that as many as 200 young men from the Maldives had gone to fight for the Islamic State in Syria and Iraq.[32] He also alleged that there were links between Islamic fundamentalists in the Maldives and the country's military and police. Nasheed also said that the country had become more conservative because of the influx of money from foundations in Saudi Arabia, which has paid for the construction of new mosques, and the recruitment to Islamist organizations of young men who resent the supposedly immoral behaviour of Western tourists.

One of the first attacks in the Maldives by Islamists took place on 29 September 2007 when a bomb exploded in a park in Male, injuring eight tourists from China, two from Britain and two from Japan. Three men were arrested and sentenced for carrying out the attack. Several other suspects fled the country and, when the police attempted to search a mosque on Himandhoo Island, they were confronted by about ninety masked and helmeted members of the mosque. The army took over from the police and established control.[33] The authorities were able to identify some of the militants as Al Qaeda associates.[34]

The most recent terrorism-linked incident of violence in the Maldives was reported on 22 August 2022, when the then minister for environment, climate change and technology, Ali Solih, was attacked with a knife and injured while he was traveling on his scooter in Hulhumale.[35]

On 8 November 2023, a militant thought to be the leader of a local faction of the Islamic State received a twenty-seven-year prison sentence on charges related to terrorism.[36] Security issues were high on the agenda when Muizzu met Xi and other Chinese officials in Beijing in January 2024, but it is not clear whether the threat of Islamic fundamentalism was mentioned during the talks.

The Seychelles is another Indian Ocean nation famous for high-end tourism, but those islands are geographically vastly different. The Seychelles, which are located closer to Africa, are not atolls like the Maldives but proper islands with tropical rainforests, hills and rivers. And they were uninhabited when they were first visited by Arab seafarers and Austronesian traders from today's Indonesia in the early Middle Ages. Records show that Vasco da Gama and his Portuguese armada sighted the islands in 1503, but it was not until the French came in the mid-eighteenth century and named them after Jean Moreau de Séchelles, King Louis XV's finance minister, that they were settled and got a permanent population. Arab pirates, who were operating from the islands, were evicted, and the French brought African slaves from the French-controlled islands of Réunion and Île de France (later British and known as Mauritius) to work the cinnamon, vanilla and copra plantations they established on the islands.

The French were also the first to recognize the strategic importance of the Seychelles and, therefore, decided to build more settlements there. If their enemies, the British, ever took charge of the islands, they would gain an ideal point from which to operate their Indian Ocean fleets. But French rule fell apart after the revolution in Paris in 1789. The British took possession of the islands in 1794 and they became a proper colony after the Treaty of Paris in 1814. Some, but not many, Indians were brought there as indentured labourers after slavery was abolished in 1835. A few Chinese also settled on the islands, mostly as shopkeepers and traders.[37]

The Seychelles also served as a kind of penal colony, but only for high-profile prisoners. The sultan of Perak in Malaya was sent there in 1877 for his alleged role in killing a British colonial officer. Others included the king of Ashanti, now part of Ghana, and his entourage as well as royalty from Uganda and British Somaliland. Some Arabs from Palestine—a British mandate under the League of Nations from the end of World War I to 1948—were also kept on the islands for a while. Winston Churchill once suggested that captured members of the Irish Republican Army should be deported to the Seychelles, but nothing came of that proposal. The best-known of all the deportees was Archbishop Makarios III of Cyprus, who was sent there for his role in fomenting communal discord between the Greeks and the Turks in the then British Crown colony.[38]

But the Seychelles, with a population of only 30,000 before World War II, was otherwise a truly colonial backwater. It was not until the early 1970s that an independence movement was formed. It coincided with the construction of an airport, which was inaugurated by Queen Elizabeth II on 20 March 1972. The Seychelles was now connected with the outside world, hotels were built and the first tourists arrived. The islands now had an income which, unlike coconuts and spices, could support the economy of an independent country. And independence was proclaimed on 29 June 1976. The Seychelles was now a republic and a free member of the Commonwealth as well as the United Nations.

But money matters and manipulations by outside forces brought instability to the Seychelles. France-Albert René, a left-wing politician, became President after a coup in 1977. The Seychelles became a one-party, socialist state under the Seychelles People's Progressive Front (SPPF), and René, assisted by Tanzania, formed a regular army to defend himself and consolidate his power. Close relations were established with the Soviet Union, Cuba and Algeria, which caused considerable concern among Western powers. It seemed as if the Eastern Bloc was gaining a foothold in the middle of the Indian Ocean. The solution, the US and its allies concluded, would be to dislodge René from power. An outright invasion would have been too provocative, so they enlisted the services of Michael Hoare, better known as 'Mad Mike Hoare', an India-born notorious mercenary of Irish origin, who had fought in civil wars in Africa.[39]

Hoare managed to put together a team of more than forty mercenaries who, on 25 November 1981, flew in on a Royal Swazi National Airways flight from Swaziland, masquerading as rugby players belonging to a beer-drinking club called Ye Ancient Order of Frothblowers. They brought an assortment of guns in their luggage hidden under toys they said were gifts for children in the Seychelles. They could have succeeded in their mission had it not been for one of the men going through the wrong counter at the airport in the Seychelles. He went to the goods declaration counter, was forced to open his bag—and the customs officer found that it contained a Soviet-made AK-47 assault rifle and ammunition. A firefight broke out between the foreign mercenaries and the airport's security personnel, killing one of Hoare's men and wounding a customs officer.

Hoare and his men then hijacked an Air India flight that was at the airport and forced it to fly to Durban in South Africa. They were arrested when they landed at Durban, but treated quite leniently. It was only after international pressure that Hoare was sentenced to ten years in prison, and the others got less than that. Hoare was released in 1985, settled in Durban and died there in February 2020, a month before he was going to turn 101.

It is not clear exactly who had ordered and financed the ill-fated coup attempt but the involvement of South Africa's security services is indisputable and it is widely suspected that the US CIA played a part in it as well. The Soviets had just invaded Afghanistan and the US had the safety of its base on Diego Garcia in the British Indian Ocean Territory to worry about. The Americans also maintained a tracking station for the air force on the main island Mahé, which they did not want to fall into the hands of some hostile power. African newspaper reports to that effect were, as expected, denied by the CIA.[40] The agency is not supposed to be involved in that kind of highly illegal operation.

After that coup attempt, René thought he needed tighter protection for himself and his increasingly authoritarian government. He turned to the North Koreans, who sent military advisers to assist René's presidential guards as well as the 750 men in the Seychelles army and 250 in the navy and air force.[41] But they could not prevent a mutiny within the armed forces. In August 1982, a group of soldiers seized the radio station in the capital Victoria, the port, some police stations and an army camp. The response was swift and harsh. Approximately 400 soldiers from Tanzania apprehended the mutineers, who had to face a court martial.

There was another coup attempt in 1986. But India sent a naval ship, the *INS Vindhyagiri*, to the islands, which was enough to scare the coup-makers and make them surrender. René seemed unwilling to soften his hold on the tiny island nation—457 square kilometres and about 100,000 people—but he could not ignore that the opposition against his rule was getting stronger. The Seychelles' growing role as a tourist destination may also have played a part in persuading him to liberalize the political system. In 1991, the one-party system was abolished, political exiles were allowed to return, and a new democratic constitution was adopted after a referendum.

Elections were held in July 1993, and René and his SPPF actually won. He had implemented a number of popular social reforms. René was re-elected in 1998 and in 2001, and it was not until then that he announced that he would step down in favour of his trusted protégé, James Michel. But René remained the head of the SPPF and, as such, the power behind the throne. The SPPF remained in power until the 2016 elections, when the Opposition took over. René died on 27 February 2019 at the age of eighty-three.

The return of reasonable political stability led to a further surge in tourism. More luxury hotels and resorts were built and the Seychelles also became a financial centre, where wealthy and often shady foreign businessmen could park their money in order to avoid having to pay taxes in their home countries, or come under unwanted scrutiny by international financial institutions. And China began to take a keen interest in developments in the Seychelles. In November 2016, General Wang Guanzhong, a leading member of China's Military Commission, paid a visit to the islands and 'enhancing the bilateral cooperation between Seychelles and China in the field of defence' was on the agenda.[42]

In June 2017, Xu Jinghu, who was identified as 'a special representative of the Chinese government on African affairs', also came for talks with high-ranking officials and stated that China enjoys 'a traditional friendship' with the Seychelles.[43] The nature of that 'traditional friendship' was not explained, only that China was now going to 'expand bilateral mutually beneficial cooperation in such areas as blue economy, tourism, health, sports and security.'[44] The visit could have been meant to promote and pave the way for the BRI, which the Seychelles joined officially on 1 September 2018.

But the Seychelles' cooperation with China before and after joining the BRI has not been without serious problems. When a new Chinese-financed, stately and white-pillared National Assembly building was going to be opened in Victoria in December 2009, the largest Opposition party, the Seychelles National Party (SNP), boycotted the ceremony. The SNP chairman, Wavel Ramkalawan, argued that such an important government building should have been built with the country's own resources, not by a foreign power. Ramkalawan also pointed out that the foundation stone for the building had an inscription only in Chinese and not in the three official languages of the Seychelles—English, French and Creole.[45]

What is often perceived as China's lack of sensitivity for feelings in countries where they have established a presence became apparent in another way in February 2018. Local truck drivers blocked a street in front of a government building in Victoria to protest against Sinohydro, a Mauritius-based Chinese company that was using its own vehicles with Chinese drivers for a project to construct a new dam at a reservoir that supplies the capital with water.[46]

The problem was eventually resolved because China has to look after its long-term interests in the Seychelles. As did the French and the British several hundred years ago, the Chinese have realized that the Seychelles' position on the equator and as the easternmost gateway to the African continent gives it a geopolitical significance that is far greater than the size of the country suggests. The Chinese authorities have invited hundreds of young people on visits and scholarships to China, and the local Confucius Institute conducts Chinese-language courses at the university in Victoria, a local adult education centre, and even in primary schools and at the Seychelles Tourism Academy.[47]

The Comoros, south-west of the Seychelles, is another sparsely populated but strategically important group of islands. Like the Seychelles, the Comoros were also uninhabited when the first seafarers, mostly Austronesians, arrived there more than 1,500 years ago.[48] Subsequent settlers came from the African mainland, Persia and the Arabian Peninsula. Zheng He visited the islands briefly during one of his voyages in the early fifteenth century, but he and his crew were the only Chinese recorded to have been there in ancient times.[49]

It is not known what religion the original islanders practiced, but by the tenth century, the vast majority had converted to Islam. Pirates ransacked the islands and warriors from Madagascar went there to capture men and women who were brought back as slaves. There was also a limited trade in minerals and tortoiseshells.

The name Comoros is said to be derived from 'qamar', moon in Arabic, and was what Arab traders, who brought Islam to the islands, named this group of islands.[50] Although outside conquerors managed to subdue one or sometimes two of the four islands of the Comoros at various times over the centuries, no foreign power brought all of them under central rule until the French arrived in the mid-nineteenth century. The islands were poor and actually of little economic value, and their main importance was as a way station for ships sailing to India and Southeast Asia. And that was why the French went there, for their strategic location in the western Indian Ocean and off the coast of Africa.

The first of the four islands in the archipelago to come under colonial rule was Mayotte, which became French in 1841. The other three islands were gradually taken over by the French and, in 1888 the entire archipelago became a single French colony and was placed under the authority of the governor-general of Madagascar. The Comoros remained poor and the colonial masters introduced sugar, vanilla, coffee and ylang-ylang, a tropical tree whose leaves can be used to make perfume, to uplift the backward economy of the islands.

Voices for independence were raised in the late 1960s and early 1970s, but the French did not want to give up such an important foothold in the region so the solution was to separate Mayotte from the other three islands. Referendums were held throughout the Comoros in 1974. Three of the islands voted overwhelmingly for independence, but Mayotte did not. Economic incentives and a long tradition of contacts with the colonial power in Europe made the people of Mayotte favour closer integration with France. When the Comoros proclaimed independence on 6 July 1975, Mayotte remained under French rule. The presence of French troops on Mayotte sent a clear message to the new rulers of the Comoros that they should not even think of occupying the breakaway island.

Mayotte became a French 'collectivité d'outre-mer', or overseas collectivity, and, after a referendum in 2009, it was declared an overseas department of France on 31 March 2011. Mayotte is thus an integral part of France and enjoys the same status as any other French department. Everyone is a French citizen, they vote in French elections and the euro is the currency. As a result, Mayotte has become far more prosperous than independent Comoros. The per capita income stands at 11,300 euros—or US$12,235—while on the Comoros it is only US$1,377. And a detachment of the French Foreign Legion is based in Mayotte to keep it well-defended.

While Mayotte has remained politically and economically stable, coups, coup attempts and assassinations have become regular features in the political life of the Comoros. The first President, Ahmed Abdallah, was ousted less than a month after the proclamation of independence and Ali Soilih, a leftist and not a friend of the former colonial power, took over. France responded by suspending all its aid to the Comoros, which amounted to 40 per cent of the national budget. As a consequence, the country's treasury was emptied because the government was unable to pay salaries to its civil servants. Economic mismanagement was also a factor, and Soilih turned to Tanzania and North Korea for support, which could provide the Comoros with only very limited aid.

Soilih became immensely unpopular, and then Robert 'Bob' Denard, a notorious mercenary, entered the scene. He had fought in Algeria and Angola as well as the Congo, Nigeria and Rhodesia before it became Zimbabwe.[51] On 12 May 1978, Denard landed with a force of forty-three mostly French mercenaries. Soilih was deposed and killed two weeks after Denard's coup while, supposedly, trying to escape from custody. France and South Africa have always denied accusations that they were involved. But suspicions remain strong that it was not Denard's own idea to launch an invasion and stage a coup in the Comoros.

Ahmed Abdallah retuned from Paris and was reinstalled as President. For eleven years, Denard headed his 300-strong presidential guard. Denard converted to Islam, assumed the name Said Mustapha Mahdjoub and took several local wives. After a while it was not clear to many in the Comoros if he or Ahmed Abdallah was the ruler of their country. Opposition grew and the economy remained as it had been under Soilih. The crisis culminated when Ahmed Abdallah was found shot dead, and, on 29 November 1989, Denard and the presidential guard seized absolute power. But that was more than what his former allies in France and South Africa could tolerate. Denard lost their support and, after he and his men had violently suppressed a demonstration of students and workers, he had to leave the country. He was flown to South Africa with a dozen of his men and placed under house arrest in Pretoria.

Denard was later allowed to return to France, but he had not given up hope of making a comeback in the Comoros. On the night of 27 September 1995, he arrived in the Comoros with thirty-three of his men aboard inflatable Zodiac dinghies. France, which by now had had more than enough of the wily and unpredictable mercenary, sent an expeditionary force to the Comoros. Denard and his men surrendered without a single shot being fired. Denard was brought back to France where he died in October 2007.

The Comoros may have recovered from those turbulent years, but relations with France did not improve. The government of the Comoros has not relinquished its claim to Mayotte, where the French have built up a loyal—and comparatively wealthy—bastion in the western Indian Ocean. Faced with economic hardships, the government of the Comoros turned to a country they had hoped would be a more trustworthy ally: China. China stepped in with help to construct a new sports stadium in the capital Moroni, a new airport, a power plant, schools and mosques.

Soldiers from the Comoros were brought to China for military training and to attend Chinese-language courses.

In December 2015, the Comoran President Ikililou Dhoinine met Xi on the sidelines of a China–Africa summit in Johannesburg, South Africa, and the Comoros then became one of the first countries to sign up to the BRI.[52] And the Chinese, like the French before them, have discovered the strategic value of those otherwise impoverished islands. Azali Assoumani, President of the Comoros since 2016, met Xi in Riyadh, Saudi Arabia, in December 2022, and the two heads of state praised each other. Xi said that, 'China supports the Comoros in playing a greater role in international and regional affairs, and stands ready to work closely with the Comoros to firmly support each other, and safeguard the common interests of developing countries and international fairness and justice.'[53] While Azali Assoumani asserted that, 'China has always stood shoulder to shoulder with the country and provided selfless help in its most difficult times.'[54] Mohamed Soilih, the director of the Comoros television station, has said: 'After 40 years [of independence], China has become the first partner. Before it was France, now it is China.'[55]

The Comoros may have benefited from its cordial relations with China, but as a study by the New Delhi-based Institute for Defence Studies and Analyses points out: '... discontent against China has started brewing. Fish stocks in the waters around Comoros are depleting and this is adversely affecting fishing—one of the three major occupations in the country. The fishing communities believe overfishing by Chinese vessels in traditionally Comorian fishing grounds is the reason. This story was reportedly suppressed by the government at the insistence of Chinese authorities.'[56] And, the study concludes: 'Debt driven infrastructure development, large-scale environmental degradation and lax regulatory standards are the side effects of engagement with China that smaller developing nations are forced to accept.'[57]

Tiny Comoros, 2,235 square kilometres and 850,000 people, is hardly in a position to challenge China on any of those issues. Partly because of French colonial ineptitude, and an internal turmoil that would make most other countries shun the Comoros, China has acquired a new, loyal ally in an important part of the Indian Ocean. Located north of the Mozambique Channel, the Comoros overlooks what for centuries has served as a transit and trade hub linking the Indian Ocean to the world—and, therefore, a potential maritime chokepoint.[58]

China has also made significant inroads in Madagascar on the eastern shores of the Mozambique Channel. Madagascar, the world's fourth largest island after Greenland, New Guinea and Borneo, joined the BRI on 1 March 2017. China had actually become Madagascar's biggest trading partner prior to that, in 2015. The huge island is rich in minerals such as gold, silver, copper, zinc, quartz, nickel and uranium. Fishing and forestry are other important sectors of the economy, which should be strong enough to support a population of twenty-nine million people. But Madagascar nevertheless is heavily dependent on foreign aid. In 2023, the European Union allocated €15.1 million in humanitarian assistance, while the US donated US$133.5 million in 2020. Since 2015, the United States Agency for International development (USAID) has provided over US$229 million for emergency and development assistance primarily to poorer communities in southern and south-eastern Madagascar.[59]

But Chinese involvement in development in Madagascar dwarfs those commitments. According to the official Chinese newspaper, *The Global Times*, the volume of bilateral trade reached US$2.08 billion in 2022, an increase of 68.56 per cent compared with 2017. Meanwhile, Madagascar's imports from China amounts to US$1.455 billion, an increase of 44.49 per cent compared with 2017, with an average annual growth rate of 7.6 per cent. Madagascar's exports to China totalled US$625 in 2022, an increase of 175.33 percent compared with 2017.[60]

In order to give trade with Madagascar some historical context, the United Nations Educational, Scientific and Cultural Organization (UNESCO), an entity not known for integrity and professionalism, has made the astonishing assertion that Madagascar had been on the 'Maritime Silk Road'. The proof, UNESCO claimed, is that 'Pottery and porcelain uncovered at archaeological sites on the island, reveal potential contacts between China and Madagascar established as early as the tenth century CE [...] These findings would indicate contacts via Silk Roads trade between Madagascar and China which pre-date the fifteenth century CE journey of explorer Zheng He to the coast of Africa.'⁶¹

There is no archaeological evidence or texts in old chronicles to suggest that Chinese traders actually visited Madagascar. Zheng He came closest, but he sailed along the upper east coast of Africa and then never south of Malindi, or modern-day Mombasa in Kenya. The Chinese porcelain and other goods from China were brought there by the seafarers from today's Indonesia who had traded with China, not directly by any Chinese traders.

Despite its size and riches, Madagascar—like the Comoros and the Seychelles, and Mauritius and Réunion in the sea east of Madagascar—had no native population when the first seafarers from what is now Indonesia arrived there more than two millennia ago.⁶² And that is the reason why at least a third of Madagascar's population even today can trace their ethnic origin to Southeast Asia, and the rest are of Bantu or of mixed Austronesian-African descent. The official name for the national language is Malagasy and it is of Malayo-Polynesian origin, but it contains many dialects which are not mutually intelligible.

Madagascar, like all the other Indian Ocean states, has had a turbulent history. In the pre-colonial era, Madagascar consisted of several kingdoms and gained infamy for being a haven for pirates. In the early nineteenth century, the island was unified under the rule of one king. The first was Andrianampoinimerina, who reigned between 1787 and 1810 and the second his son and successor Radama I, who remained on the throne until his death in 1828. Radama I sought to modernize Madagascar along Western lines. Missionaries from the London Missionary Society established schools on the island and brought in a printing press, which resulted in the Merina dialect becoming the official language, written with the Roman alphabet.

French colonizers were the next to arrive, who managed to sideline the British and, in 1894, they declared a protectorate over the entire island. But Queen Ranavalona III, then ruler of Madagascar, refused to recognize the proclamation. The French responded by sending an expeditionary force, which occupied the capital Antananarivo in September 1895. The following year, the French declared Madagascar a colony and deported the queen and her Prime Minister first to Réunion and later to Algeria. French colonial officials arrived to take over the administration from the native civil servants who had served the indigenous monarchy.

Madagascar remained a French colony until 26 June 1960, when it became independent after a referendum and a national election, which had been held the year before. Philibert Tsiranana, a cattle farmer's son who was educated in France, was sworn in as the first President of the republic. He introduced what was called 'Malagasy socialism', a form of social democracy combined with private enterprise. At first, Madagascar experienced political stability and economic growth but, as the years went by, Tsiranana became increasingly authoritarian. Anti-government demonstrations rocked Antananarivo and, in May 1972, Tsiranana tried to defuse the crisis by handing over power to the military under General Gabriel Ramanantsoa. Chaos ensued and Ramanantsoa, in turn, handed power to another officer, Colonel Richard Ratsimandrava, who was assassinated after only five days in office.

A semblance of order was restored after yet another military takeover in 1975 under Lieutenant-Commander Didier Ratsiraka, who was elected to a seven-year term as President and changed the name of the country to the Democratic Republic of Madagascar. Madagascar did not technically become a socialist one-party state, but it was governed by a coalition of six parties called 'Front National pour la Défense de la Révolution', or the National Front for the Defence of the Revolution. It established close relations with the Soviet Union, Cuba, North Korea and China. Soviet military advisers arrived in Madagascar, while the North Koreans provided training for Ratsiraka's personal security guards. Cuba provided assistance in the educational field, and China entered into a trade, economic and technical cooperation agreement with the country.

This was actually not a new development. Since the fall of Tsiranana in 1972, Madagascar had been drifting away from France and other allies in the West. But this time, a more austere form of socialism was introduced, which put Madagascar firmly in the Eastern Bloc. However, strict socialist policies also resulted in a severe economic crisis that forced Ratsiraka to turn to the IMF to get assistance. Further economic mismanagement drove people out into the streets of major cities. In November 1992, Ratsiraka agreed to hold elections, which he lost. Albert Zafy, a French-educated university lecturer, became President, though even he proved unable to solve the country's economic woes. He was forced to resign in 1996, and Ratsiraka returned to power. His second term in office lasted until 2001, and he was succeeded by a series of ineffectual Presidents.

After elections were held in December 2013, a former finance minister called Hery Rajaonarimampianina became President in January 2014. His full name was Hery Martial Rajaonarimampianina Rakotoarimanana and apart from being known for having the longest name of any head of state in the world, he was also the architect of Madagascar's current close relationship with China. However, this time, the attraction was not socialism but Deng Xiaoping's free-wheeling capitalism—and the lure of Chinese money. It was during a visit to Beijing in March 2017 that Madagascar joined the BRI. Rajaonarimampianina praised the scheme as 'a wise and visionary strategy'.[63]

But Rajaonarimampianina's reform-minded government could not escape a perennial problem of Madagascar politics and governance: corruption. Rajaonarimampianina was also accused of undermining Madagascar's secular constitution by favouring Christianity. According to the official census, 58.09 per cent of the population is Christian, either Roman Catholics or Protestants, while 39.22 per cent practice indigenous beliefs and 2.12 are Muslims.[64] Rajaonarimampianina was forced to resign in 2018.

Close cooperation with China has continued under the current President Andry Rajoelina, a politician and businessman who assumed office in December 2023. But, as elsewhere, the BRI has not been without problems. According to the Prague-based China Observers in Central and Eastern Europe (CHOICE), the number of projects proposed under the BRI remains limited. All five projects focus on road construction, including a 20-kilometre road leading to the Antananarivo's airport and a 10-kilometre road connection to Tamatave, the country's major port.[65]

CHOICE points out that China has so far not been involved in bigger infrastructure projects, such as ports and airports, as has often been the case in other African countries. But indications suggest that China is interested in similar projects, which could be crucial for its long-term strategic objectives in the Indo-Pacific.

Given widespread poverty in Madagascar, it would be expected that China and its construction projects and activities in the country would be considered positively. Nevertheless, the Afrobarometer data gathered in 2022 and presented by CHOICE shows that only about 35 per cent consider China's influence in the country as positive, putting Madagascar among the countries with the least positive views towards China from the twenty-eight African countries surveyed.[66]

A major reason for the discontent with China is the migration that has followed in the wake of Chinese investment and the BRI. The first Chinese immigrants arrived in Madagascar as labourers working on French-owned plantations. Later, many became shopkeepers and craftsmen but, upon independence in 1960, they numbered only about 8,000. Today, between 60,000 and 100,000 Chinese are believed to be residing in Madagascar, representing the second largest Chinese community in Africa after South Africa. And they show little desire or willingness to integrate into local communities.[67]

The Indian Ocean islands immediately east of Madagascar—Mauritius and Réunion—have seen a very different development from those of the Comoros and Madagascar. Mauritius, a former British colony, has always been politically stable and, by regional standards, is quite wealthy. Réunion, with an even higher living standard, is a French overseas department and has held that status since 1946. Both islands were once ruled by the French, who built up plantation economies based on sugarcane and a labour force consisting of slaves brought in from Africa.

The French ruled Mauritius, then Île de France, from 1715 to 1810 when it was captured by the British and formally ceded to them in the 1814 Treaty of Paris. The British renamed it Mauritius, which was what the Dutch had called the island before it was taken by the French, and English became the official language.[68] But English never fully replaced

French and Creole, and all three languages are still spoken by a majority of the island's population.

British colonial rule led to great changes in other fields. In 1833, the British abolished slavery and about 70,000 African slaves were freed.[69] Few of the freed slaves wanted to continue working on the sugarcane plantations so the British decided to solve the problem of a severe shortage of workers by importing so-called 'indentured labourers' from India. Most of them came from Bhojpur, an impoverished area in northern India.

The Indians soon came to make up the majority of the population of Mauritius and with the introduction of British-style education, a new predominantly Indian middle class emerged. Seewoosagur Ramgoolam, a graduate of University College London and the son of an indentured labourer who had arrived in Mauritius at the age of eighteen in 1896 onboard a ship from Calcutta, began campaigning for independence. It was finally achieved on 12 March 1968, and Ramgoolam became the first Prime Minister of independent Mauritius.

Réunion, like Mauritius, was uninhabited when the first Europeans arrived there in the early sixteenth century. The first to spot the islands were the Portuguese but they never established a settlement there. That came with the French, who took possession of the island in 1642 and named it Île Bourbon after the royal family who at that time ruled France. The population consisted of French plantation owners and African slaves. Some coffee was produced for export, but the population, white as well as black, remained poor.

The name was changed to Île de la Réunion in 1793 by a decree issued by the revolutionary constituent assembly in Paris. The name alluded to the union of revolutionaries from Marseilles with the National Guard in Paris. After a brief occupation by the British during the Napoleonic wars in Europe, sugar was introduced and, as a result, Réunion prospered. When slavery was abolished in 1848, the French also began importing labour from India. This was possible because France still had some enclaves on the coasts of otherwise British India: Pondicherry (now Puducherry), Karikal (now Karaikal) and Yanaon (now Yanam) on the eastern Coromandel coast, and Mahé on the western Malabar coast as well as Chandernagore (now Chandannagar) near the Hooghly river north of Calcutta (now Kolkata).

Unlike Mauritius, Réunion never had any really strong independence movement. The major reason was that the inhabitants of Britain's colonies were subjects of the crown, while France made everyone a citizen of the French republic. The relationship between Paris and its overseas territories was cemented when Réunion along with some French possessions in America—Guadeloupe, Martinique and French Guiana—were declared to be overseas departments, a status also enjoyed by Mayotte since 2011.

There is no reason for Réunion to even contemplate joining the BRI; Mauritius has not done it either. Mauritius' wealth is based on luxury tourism and the manufacturing of high-tech goods. Banks and financial institutions are also able to provide the kind of sophisticated services that are hard to come by in mainland Africa. China, naturally, has shown interest in what Mauritius has to offer. The two countries signed a free trade agreement in January 2021 and, after that, data published by Chinese sources suggest that Mauritius' exports to China increased by 148 per cent.[70] Chinese direct investment in Mauritius in 2020 was estimated at US$45.77 million according to the same source, with Chinese cumulative investment in Mauritius amounting to approximately US$887 million, 'mainly in the finance, real estate, manufacturing and tourism sectors.'[71] Air Mauritius has started direct flights to Shanghai and Chinese businessmen have become a familiar sight in Port Louis. Chinese tourists flock to the island's beach resorts.

Without being a member of the BRI, Mauritius has become a vital link in Xi's vision of the BRI, which the Indians see as a threat to their interests in the Indian Ocean. Ties to India have always been close because of the number of people in Mauritius who are of Indian ancestry. Naval cooperation between India and Mauritius is especially strong and, in a show of force, India sent *INS Teg*, a guided missile frigate that towed *Valiant*, a newly built coast guard ship to the island. On arrival at the capital Port Louis, *Valiant* was handed over to the Mauritian government for use by its coast guards.[72]

After having been a realm of the Commonwealth with the British monarch as head of state, Mauritius became a republic with its own President on 12 March 1992. But it was revealed much later that independence had not been without conditions. The colony of Mauritius consisted not only of the main island but also Rodrigues plus some scattered islets in the Indian Ocean, among them the Chagos Archipelago to the north. During talks in London in the mid-1960s, Ramgoolam, then chief minister, had been told that Mauritius would not be granted independence unless he agreed to separate the Chagos Archipelago from Mauritius.

Reluctantly, Ramgoolam agreed and the Chagos Archipelago became part of the British Indian Ocean Territory (BIOT). Between 1967 and 1973, the entire population of BIOT—1,500 to 2,000 people, mostly a Creole-speaking mix of Indians and Africans who survived by growing coconuts and collecting guano—was deported, mainly to Mauritius but also to the Seychelles.

Military personnel from the US arrived on the main atoll Diego Garcia in March 1971, bringing with them earthmoving gear, building materials and workers, of whom many were Filipinos, to build a military base which is now among its most important worldwide.[73] The US military, which leases Diego Garcia from the British, has coordinated most of its military operations in the Middle East from this tiny, subequatorial atoll. It also uses Diego Garcia to monitor sea traffic between Asia, Africa and Europe, including keeping a close watch on China's increased presence in the Indian Ocean region. Moreover, Diego Garcia earned notoriety during President George W. Bush's so-called 'war on terror' when it was revealed as one of the 'black sites' where terror suspects, many from Afghanistan, were detained and interrogated.[74]

Diego Garcia has been front-page news in the international media for another reason as well. The Chagossians, those who were expelled from the islands, and their descendants have for years been involved in a campaign for the right to return to their islands—and won a hearing for their demands in the International Court of Justice (ICJ). The court delivered what is called an 'advisory opinion' on 25 February 2019, concluding that 'the process of decolonization of Mauritius was not lawfully completed when that country acceded to independence' and that 'the United Kingdom is under an obligation to bring to an end its administration of the Chagos Archipelago as rapidly as possible.'[75] The ICJ's judges said as part of their advisory opinion that all United Nations member states, including the US, are obliged to cooperate 'to complete the decolonization of Mauritius.'[76] Mauritian politicians have also started to grandstand on how their predecessors were forced to give up the Chagos Archipelago in what they view as Britain using political blackmail to retain control of the islands.

The Chagossians, who now number about 6,000 if those born after the eviction are included, have stated that they only want to return to now uninhabited islands and the part of Diego Garcia where the US has no military installations, and have no interest in the base being shut down. But the likelihood of such a return taking place is virtually nil. The set-up at Diego Garcia is far too important to be tampered with in any shape or form, and the China factor has made it outright improbable that the UK and the US will change their minds. In January 2024, UK foreign secretary, David Cameron, caused an uproar from Opposition politicians and human rights advocates by ruling out the resettlement of the Chagossians.[77]

The UK and the US are not the only Western powers with an interest at preserving the status quo in the Indian Ocean. It is often lost on international observers that France is an Indian Ocean power. Apart from the detachment of the French Foreign Legion in Mayotte and the base in Djibouti, France also has some 2,000 troops in Réunion—and it controls more maritime territory in the Indian Ocean than any other country.

France's exclusive economic zone in the Indian Ocean encompasses altogether 2,650,013 square kilometres, which is possible because of all the scattered islands that are under French control. In addition to Réunion and Mayotte, France also controls the Kerguelen Islands, the Crozet Archipelago, the St. Paul and Amsterdam islands, and a string of smaller islands around and near Madagascar: Juan de Nova, Europa, Bassas da India, Gloriosa and Tromelin. None of those islands have any permanent population, but French scientists and researchers stay on some of them on a rotational basis. Together, all those islands form the French Southern and Antarctic Lands, an overseas territory.

Most of those islands are small, but the largest and most mountainous is Kerguelen, 7,215 square kilometres, where more than 100 French scientists are based during the summer, with somewhat fewer in winter. There is also a French satellite tracking station and installations which are believed to be of military significance. In September 2021, it was announced that the construction of a new Galileo Sensor Station, which can establish satellite orbits more precisely, had been completed.[78]

Further to the east in the Indian Ocean are two Australian external territories: Christmas Island and the Cocos (Keeling) Islands. Small and insignificant as they may be in terms of size and population, those islands extend Australia's reach into the region for surveillance, air defence and maritime and ground strike operations. The importance of Christmas Island and the Cocos (Keeling) Islands—both of them originally British possessions—became apparent during the World Wars of the twentieth century. One of the first naval battles of World War I was fought near the Cocos between the British and the Germans. During World War II, Japan invaded Christmas Island and bombarded the Cocos. The first airstrip on the Cocos (Keeling) Islands was built in the early 1940s and played an important role in the defence of Australia.

Today, neither Germany nor Japan poses a threat to Australia and the regional order, but China's involvement in upgrading ports in Cambodia, Myanmar, Bangladesh, Sri Lanka and Pakistan has prompted Australia to pay more attention to those islands. Christmas Island does not have any defence installations but there are signals intelligence facilities on the Cocos (Keeling) Islands. In July 2023, aircraft from India's navy and air force made a groundbreaking visit to the Cocos (Keeling) Islands, which David Brewster, the Australian defence expert, said 'represents an important step in the bilateral relationship as the two countries increasingly give each other access to their military facilities in the Indian Ocean.'[79]

Efforts are underway to further strengthen defence cooperation between Australia and India, and, according to a paper produced by Radhei Tambi, a research associate at the Centre for Air Power Studies in New Delhi, for the Lowy Institute in Australia: 'the growing number of Chinese research vessels, submarines and underwater drones operating in the Indian Ocean has raised concerns. This is where the island territories of India and Australia offer the chance to strengthen maritime surveillance in the region, as well as develop ties with other partners.'[80]

Tambi mentions India's Andaman and Nicobar Islands, which lie close to the Strait of Malacca and Australia's Cocos (Keeling) Islands in the strategic waters leading up to Indonesia. 'Taken together, these territories cover the entry and exit points of the Indian and Pacific Oceans,' Tambi argues.[81]

Military cooperation between France and India has also seen a marked increase in recent years. French President Emmanuel Macron has visited New Delhi on several occasions for talks about regional security; and, in October 2023, India announced that it wants to purchase Rafale Marine aircraft worth US$6 billion from France to be used by the Indian Navy.[82] Although China has never been mentioned as the common adversary, it is quite clear that India and France share the same concerns about the new role that the Chinese are playing in the Indian Ocean.

International security analysts usually assume that an armed conflict between China on one side, and the US and its defence-partners Japan and Australia and possibly also India on the other, would begin in the South China Sea. But nothing can happen there without spy satellites zooming in on any new development, and some kind of negotiations would immediately be underway to defuse a particularly critical situation.

An armed confrontation is still possible in the South China Sea, but it is far more likely that something could go fundamentally wrong in the Indian Ocean, where the battle lines are less clear. Moreover, the region's small island states where corruption is a major problem are vulnerable to manipulation by outside powers. All of them also have long histories of political instability and exploitation by colonialists, pirates, mercenaries and fraudsters, and, in the case of the Maldives, the additional threat posed by Islamic extremists. A similar situation prevails in the Pacific Ocean, where China is also making its presence felt in a way that has created concern. And, even there, the BRI is having an impact that could have far-reaching geopolitical consequences.

6

PEARLS OF THE PACIFIC

CHINA'S LEADERS HAVE NOT YET COME UP WITH A NEW, FANCY name for their interactions with the many island nations across the Pacific Ocean. A 'Pacific Silk Road' would have sounded a bit too incongruous as no noteworthy number of Chinese traders or migrants went there before the advent of the European colonial powers in nineteenth century. Some Chinese traders settled in Fiji after the British conquest in the 1870s, while others came as cooks and carpenters. But Fiji's immigrant community has always been overwhelmingly Indian, not Chinese. The French brought Chinese to Tahiti as indentured labourers for their cotton plantations on the island rather than employing local people. The Germans preferred to import Chinese to work on their copra plantations in Samoa and the north-eastern part of New Guinea, two territories that they controlled until World War I.[1] But all that history has not prevented today's Chinese leaders from using the 'Silk Road' analogy even here. In November 2014, President Xi Jinping stressed that the South Pacific region was a natural 'extension of the twenty-first century Maritime Silk Road initiative put forward by China.'[2]

Many of the islands in the Pacific Ocean were first populated by aboriginals from Taiwan; but they were Austronesians, not Chinese. The only exceptions would be some Chinese traders who made it to the northern coast of New Guinea before the earliest Europeans arrived on the scene, and the Polynesian island of Futuna, where a Chinese ship was wrecked several hundred years ago. Some mixed-race descendants of theirs are still living on Futuna, which, together with the nearby island of Wallis, is now a French collectivité d'outre-mer, or overseas collectivity.[3]

But despite the lack of any historical links to the Pacific region comparable with those to the Russian Far East and Southeast Asia, the Chinese have made having influence over the scattered islands of Polynesia, Melanesia and Micronesia a priority in their foreign policy, and that includes promoting the BRI. In 2018, at a meeting of Chinese so-called 'friendship associations' in Hainan, China, Tonga's Princess Royal Salote Mafile'o Pilolevu Tuita proposed establishing what she called a Pearl Maritime Road Initiative, extending the BRI into the Southwest Pacific.[4] Soon after that, all the countries in the Pacific region, which maintain diplomatic relations with Beijing, signed agreements on the BRI.

China's interests in the Pacific islands are threefold. The first is purely economic: to exploit the natural resources of Papua New Guinea and the fish-rich waters of the Pacific Ocean, the world's most fertile fishing ground. The second is to deprive Taiwan of recognition from some of the island nations, which have diplomatic relations with the authorities in Taipei, but not Beijing. Beijing considers Taiwan a 'breakaway, renegade province', while the official name of the island nation is still 'the Republic of China', a leftover from the days when it purported to be the legitimate government of the whole of China. In recent years, 'the Republic of China' has adopted a more 'Taiwanese' identity and no longer claims territories on the mainland. Today, only twelve countries worldwide afford full recognition to 'the Republic of China' on Taiwan, and 'the People's Republic of China' has used pressure and bribes, in the Pacific and elsewhere, to make them switch recognition from Taipei to Beijing. It is still not possible to have diplomatic relations with both the People's Republic of China and the Republic of China, Taiwan.

The third and most important interest is to challenge and eventually replace the US as the self-proclaimed 'guardian and protector' of the Pacific and shift the region's geopolitics in favour of Beijing. The vast expanse of the Pacific Ocean forms a buffer between East Asia and North America. Before and during World War II, Japan sought to establish a presence there to be able to confront the US from an advantageous position. Now and for the same reason, it is China that is pushing into the region to recalibrate the power balance in the Pacific. And it is in this context that China's BRI projects in the Pacific should be seen, and not as unselfish attempts to reduce poverty and mitigate the lack of infrastructural developments on the islands.

As for the first motivation for moving into the Pacific, Papua New Guinea with its reserves of minerals, timber, oil and gas has attracted not only private businessmen from China but state enterprises as well, which precede the BRI by several decades. In the mid-1990s, only 0.5 per cent of Papua New Guinea's log exports went to China. Today it is 90 per cent.[5] A similar rape of the forests on the Solomons may lead to the total deforestation of those islands within less than two decades. In the 1990s, Papua New Guinea's mining sector was dominated mainly by Australian, British and Canadian companies. Today, China is there as well. Papua New Guinea has nickel, cobalt, copper and, in the highlands, even gold. In 2003, the China Metallurgical Group became the majority shareholder of Ramu NiCo, which owns a nickel mine near Madang on the country's north-eastern coast.

As Geoffrey York, a Canadian journalist, reported in January 2009: 'With a planned investment of US$1.4 billion and an expected lifespan of twenty to forty years, Ramu is one of the biggest mining projects China has ever attempted overseas. And China Metallurgical is determined to do it right.'[6] The Chinese investment turned out to be US$2 billion. Zeng Fanhua, Chinese ambassador to Papua New Guinea, confirmed in a statement in May 2023 that 'the Ramu nickel and cobalt mine in Madang is the single largest Chinese investment in the Pacific.'[7]

But the Chinese company has not always 'done it right'. When then Papua New Guinean labour minister, David Tibu, visited the mine in early 2007, he found that the local workers were treated like slaves. They were paid less than US$3 a day and given tins of fish as compensation for overtime work. Christianity is strong in the area, but the workers were not allowed to go to church on Sundays. When they went anyway, the company deducted a day's work from their pay. The canteen where the workers ate, the minister said, was 'not fit for pigs or dogs', and the toilets were filthy.[8] Tibu's findings made headlines in the country's newspapers and prompted the Chinese to embark on a vigorous PR drive. The Chinese-owned company pledged to set aside millions of dollars to build clinics, schools and churches, and to sponsor rugby and basketball teams, festivals and farms managed by local people.

But all that did little to alleviate the tense relationship between the company and the locals. In February 2020, a coalition of more than 5,000 villagers and the provincial government sued the company, demanding that it stop dumping millions of tons of mine waste into the ocean near the mine.[9] They also asked for US$5.2 billion in restitution. Half a million people in the area rely on fishing, and the plaintiffs argued that their lives and food supply were at stake as the waters had become polluted and the fish had died.

When it comes to large-scale commercial fishing by foreign companies, Chinese fleets may not be the only ones active in the Pacific. Industrial-scale fishing in the region began after World War II, and the business was long dominated by companies from the US, South Korea, Taiwan and Japan. But in the past two decades, China has dispatched wave after wave of fishing boats, mainly longliners and purse seiners, which scoop up almost everything. China's Pacific fishing fleet has grown by 500 per cent since 2012 and the amount they catch, especially tuna, may soon surpass that of all other countries combined. A May 2021 report by the Australia-based Judith Neilson Institute, which supports quality journalism around the world, reported, 'a survey of boats operating in the Pacific in 2016 found that Chinese-flagged vessels far outstripped those of any other country. China had 290 industrial vessels licensed to operate in the region at the time, more than a quarter of the total, and more than the 240 from all the Pacific nations combined.'[10]

Although many countries across the world maintain unofficial relations with Taiwan through 'trade representatives', 'economic and cultural offices' and other euphemisms for de facto diplomatic missions, three of the twelve full-fledged embassies of 'the Republic of China' are located in the Pacific: in the Marshall Islands, Palau and Tuvalu. The other nine are the African kingdom of Eswatini (formerly known as Swaziland), Belize, Guatemala, Haiti and Paraguay in Central and South America, the smaller Caribbean Island nations of St. Kitts-Nevis, St. Lucia, St. Vincent and the Grenadines, and finally the Vatican in Europe.

The 'Republic of China', then representing the entire nation, was a member of the United Nations and its Security Council until 1971, when the People's Republic of China was recognized by the United Nations as the sole legitimate government of China. Following Taiwan's ouster from the United Nations, its remaining allies have pledged to promote Taipei's interests in the United Nations, and do so actively. And, in the United Nations, every member state has one vote, so that applies equally to countries with millions of inhabitants as well as tiny island nations such as Nauru (21 square kilometres and 12,500 inhabitants in 2019) and Tuvalu (26 square kilometres and 11,200 inhabitants in 2012).

Both China and Taiwan have resorted to what is called 'chequebook diplomacy' to further their respective interests: China to deprive Taiwan of diplomatic recognition, and Taiwan to maintain its status as an independent nation and recognized as such by others. This had led to certain resource-starved Pacific nations shifting recognition back and forth depending on which 'Chinese side' offered more aid.

Tiny Nauru is a case in point. The minuscule island became independent in 1968 after having been under a joint British–Australian–New Zealand trusteeship since World War I, before which it was a German colony. Once immensely rich from phosphate mining, it turned poor because of mismanagement and, for a while, tried to survive as a tax haven and resorted to selling its passport in order to cover government expenses. In 1980, Nauru first established diplomatic relations with Taiwan, which offered generous aid in return. In 2002, however, it decided to recognize China and proclaimed that it supported its 'one China principle'.

Beijing had offered Nauru US$100 million, which was more than Taiwan had given the country in aid. But then, in 2003, Nauru closed its newly established embassy in Beijing. In May 2005, Nauru re-established diplomatic relations with Taiwan, which sent doctors to the island republic's only hospital as well as money and other gifts to its officials and politicians. But after the January 2024 elections in Taiwan, which saw yet another victory for the pro-Taiwan independence Democratic Progressive Party—Nauru once again recognized the People's Republic of China.[11]

The Republic of Kiribati, which was part of the British crown colony the Gilbert and Ellice Islands until independence in 1979 (the smaller Ellice Islands became Tuvalu), established diplomatic relations with China in 1980. But in 2003, Kiribati shifted recognition to Taiwan only to break relations with Taipei in 2019 and re-recognize Beijing as the sole legitimate government of China. Nearby Tuvalu, though, continues to recognize Taiwan.

The first major turning point in the fight for control over the Pacific islands came when Tonga decided to sever ties with Taiwan in 1998—and recognize China. Until then, Tonga had been Taiwan's staunchest ally in the Pacific. Tongan ministers were wined and dined in Taipei, and treated much like leaders of some bigger and much more important nation. It is not certain how China managed to win over Tonga, but on 1 November of that year, the Taiwanese were suddenly, and for many—unexpectedly, told to evacuate the rented building near the waterfront in the capital Nuku'alofa that had served as the embassy of the Republic of China. A day later, it was announced that Tonga and China had established diplomatic relations.

In October 1999, Tonga's then king, Taufa'ahau Tupou IV, received a red-carpet welcome in Beijing along with promises of aid. Significantly in a broader context, in July 2000, Wu Quanshu, deputy chief of general staff of China's People's Liberation Army, visited Tonga, followed in 2001 by another army deputy, Wei Fulin.[12] Tonga is one of very few Pacific island countries with a military force, and its links with China have grown steadily since the two countries established diplomatic relations.

In October 2004, the Tongan king paid another visit to China at the invitation of then President Hu Jintao. Taufa'ahau Tupou IV passed away in September 2006 at the age of eighty-eight, and was succeeded by his eldest son, Siaosi, or George, Tupou V, who paid a state visit to

China in April 2008. He died in March 2012, and his younger brother and successor, Aho'eitu Tupou VI, visited China in March 2018.

In February 2022, after an underwater volcano had erupted near Tonga and set off a tsunami, two ships from the People's Liberation Army Navy delivered relief supplies to the island nation.[13] And, in May that year, the Chinese foreign minister Wang Yi was received in the royal palace in Nuku'alofa. The new Chinese ambassador Liu Weimin stated when he arrived in Tonga on 18 April 2024 that he 'will spare no effort to work with friends from all walks of life in Tonga to promote China-Tonga comprehensive strategic partnership based on mutual respect and common development.'[14]

Evidently, Tonga is important to China, and Beijing spares no effort to maintain friendly relations, including military cooperation, with the small but strategically located Pacific kingdom. There is no other reason beyond geostrategic considerations that China would befriend Tonga and court its royalty. It may be hard to find a more odd couple anywhere in the world: China, atheist and still ruled by an omnipotent Communist Party—and Christian fundamentalist Tonga, where the king wields great political authority over an essentially feudal system of government controlled by noble families, and where it is illegal to do any work on a Sunday, even mowing the lawn in the yard outside one's house. But the Chinese authorities have treated the kings, princes and princesses of Tonga with more respect than they have any other royal family in the world.

The Solomon Islands used to be another Taiwan ally in the Pacific and a recipient of generous aid from Taipei. But in September 2019, Prime Minister Manasseh Sogavare announced that the Solomon Islands had decided to recognize China. It was reported at the time that Beijing had offered huge bribes to Solomon Islands politicians to get them to agree to the switch. Taiwan had also offered them bribes, but lost out in the bidding contest.[15] The shift in alliances came with a security pact, which caused sharp reactions from the US, Australia and New Zealand. The government in Honiara has since tried to downplay the importance of the pact, but suspicions remain that it will lead to some kind of military cooperation between the Solomon Islands and China.[16]

The tiny Micronesian Republic of Palau recognizes Taiwan and maintains an embassy in Taipei. In recent years, Palau has come under heavy pressure from China to switch recognition and, for the first time in the Pacific, the authorities in Beijing have used tourism as a weapon to get what they want. In 2017, China decided to restrict group travel to the island country, which is heavily dependent on tourism. According to official figures, more than 91,000 people from China visited Palau in 2015, accounting for 54 per cent of all visitors. By pre-Covid-19 2019, that number had already fallen to about 28,000, causing a significant drop in tourism revenue.[17] But Palau has persevered and its President, Surangel Whipps, has said that there will be no changes in the arrangement as long as he is in office.

But for China, much more is at stake than depriving Taiwan of diplomatic recognition. There is a strategic dimension to China's interest in Polynesia as well as in Micronesia. These islands have tiny land areas and lack the mineral resources and forests of Melanesian countries such as Papua New Guinea and the Solomon Islands, but their sea areas and exclusive economic zones are huge. The 119,000 inhabitants of Kiribati live on 811 square kilometres of land, but its thirty-two atolls and one raised coral island are dispersed over 3,441,810 square kilometres of ocean, a strategically located exclusive economic zone in the middle of the Pacific Ocean, straddling the equator. Tonga has about 100,000 inhabitants and 748 square kilometres of land, and an exclusive economic zone measuring around 700,000 square kilometres.

Approximately 104,000 people live on 702 square kilometres of land in the Federated States of Micronesia—and it occupies 2,780,000 square kilometres of ocean, giving the country the fourteenth largest exclusive economic zone in the world. The Cook Islands, still not fully independent but a territory in 'free association' with New Zealand, has an exclusive economic zone covering 1,960,027 square kilometres, while only 15,000 people live on 236 square kilometres of land. The outside power that wins over these small island nations can control the Pacific, the world's largest ocean, and the coveted buffer between Asia and America.

China's growing influence in the Pacific comes in the shape of loans to governments, bribes to officials, investment in mining, logging and fisheries, tourism and, especially alarming for many in these small island nations, migration. The loans-and-grants side of China's involvement, though, has worked quite well for Beijing, at least in the short term. A major reason is that China, for whatever reasons, has shown more interest in developing ties with the Pacific islands than the West—and the West has neglected the importance of the small and largely impoverished nations in this mighty and strategically important ocean.

Dorothy Wickham, a Solomon Islands' journalist and editor of the Melanesian News Network, wrote in an opinion piece for the *The New York Times* on 27 June 2022: 'For decades, we identified with the West, a legacy forged when the United States, Australia and their allies halted Japan's imperial advance during World War II in the Battle of Guadalcanal. But that was long ago. There is a creeping sense today that we are being ignored, if not forgotten. So who can blame us if we open the door to new friends who can help with our needs?'[18]

The Solomon Islands' switch of recognition from Taipei to Beijing has also had some other positive outcomes, according to Wickham: 'At least one politician fretted that the Solomons may become a "little Cuba off our coast", [so now], at the very least, the United States and Australia have been forced to notice us again. They are pledging to be more involved, there are plans to reopen the US embassy in Honiara, and Peace Corps volunteers are returning.'[19] Wickham also writes that 'to be fair, Australia, New Zealand and the United States have provided much-needed assistance over the decades.'[20] But that has not been enough to satisfy many politicians in the Pacific. China has promised to be more generous.

Another reason why several Pacific island countries like the Solomon Islands are turning to China for support is that Western aid always comes with conditions such as demands for good governance and democracy. China has no such qualms. A series of military coups in Fiji—two in 1987, and then in 2000 and 2006—prompted Australia, New Zealand, the US and Britain to suspend their aid and, after the 1987 coups, the Australian labour movement instituted an embargo on shipments to the islands. The Commonwealth of Nations, an association of mostly former British colonies, decided to suspend Fiji's membership. Fiji was readmitted to the Commonwealth in 2001, suspended again following the 2006 coup, and readmitted a second time after elections were held in 2014.

Qian Bo, the Chinese ambassador to Fiji, commented on those moves in an article published in the *Fiji Sun* on 26 May 2022: 'China has always supported Fiji in pursuing its own development path and stood firmly with the Fijian people at the most difficult time when Fiji was subjected to unreasonable sanctions by the West.'[21]

When James Marape, the Prime Minister of Papua New Guinea, attended the BRI Forum in Beijing in October 2023, Xi Jinping told him: 'China's assistance to Pacific island countries does not attach political conditions, does not seek exclusive rights, does not impose on others, does not write "empty promises", and fully respects the wishes and actual needs of Pacific island countries.'[22]

By contrast, corruption has been a common theme in many academic papers and public disclosures in Australia and the West, among them a 2013 report from Transparency International: 'Corruption in Papua New Guinea is widespread and endemic, penetrating all levels of society. This situation is reflected in Papua New Guinea's poor performance in most areas assessed by governance indicators. Official corruption and the misappropriation/theft of public funds are seen as the most significant governance issues of the country.'[23] The situation has hardly improved since that report was written, but such issues are of no concern to Chinese investors and government officials.

Lots of money has changed hands between private as well as official Chinese interest groups—and government officials and politicians in the Pacific. But there is little to indicate that China's BRI projects have improved the living conditions of ordinary islanders. A columnist for the official Chinese newspaper, *Global Times,* asserted in 2023 that China's cooperation with Pacific island countries over the last ten years has focused on areas 'such as humanitarian assistance, disaster response, and training. Most of the cooperation is reflected in infrastructure construction, tourism promotion and economic as well as trade issues under the BRI framework.'[24]

But as journalist William Yang put it in a 13 October 2023 report for Voice of America: 'Where Beijing sees progress and success, Western think-tanks and Pacific experts say the facts on the ground paint a different picture.'[25] According to the International Institute for Security Studies, a London-based security think-tank: 'Exports from China to the South Pacific have increased twelvefold in value between 2000 and 2018, though the numbers for exports from Pacific island countries to China have grown at a much less impressive rate [...] further major Chinese investment in the form of large-scale physical-infrastructure projects is unlikely given the existing debt burdens and the lack of demand for Chinese loans.'[26]

Roads have been upgraded in the Federated States of Micronesia, Fiji, Vanuatu and Papua New Guinea; bridges have been built in the Federated States of Micronesia, Kiribati and Fiji. A street in Nukuʻalofa has got a new sidewalk, a solar plant and a government building; there is a new government building in Chuuk in the Federated States of Micronesia; and a civic centre and a sport facility for a school in Fiji. New school buildings have been constructed in Papua New Guinea and Vanuatu; Papua New Guinea has new hospitals; and an airport has been built at Tari in its Hela Province. There is a new Confucius Institute in Samoa, and young students from Niue and the Cook Islands have attended camps in Zhuhai in China's southern Guangdong Province. The Solomon Islands got a new sports stadium for the 2023 Pacific Games.[27]

But very little of that is free. Several small island nations have been forced to borrow money from Chinese banks to pay for the projects and the main beneficiaries have been the Chinese conglomerates that have built those new roads, bridges and official buildings. According to a study by Carol Li at the University of Hawaii at Manoa: 'Many small nations [in the Pacific] take on a great deal of risk when signing on those concessional loans. If the investments do not yield gains, these loans become a burden on the country's economy. This situation has raised concerns among leaders in the Pacific.'[28] As an example of such concerns, Li mentions for example how Tongan Prime Minister Akilisi Pohiva in 2018 publicly urged the Pacific Islands Forum, an inter-governmental organization that aims to enhance cooperation between countries and territories of the Pacific Ocean, to collectively lobby China to forgive hundreds of millions of US dollars in debt. He questioned specifically whether Samoa, Tonga and Vanuatu could pay off the high levels of debt they had already incurred to China.[29]

Also according to Li: 'Another set of concerns about BRI projects has to do with the lack of return on investment. The PRC [People's Republic of China] is known to build grand infrastructure projects, but there are several well-publicized cases in which projects have been left incomplete for years. For example, the twenty-eight-storey Wangguo (WG) Friendship Plaza in Suva, Fiji, was supposed to be the tallest building in the South Pacific and to employ hundreds of Fijians. However, due to transport restrictions during the Coronavirus Disease 2019 (Covid-19) pandemic, construction was delayed. The multi-million-dollar project was stopped by the government of Fiji because of safety concerns.'[30]

Another project, the US$240 million Silkroad Ark Hotel, which promised to create jobs for about a thousand Fijians, remains incomplete. According to Li: 'The lack of return on investment of these projects has led many locals to develop negative perceptions of the Chinese presence and investments.'[31]

Realizing that the construction of large-scale buildings and other vanity projects was not the way to win sympathy for China, Xi said when addressing a high-level BRI meeting in Beijing in November 2021 that the emphasis should be more on 'high-quality development.'[32] He also emphasized the importance of 'small and beautiful projects' that would 'touch people's hearts'.[33] Xi was also apparently aware of the reputation Chinese officials and businessmen were getting in poor countries because he went on to state in no uncertain terms that, 'China will educate and guide its citizens and enterprises abroad to abide by local laws and customs and step up efforts to combat cross-border graft [and] enterprises should regulate their business activities and will not be allowed to damage the country's prestige.'[34]

But there is also another, much uglier side to China's newly established footholds in the Pacific. With diplomatic relations with China, increased trade and the implementation of BRI projects, large numbers of businessmen and traders have moved into small, vulnerable communities. It has led to a collision of two fundamentally different cultures. This is a problem that is only going to get worse as more Chinese arrive on the Pacific islands—and the number is increasing steadily.

The Solomon Islands was the first country where anti-Chinese sentiment degenerated into serious violence. For more than a century, the capital Honiara has had a small Chinatown and about 2,000 of its 50,000 inhabitants were ethnic Chinese. Most of them lived there peacefully, managing their stores and small businesses. Some had moved there from New Guinea in the early twentieth century or had come directly from Australia and China. During the colonial era of the Solomons, they worked as labourers, cooks and laundry boys for British administrators and plantation owners. Over the years, they worked hard and managed to set up retail stores and other businesses and eventually came to dominate both wholesale and retail trade in Honiara. Even though the Solomon Islands maintained diplomatic relations with Taiwan until 2019, large numbers of new settlers began to arrive from mainland China as early as the 1990s. The Solomons were soon ripe for an ethnic explosion on a scale it had never before experienced.

In April 2006, long-simmering discontent with the economically more powerful Chinese—old-timers as well as newly arrived Chinese—erupted into violent riots. The trigger was allegations that the newly elected Prime Minister Snyder Rini had used bribes from Chinese businessmen to buy votes from members of the country's Parliament.

Protesters armed with knives and daggers threatened to destroy the entire capital unless Rini stepped down. Inevitably, Honiara's Chinese were the main targets and victims of the riots. The capital's Chinatown was almost levelled following looting and arson. The rioters also attacked the Pacific Casino on the waterfront between downtown Honiara and the airport, which was renowned for Chinese—in this case Taiwanese—money laundering.

But many victims were from mainland China, and since Taiwan, not China, then had an embassy in Honiara, the Chinese from the mainland appealed to Beijing's mission in Papua New Guinea for help. Four chartered planes were sent to evacuate several hundred Chinese citizens, who were airlifted to Papua New Guinea's capital Port Moresby, and then flew on to Guangzhou in China.[35]

Australia, New Zealand and Fiji sent troops to Honiara to help restore peace, and the Solomon Islands' governor-general, Sir Nathaniel Waena, the local representative of the British monarch, officially apologized to the local Chinese community. He also appealed to those who had left to return if they still regarded the islands as their home. Rini was forced to resign. The Taiwanese, on their part, denied any political interference in the events. But it is undeniable that 'cheque-book diplomacy' by Taiwan and mainland China then as well as now has fuelled corruption not only in the Solomons but all over the Pacific.

After the evacuation of the Chinese to Guangzhou, the Guangdong Overseas Chinese Affairs Office sent staff to the Solomon Islands to find out why the rioters had targeted ethnic Chinese in Honiara—and the report they compiled after the visit was unusually frank for one issued by a Chinese government entity. They did not blame the opportunism of local politicians or, as one would have expected, Taiwanese money, but rather the newly arrived Chinese migrants themselves: 'Over the past ten years, nearly 1,000 new immigrants have arrived from Guangdong ... most do not understand foreign languages and have no knowledge of foreign trade ... they lack the calm and patience of the previous generation of migrants, often grasping for money with no thought to the consequences, and they are happy to use cash to grease all transactions. "Improper" behaviour has drawn the contempt not only of the old overseas Chinese community, but more seriously it has transformed local people from respecting the Chinese to resenting their presence.'[36]

Next in turn was Tonga. Before Tonga and China established diplomatic relations in 1998, there were only a handful of Chinese shopkeepers on the islands and, unlike Honiara, Nuku'alofa did not have any actual Chinatown. In the early 2000s, more than 70 per cent of all stores in Nukuʻalofa and other towns were owned by newly arrived Chinese migrants, who by then made up 3,000–4,000 of Tonga's population of 100,000.

In 2001, Tonga began to expel hundreds of Chinese who had become victims of a wave of ethnic violence. In that year, there had been about a hundred cases of assault, armed robbery, burglary and arson of Chinese-owned shops carried out by native Tongans.[37] The Chinese embassy in Nukuʻalofa expressed concern about the level of violence against its nationals, while Tonga's chief immigration officer, Susana Fotu, said the expulsions were in response to 'widespread anger at the growing presence of the shopkeepers', and the fear that the Chinese had come to dominate the economy.[38]

It was again a clash between two seemingly incompatible cultures: Tongan shopkeepers were laid-back and relaxed, and their stores served more as meeting places for locals than actual commercial outlets; the Chinese had come to make money, and kept their stores open all day and night, except, of course, on Sundays when they had to be closed. The Chinese were also able to bring in Chinese consumer goods, which were much cheaper than New Zealand and Australian ones sold by Tongan shopkeepers, who were soon put out of business.

The expulsions of the Chinese did not put an end to the conflict. In November 2006, years of simmering discontent reached a new breaking point. Ostensibly demonstrating for democratic reforms, angry mobs looted and burned at least thirty Chinese-owned stores. Cars were overturned and a reporter from the local new agency, *Tonga News*, described the rioting: 'Nukuʻalofa is an inferno … and major Chinese outlets are up in smoke. Chinese stores were smashed and empty, save for mobs to carry booty of everything from toilet paper to boxes of chicken.'[39]

The official Chinese news agency, Xinhua, reported that the Chinese embassy in Nukuʻalofa had tried to contact all Chinese residents in the capital to make sure they were safe. But it did little more than that, and the mayhem did not end until Australian and New Zealand peacekeepers arrived, as they had done in the Solomon Islands a few months earlier.

Papua New Guinea, by far the largest country in Melanesia, has one of the oldest Chinese communities in the Pacific. In the late nineteenth century, the island of New Guinea was divided between the Netherlands, which controlled the western half, Germany took over the north-eastern, and Britain, from Australia, ruled the south-eastern part called Papua. It was an artificial colonial division where borders were straight lines on a map drawn up in Europe.

Britain and the Netherlands were not keen on encouraging Chinese immigration, but the Germans imported hundreds of Cantonese-speaking Chinese workers from the southern province of Guangdong to work on tobacco and coconut plantations, and as cooks and domestic servants for German officials and entrepreneurs. Some Chinese later became mechanics, carpenters and tailors as required in the colonial economy.

When World War I broke out in Europe in 1914, British–Australian forces took over the German colony. Some Chinese were repatriated and restrictions were imposed on those who remained. But most of them were not sent back to China, and some moved to other parts of the now combined territory of Papua New Guinea.

About 3,000 Chinese and part-Chinese lived in Papua New Guinea before independence in 1975, mostly locally born descendants of those who had come before 1914 to work in the German part of New Guinea.[40] But they were worried about their future in a Papuan-ruled nation, and it was even unclear if they were going to be given Papua New Guinean citizenship. As a consequence, most of them emigrated to Australia. A thousand or so stayed behind, and one of those of mixed blood, Julius Chan, served as the country's Prime Minister in 1980–82 and again in 1994–97. But descendants of the early Chinese settlers were and still are a tiny minority in a country of more than nine million people. Then came the newcomers.

At the time of Papua New Guinea's independence, there were nearly 50,000 non-citizens in the country. Now, only a few thousand Australians, New Zealanders and Britons remain—and Chinese migrants are replacing them as businessmen, contractors and importers-exporters. General Jerry Singirok, a former Papua New Guinea Defence Force commander, wrote in a local paper in 2005: 'Australia has always considered Papua New Guinea as its backyard [but] since 2000, Papua New Guinea has increased its bilateral relations with China in areas of trade, investment and the military ... China is here to stay.'[41]

But there is here, as in the Solomon Islands, a wide gap between the newcomers and the Chinese who have been in Papua New Guinea for generations. According to Graeme Smith, an associate professor at the Australian National University in Canberra: 'Unlike the old Chinese, who tend to follow Christianity and can barely speak their original local [Chinese] dialect, let alone passable Mandarin, many recent migrants remain immersed in Chinese media and popular culture, through the internet, satellite television and frequent return travel to China.'[42]

Resentment of the migrants grew as more arrived to seek their fortunes in Port Moresby and other towns in Papua New Guinea. The first riots occurred in Mount Hagen in the Western Highlands in September 2007. At the forefront were local youth gangs, unemployed and angry young men—not unlike the situation in Tonga and the Solomon Islands. Even schoolchildren were reportedly seen running away with clothing, food and kitchenware. Several shops and warehouses were burnt to the ground, the police fired warning shots, and gangs of looters hit back with a barrage of stones.

The rampage in Madang in 2003 was a local outburst of anger against the newly arrived Chinese migrants; but in May 2009, anti-Chinese riots broke out across Papua New Guinea. It began with a demonstration in Port Moresby, and the organizer, Noel Anjo Kolao, explained why people had taken to the streets: 'We want investors but we don't want robbers ... they don't have any respect for our laws, they don't have any respect for our customs, for our people. They are mafia. We don't need them.'[43]

Fights erupted between Chinese and Papuan workers at the controversial Ramu nickel refinery, while riots broke out in upcountry towns such as Lae, Madang, Goroka, Kainantu and Mount Hagen. The targets were Chinese-run stores and bars, which were ransacked and looted. Veteran Papua New Guinea watcher Rowan Callick reported in the 23 May 2009 issue of *The Australian*: 'Fast-food outlets known as "tucker boxes" and other small businesses run by Asians [Chinese] were swiftly closed down in Port Moresby and other cities as the protests spread. Such retail operations have typically provided the main channel for Papua New Guineans to set up in business. But they have been largely taken over by Asian operators with access to much cheaper products.'[44] Before the police could restore order, three looters had been shot dead and a fourth was trampled to death in a stampede. Three Chinese were also killed, but the circumstances surrounding their deaths are not clear.

In November 2021, another bout of violence shook the Solomon Islands. It began with a peaceful protest against the government's decision to recognize China instead of Taiwan, but soon turned into riots targeting businesses in Honiara's Chinatown. Underlying factors such as unemployment and poverty were seen as the actual reasons for the unrest, and Chinese businessowners were accused of hiring foreigners rather than locals. Stores were burnt and looted, and the government had to ask police and troops from Australia, New Zealand, Papua New Guinea and Fiji to step in and restore order. The protesters had demanded the resignation of Prime Minister Manasseh Sogavare, but he survived a vote of no confidence in the Parliament and warned that those who had rioted 'would face consequences'.[45]

The Chinese government expressed 'concern about the attacks' and declared its support for the attempts of the Sogavare government to 'restore order and stability quickly'.[46] Sogavare, who was behind the 2019 switch of recognition from China to Taiwan, claimed that the riots were 'politically motivated' and blamed unnamed foreign powers for the unrest. Taiwan, which most probably was the 'foreign power' Sogavare alluded to, denied any involvement in the events. Joanne Ou, a spokesperson for Taiwan's foreign ministry, stated that, '... we have nothing to do with the unrest.'[47]

But China has not been deterred by such incidents, and its growing influence has been especially noticeable in Fiji. Migrants and businessmen from China are rapidly replacing the old Asian community on those islands: the Indians, who were brought in as indentured labour by the British colonial power in the late nineteenth and early twentieth century.

Most of the Indians came from Bengal and Bihar and worked in sugar plantations, and brought with them Indian culture, religion and social structures to the South Pacific. The Indians may have come as labourers and many of them still are, but like their Chinese counterparts elsewhere in the Pacific, they soon came to dominate trade and commerce in Fiji. This was not a major problem till the Indians began to enter politics, and were in direct conflict with the native Fijians. This, in turn, led to the coups—and the off-and-on suspension of aid from its traditional Commonwealth allies.

More significantly at home on the islands, it resulted in demographic changes as many businessmen, shopkeepers and professionals of Indian origin emigrated to Australia and New Zealand. Many of Fiji's old Chinese residents also left after independence in 1970 as well as the political turmoil in the 1980s, and they and the Indians were soon replaced by new migrants from China.

Before independence, there were about 5,000 people of Chinese descent in Fiji, and almost all of them lived in and around Suva. They had come as workers and small-scale traders and were never nearly as numerous as the Indians. But, after generations of hard work, most of them became relatively wealthy—and loyal to the Nationalist Chinese Kuomintang, which even had an office in an old colonial mansion in downtown Suva that long doubled as a consulate for the Republic of China, Taiwan. But that function of the Kuomintang office had to close when Britain established diplomatic relations with Beijing in 1951. It continued, however, to function as a community hall for the local Chinese.

Independent Fiji recognized the People's Republic of China in 1975, and relations with the mainland became close. The 'new' migration began in the early 1990s, when Chinese-owned garment factories brought in several hundred workers, of whom most were women, who had been recruited by labour agencies in various parts of China. All of them were Mandarin speakers, unlike the old-timers, the great majority of whom are Cantonese with a minority of Fujianese.

As more Indians were leaving, Major-General Sitiveni Rabuka, who staged the two coups in 1987, suggested in January 1995 that the country should bring in 28,000 Chinese immigrants to foster investment and economic development.[48] The proposal was met with serious objections from various sectors of society, including the local Chinese community. According to William E. Willmott, an associate professor of anthropology and lecturer in Asian studies at the University of British Columbia, Canada: 'It became one of the issues that sparked a mass demonstration in February, when 12,000 Fijians marched on Suva's main street. Nothing came of the scheme, but Chinese migration continues unabated.'[49]

No exact figure has been mentioned, but the number of Chinese migrants in Fiji, legal and illegal, is significant, and growing. Estimates vary between 5,000 and more than 20,000. Already in the early 2000s, Fiji authorities privately put the figure at about 15,000, but according to Robert Keith-Reid, editor of *Islands Business* until his death in May 2006: 'The government doesn't want to mention the actual figure publicly because of fear of a backlash.'[50]

The total population of Fiji is about 900,000, so the Chinese may be a small minority, but they are an economically powerful one. And not all Chinese migrants have turned out to be law-abiding business people and factory workers. With the first wave of Chinese migrants in the late 1990s came Chinese criminal gangs and they became engaged in prostitution, gambling, drugs, passport fraud, corruption in the fisheries' industry and corrupting local officials.[51] In November 2000, a shipment of 357 kilograms of heroin was seized in Fiji, not for local consumption but to be smuggled on to Australia and North America. The heroin came from Southeast Asia's Golden Triangle, and the gangs thought that Fiji would be a convenient transhipment point for drugs destined for world markets. Who would suspect that a container arriving from Fiji would contain Golden Triangle heroin?

This has caused concern among Fiji's old-time Chinese population. Bessie Ng Kumlin Ali, a Fijian-Chinese, wrote in her very personal book, *The Chinese in Fiji*, about Rabuka's scheme to invite Chinese to settle in the country: 'Leaders of the Chinese community themselves have voiced their reservation about an influx, which had the potential to spoil long-established, hard-won relations with other communities.'[52]

And that is already happening. There have been assaults on ethnic Chinese in Fiji, not as severe as in Papua New Guinea, the Solomon Islands and Tonga, but nevertheless an entirely new phenomenon. In December 2005, Dixon Seeto, president of the Chinese Association of Fiji, stated publicly that there had been violent attacks made against Chinese market gardeners and farmers, presumably well-settled Fijian Chinese. Seeto claimed that both men and women bringing their produce to local markets were targeted by Fijian youths seeking cash, and he urged the police to increase their patrols to prevent such violence. Whether that put an end to the attacks is hard to say, but some reports indicate that we have not seen the end of it.

It can be hard for locals to distinguish between 'old' and 'new' Chinese. But Chinese like Bessie Ng Kumlin Ali, whose families have been in Fiji for generations, know the difference. The commissioner of police, Andrew Hughes, has echoed her words: 'Chinese old-timers are worried, especially about the influx of shady newcomers.'[53] Even the Chinese authorities were, in the end, forced to move against Fiji-based, Chinese organized crime. In August 2017, Fiji deported seventy-seven Chinese nationals accused of running a phone and online scam targeting victims in mainland China.[54] The operation involved Fijian as well as Chinese law enforcement agencies, and similar joint operations were also carried out in Indonesia and Cambodia. The French news agency AFP reported: 'Cyber criminals targeting victims in China have increasingly exploited technological advances to operate from abroad in a bid to evade authorities. The Fiji-based ring is suspected of involvement in more than fifty telecom and online fraud cases, and cost victims in China more than six million yuan (US$892,000), Fijian police said [...] without giving precise details of the scams.'[55]

The cooperation of Fijian and Chinese law enforcement agencies shows that the relationship between Suva and Beijing has reached new heights, and that is hardly surprising given Fiji's troubled relationship with its old Commonwealth partners. Long before Chinese ambassador Qian Bo made his comment about 'unreasonable sanctions by the West' in May 2022, Fijian leaders had expressed similar sentiments. When Frank

Bainimarama, a former naval officer who served as Prime Minister from 2007 to 2022, visited Beijing in August 2008, he told his Chinese hosts: 'Fiji will not forget that when other countries were quick to condemn us following the events of 1987, 2000 and 2006, China and other friends in Asia demonstrated a more understanding and sensitive approach to events in Fiji. The government of the People's Republic of China expressed confidence in our ability to resolve our problems in our way, without undue pressure or interference.'[56]

When Western countries make 'unreasonable' demands for democracy and good governance and criticize corrupt practices, China is always willing to step in—in Fiji, the Solomon Islands and Papua New Guinea. China is indeed in the Pacific to stay, anti-Chinese riots or not.

In 2018, China and Fiji signed a memorandum of understanding on Belt and Road cooperation. But according to Henryk Szadziewski at the University of Hawaii in Manoa: 'Although the precise details of the agreement remain undisclosed, Chinese state media revealed the document included BRI buzzwords of exchange, networks, and infrastructure.'[57] The memorandum, according to Szadziewski, 'was a formality, codifying over a decade's worth of increasing migration, aid, trade, and investment. Chinese companies, such as China Railway First Group, China Railway No5 Engineering Group, China Railway 14th Bureau Group, and Yanjian Group, have been active in constructing roads, bridges, and buildings, often getting a foothold in the local market through BRI funding in the form of grants or loans.'[58]

In Polynesian states other than Tonga, China's relations with governments and local populations have been smoother than in Melanesia. Samoa, a German colony before it was taken over by New Zealand during World War I and became independent in 1962, is neither a republic nor a hereditary monarchy. Two of Samoa's paramount chiefs at the time of independence, Tuopua Tamasese Mea'ole and Malietoa Tanumafili II, were appointed joint heads of state for life. But Tuopua Tamasese Mea'ole died in 1963, leaving Malietoa Tanumafili II as the only head until his death at the age of ninety-four in June 2007. He was, in effect, a constitutional monarch, but none of his sons succeeded him.

Instead, the Parliament elected another chief, Tuiatua Tupua Tamasese Efi, as head of state for a five-year term, thus introducing a more republican form of government. The present head of state, or O le Ao o le Malo, is Afioga Tuimaleali ifano Va aleto a Eti Sualauvi II, and he has served in that post since 2017. In 2022, he was reappointed as O le Ao o le Malo for a further five-year term. At first, the country was known as 'Western Samoa' to distinguish it from nearby American Samoa, but it is now officially known as 'The Independent State of Samoa'—to make an even stronger statement to its non-independent neighbour.

In 1976, a year after Samoa and China established diplomatic relations—Samoa was the first of the Pacific nations to recognize China after Fiji—Malietoa Tanumafili II travelled to Beijing on an official state visit, the first by the head of state of any Pacific nation. He was given a red carpet welcome, emphasizing the importance Beijing places on relations with the small Pacific states. Malietoa Tanumafili II held talks with the then Chinese premier Hua Guofeng and, according to an announcement at the time, an agreement was signed 'on economic and technical cooperation between the two countries', which, in effect, meant Chinese aid to Samoa as the country had nothing to offer China other than its strategic location in the middle of the Pacific Ocean.[59]

Samoa was also one of the first Pacific nations to get substantial grants from China. In April 1985, then Chinese leader Hu Yaobang even visited the island nation and it was then he promised to provide a grant of US$500,000 for unspecified development. Nine years later, a new, imposing government building was erected on Beach Road, the main street through the capital Apia, with a multi-million-dollar interest-free loan from China. Such generosity could explain why the speaker of the Parliament, Tolofuaivalelei Falemoe Leiataua, said after China's brutal crackdown on protesters in Tibet 2008 that, 'the Tibet issue is China's internal affair, and foreign governments have no right to interfere, nor should its leaders meet the Dalai Lama.'[60]

In 2018, China's Liaocheng University and the National University of Samoa jointly set up a Confucius Institute, a BRI project, in Apia. And in 2021, the Ministry of Education Sports and Culture asked the institute to offer more, free Chinese-language lessons across the nation's secondary schools.[61] During the Covid-19 pandemic, China sent medical supplies to Samoa, which has become China's closest and most trouble-free ally in the Pacific.

China has also quite successfully managed to court the Cook Islands, tiny pearls in a huge ocean and hundreds of kilometres away from the nearest land, French Polynesia in the east and Samoa in the west. New Zealand remains its closest political and economic partner and the Cook Islanders are New Zealand citizens, but the newest and biggest buildings in the one-street capital Avarua are the courthouse and a police station, both built with Chinese grants and by workers brought in from China. According to Ron Crocombe, the New Zealand-born dean of Pacific studies who remained a permanent resident of the Cook Islands until his death in June 2009: 'Such structures are fairly typical of Chinese aid to the Pacific. China builds symbols of power and authority for the government leaders, and huge sport stadiums for the public at large.'[62]

And then there have been 'friendship tours'. Government officials as well as journalists from the local papers, *Cook Island News* and *Cook Islands Times/Herald*, have been invited to China and have toured Beijing and other cities. Under the aegis of the BRI, young Cook Islanders have attended a winter camp for students in Zhuhai and the Guangdong International Tourism and Cultural Festival in January 2018. China's special envoy for Pacific island countries affairs, Qian Bo, attended the 52nd Pacific Islands Forum Leaders Meeting, which was held in Avarua from 6–10 November 2023. He took the opportunity to tell the audience that 'China will stay committed to a high-level opening-up to the outside world, and is willing to strengthen cooperation with Pacific island countries within the framework of the BRI.'[63]

China has also used generosity to try to gain influence in French Polynesia, which has the largest of the old Chinese communities in the Pacific after that in Hawaii. Numbering nearly 10,000, most of them live in the capital Papeete on the main island Tahiti. But there are also Chinese-run retail stores and small businesses elsewhere in French Polynesia, which consists of five archipelagos with altogether 118 islands and 280,000 inhabitants. And its exclusive economic zone measures 4.5 million square kilometres.

Like the much smaller Wallis and Futuna, French Polynesia is a collectivité d'outre-mer, but is even more self-governing. French Polynesia has its own President and legislative power is vested with the government and the elected territorial assembly. There is a strong movement for complete independence, but the territory is so heavily dependent on financial assistance from France that it would face serious hardship if it decided to go its own way and break with Paris. Subsidies from France combined with income from tourism and the export of black pearls, noni juice and high-quality vanilla gives it one of the highest GDP per capita in the Pacific region, which is another incentive to remain a self-governing territory of France.

New Caledonia, the third French territory in the Pacific, is bigger in land area than French Polynesia and is more developed economically. But New Caledonia has no significant Chinese community, which may be the reason why Chinese efforts to win influence in the 'French Pacific' have been concentrated not on that territory but French Polynesia.

As in other parts of the Asia-Pacific region, the Chinese in French Polynesia, most of whom are Hakka from southern and coastal China, progressed from having been groups of imported labourers and craftsmen into a prosperous business community. Nothing remains of the old cotton plantations, and the fact that the Chinese like the native Polynesians are now citizens of France allows them to freely engage in any kind of business and take part in local politics. French sovereignty also means that immigration, legal and otherwise, is strictly controlled and citizenship cannot be bought. Consequently, there has been no influx of 'new' Chinese to French Polynesia. The 'old' Chinese are well-established and some of the richest people in French Polynesia are of Chinese descent. French Polynesia's booming black pearl industry was founded by second-generation Chinese and several of them have also entered territorial politics. Their celebrations are often held in the local hall of the Kuomintang in downtown Papeete.

The Chinese in French Polynesia have traditionally been loyal to the Chinese Nationalists, and therefore Taiwan. But the rivalry between China and Taiwan, and Beijing's desire to make inroads even into French Polynesia, became obvious when the largest Chinese place of worship in the Pacific, the Kanti Temple, was built in Papeete in the late 1980s. Taiwan donated a pair of carved dragons on the pillars as well as carvings and a plaque—while China's contribution was a pair of stone lions.[64] It was a first and obvious gesture from Beijing to improve its standing among the Chinese in French Polynesia.

Paco Milhiet, who holds a PhD in international relations from the University of French Polynesia and the Catholic Institute of Paris, and currently is a visiting fellow at the S. Rajaratnam School of International Studies, pointed out in an article for *The Diplomat* on 23 June 2022 that French Polynesia may be a French overseas territory, but its enlarged status of autonomy and its own institutions (President, government and legislative assembly) makes it possible for it to establish external relations: 'The territory is a member of international organizations such as the Pacific Islands Forum and the Pacific Community. In addition, Polynesian leaders have regularly met with top international political authorities: then-Chinese Vice President Xi Jinping in 2011, US President Barack Obama in 2016, UN Secretary General Antonio Guterres in 2019.'[65]

Also according to Milhiet: 'In a context of China's growing influence in the Pacific region, French Polynesia, like other island states or territories, seeks to develop its own balance of power [...] The Polynesian executive notably maintains strong bilateral relations with China, without necessarily involving the French state. Beyond official institutions such as the Chinese consulate (2007) and the Confucius Institute (2013), soft power initiatives led by official authorities or by mandated associations are used locally to promote Beijing's influence.'[66] In November 2019, French Polynesia's President Edouard Fritch stated that the territory was part of China's BRI: 'It is therefore by the common interest shown by Chinese private investors and by all Polynesian governments on all sides that China has chosen to place French Polynesia on the Silk Road.'[67]

But France is not going to let China's newly won influence jeopardize its own strategic interests in the Pacific. The Indian Ocean is not the only maritime area outside Europe where France maintains a military presence. There are nearly 2,000 French soldiers and naval personnel in New Caledonia, and Paris is also responsible for the defence of French Polynesia where about 900 military personnel are deployed in the territory. The French Foreign Legion was stationed on Moruroa and Fangataufa, where France carried out nuclear tests between 1966 and 1996, but they were withdrawn in 2000. There is no military presence on Wallis and Futuna, but it has ports and airports that could be used in case of a strategic emergency.

With almost 3,000 military personnel stationed in New Caledonia and French Polynesia, France is the only European country with a capacity to make a substantial contribution to security in the South Pacific.[68] Britain has given up all its former colonies in the Pacific—except for the island of Pitcairn with only about fifty inhabitants, most of whom are descendants of English and Irish sailors who staged a mutiny on the ship *HMS Bounty* in 1798 and their Tahitian common-law-wives.

The situation is more complex in Micronesia, where the independent states of the Marshall Islands and Palau recognize Taiwan (Tuvalu is the only Polynesian country that has diplomatic relations with Taipei). Kiribati, Nauru and the Federated States of Micronesia have sided with China in the diplomatic tug of war in the Pacific. Then there are Guam and the Commonwealth of Northern Mariana Islands, which are unincorporated territories of the US. Together with Hawaii, which is Polynesian, these islands form the pillars of American influence in the Pacific Ocean. Naval Base Guam is a strategic US base, which, in 2009, was combined with Andersen Air Force Base to form Joint Region Marianas, a Navy-controlled joint base for multiple military services.

More importantly, there are twelve key military installations in Hawaii, where all branches of the US armed forces have a presence, including the US Army, the Marine Corps, the Navy, the Air Force, the Coast Guards and the United States Space Command. The Army

National Guard and the Air National Guard are there as well but operate in part under state authority. The Department of the Navy is the largest contracting entity in Hawaii, followed by the Department of the Army and the Department of the Air Force.[69]

It is evident that the two military powers, the US in the North Pacific and the French in the South Pacific, together with their strategic allies Australia and New Zealand, still have the upper hand in the Pacific. But the 2019 security pact between the Solomon Islands and China sent alarm bells ringing in Western circles. It came a year after Australian media had suggested that China aims to establish a naval base on the Vanuatu island of Espiritu Santo. The Vanuatu government was quick to deny that any such plans were afoot, but the fact is that China has already built a new wharf on Espiritu Santo, which is far too large for the mere commercial purposes of the 40,000 people who inhabit that island and its occasional tourists.[70] Whatever the facility's ultimate intent, the controversies surrounding the port on Espiritu Santo and the Solomons' security pact have shone a new spotlight on China's expanding influence in the Pacific, a challenge not only to nearby Australia but, specifically, the US as the prime power in the region.

China did suffer a major reversal in fortunes back in 2003 when Kiribati decided to shift recognition from Beijing to Taipei. The Chinese had not only to close their embassy but also dismantle a satellite-tracking station that they had established in 1997 on Tarawa atoll in Kiribati. The station was the only one of its kind outside China, and Kiribati, which straddles the equator, is an ideal place for satellite-tracking. Furthermore, defence experts had long suspected that China's Tarawa station also monitored American missile tests at Kwajalein in the Marshall Islands, which are vital for the development of the US missile-defence system.

Other observers argued that the satellite dishes at Tarawa were too small for such advanced operations. Des Ball, professor at the Australian National University and an expert on signals intelligence, said at the time that China's Yuan Wang tracking ships here as well as in the Indian Ocean were far more useful for intelligence gathering.[71] But the Tarawa station was significant for another reason: it was a land base from where the movements and the activities of the Yuan Wang ships could be coordinated. Be that as it may, in September 2019, Kiribati re-established relations with Beijing. There is nothing to indicate that the tracking station has been rebuilt; but, on 15 July 2023, the Chinese military hospital ship 'Peace Ark' docked at Tarawa, the first Chinese military vessel to visit Kiribati since the re-establishment of diplomatic relations. The week-long visit came with humanitarian and medical assistance, part of China's effort to expand its influence in the Pacific, and was followed by stops in Tonga, Vanuatu and the Solomon Islands as well as East Timor in South East Asia.[72]

Rajaram Panda, a senior fellow at the Prime Minister's Museum and Library, formerly known as Nehru Memorial Museum and Library, New Delhi, pointed out in an article for *Global Asia* in June 2022, that, 'China has taken advantage of the ongoing Russia-Ukraine crisis and continuing tensions with the United States to expand its maritime and strategic footprint in the South Pacific.'[73] A main concern about the agreement between China and the Solomon Islands, according to Panda, is that it 'is not transparent, and there are ambiguities over its content and intentions'.[74]

It is not known what the exact nature of the security cooperation between Asia's main superpower and a remote group of islands in the Pacific entails, but a draft document was leaked in March 2022 and, reading between the lines, it indicated that a Chinese military presence may be a possibility and even that a Chinese military base could be established on the Solomons. The Solomon Islands government has insisted that the fears are unjustified because there are no such plans, but Panda argues that 'in the event that China establishes a naval base in the Solomon Islands following the security pact, it will be necessary for Australia to revamp its defence posture with urgency [...] the plethora of uncertainties emerging from the China–Solomon Islands security pact demand coordinated responses from many stakeholders committed to maintaining peace and stability in the entire Indo-Pacific region.'[75]

The news about the security pact made the Western powers realize that they had taken old arrangements for granted and not paid enough attention to relations with countries such as the Solomon Islands. New Zealand, long a moderate voice on China, toughened its stand almost immediately. In May 2022, Prime Minister Jacinda Ardern described the pact as 'gravely concerning', and called on the Solomon Islands to discuss it within the Pacific Islands Forum. She went on to state that 'what is really changing around us is the level of assertiveness and aggression we see in the region.'[76] New Zealand as well as Japan announced plans to increase security ties with not only the Solomon Islands but also other Pacific Islands states. On a softer note, the New Zealand government said that a tuna processing plant would be established in the Solomon Islands, which is set to create 5,500 new jobs.

In June 2023, Australia's Deputy Prime Minister Richard Marles travelled to the Solomon Islands to push for an enduring security presence in the country. He held talks with Prime Minister Manasseh Sogavare. Before the visit, Marles said that '... we'll continue to focus on the way Australia can contribute to Solomon Islands development ... our focus needs to be on improving the development outcomes of all countries around the Pacific.'[77] But when US congressman Neal Dunn and other members of the US select committee on the Communist Party of China went to the islands two months later, Sogavare gave them the cold shoulder and declined to see them. He was 'busy', it was claimed.[78]

A victory for the West was scored in January 2023 when Fiji's Prime Minister Sitiveni Rabuka, the old coup-maker, announced that there was no need for Chinese state security personnel to continue working with the country's police force. 'Our system of democracy and justice systems are different so we will go back to those that have similar systems with us,' he said, referring to Australia and New Zealand.[79] A previous memorandum of understanding between Fiji and China allowed Chinese policemen to be deployed in the country and it also saw Fijian policemen undergoing training in China. That memorandum was scrapped after Rabuka made his statement. In March 2022, New Zealand's then foreign minister, Nanaia Mahuta, had visited Fiji and signed an agreement that would facilitate the exchange of intelligence information on regional security challenges.[80]

The battle for the Pacific has already begun and, despite setbacks, the various BRI projects remain vital elements in this new 'great game'. The West has at long last woken up to the new realities and begun to show an active interest in countering China's economic and diplomatic forays into the region. Caught in the middle are small, poor and potentially vulnerable island nations that are only looking for assistance so they can achieve some degree of noteworthy development.

7

WHOSE ASIA–PACIFIC CENTURY?

It is too early to say whether President Xi Jinping's BRI has been a complete failure or, perhaps, a partial success. Although it has come at a price in terms of huge debts, it has brought some development to countries such as the Maldives, the Comoros and Samoa. It is clear that Xi was aiming too high when the first megaprojects were launched in countries that could ill afford them or where China did not have the means and resources to complete them. Chinese interests may have taken over assets in countries like Sri Lanka and Laos when loans could not be repaid, but that also means that billions of dollars have been flowing out of China. The newly acquired assets are unlikely to generate enough revenue to compensate the losses.

China has obviously overstretched itself and, at the tenth anniversary summit in Beijing in October 2023, the BRI was rebranded with an entirely new slogan: Small is beautiful. There will be new investment under the umbrella of yet another 'Silk Road': 'The Digital Silk Road', with a focus on science and technology, innovation and e-commerce.[1] Strategic port and railway projects will also continue, but with faster implementation and at lower risk.[2] Xi has not given up his ambitions to make China the dominant power in Asia, perhaps even in the world. The continued existence of the BRI is testament to that. One of the most notable announcements made at the meeting in Beijing was the launch of what the Chinese hosts called the 'Artificial Intelligence (AI) Governance

Initiative'. China apparently hopes to shape the global rules for AI and other cutting-edge technology—and that could be even more menacing when it comes to attempts to dominate the world than the original BRI.[3]

No Chinese official at the meeting indicated that the downsized BRI will focus on China's immediate neighbourhood, but it seems obvious. Deals with Myanmar, Laos, Nepal, Sri Lanka, Pakistan, the Russian Far East and the island nations of the Indian and Pacific Oceans seem to be largely unaffected by the new direction. And it also makes perfect sense from a security point of view—it is in the Indo-Pacific region that Beijing's adversaries are forging blocs and alliances to counter the rise of China.

The strongest argument against those who have criticized the BRI and China's new role in world trade and politics is that the old Western colonial and imperialist powers were much worse. Britain, France and the Netherlands conquered territory, established colonies and plundered them more ruthlessly than China is doing today. In order to protect its strategic and economic interests, the US has intervened militarily in many countries all over the world, among them Haiti, the Dominican Republic, Cuba, Honduras, Guatemala, Vietnam, Panama, Grenada, Afghanistan, Iraq and Syria. Washington's security agencies have backed coups that saw the overthrow of elected governments such as those of Mohammed Mossadegh in Iran in 1953, João Goulart in Brazil 1964, and Chile's Salvador Allende in 1973. France fought bitter colonial wars in Algeria and Vietnam, and frequently intervenes militarily to quell crises in its former African colonies. In recent years, Britain has sent troops to fight in wars in Afghanistan and Iraq.

But the wrongs of Western powers do not justify Xi's imperialist policies, and China's global outreach is bound to change the map of the world. After the collapse of the Soviet Union in 1991, the US emerged as the world's only uncontested superpower and it could be argued that the rise of China has created some badly needed counterbalance to the American dominance of many parts of the world. China, like the erstwhile Soviet Union, is certainly not a beacon of freedom and democracy, but a bipolar world may be better than one dominated by a single power.

And as a consequence, the US has to take China's new policies and actions worldwide into consideration—as it had to consider Soviet interests during the Cold War—and that requires checks and balances that are in the interests of the world's smaller nations, which would want to, but often cannot, maintain their neutrality and independence from any superpower dominance.

On the other hand, stressing the importance of a bipolar world should not lead to the acceptance of a new form of imperialism only because the new superpower happens to be Asian. This uncritical attitude echoes the sentiments of pre-World War II, when many Asian nationalists saw Japan as a flag-bearer for Asian peoples because it dared to challenge British, French, Dutch and American imperialism. Myanmar nationalists, led by that country's independence hero, Aung San, formed a group of thirty young men who underwent training in Japan—and returned home as the Burma Independence Army when the Japanese invaded Burma in January 1942. With Japanese assistance, India's Subhas Chandra Bose organized the Indian National Army (INA) to fight the British. Indonesian nationalists like Sukarno and Mohammed Hatta openly stated that a Japanese advance in the then Dutch East Indies would be advantageous to their struggle for freedom.

In the beginning, it was only countries that suffered from the onslaught of Japanese imperialism, such as Korea and China, that viewed the rise of Japan differently. In Myanmar, the nationalists soon discovered that the Imperial Japanese Army was even worse that the British in their treatment of the native population. In March 1945, Aung San and his comrades broke with the Japanese and forged an alliance with the British. Three years later, Myanmar became an independent republic, free of any imperialist dominance.

The Japanese invaded the Andamans in March 1942, and, on 30 December 1943, the INA hoisted the Indian tricolour over the islands, which were declared to be 'Free India'. But that freedom meant only that British brutality had been replaced with Japanese brutality. Suspected 'British spies', guilty or not, were stripped and caned in public. Others were executed or tortured to death. Nearly half the population starved during the Japanese occupation and hundreds of innocent people were killed for no obvious reason. 'Freedom' for the Andaman Islands meant just another kind of barbaric foreign rule.

In Malaya and the Philippines, local communist forces fought against the Japanese and, in the beginning, received support from their respective colonial powers—but then turned against them once the Japanese had been driven out. The US Office of Strategic Services, the forerunner to the CIA, maintained close contacts with Ho Chi Minh's forces as long as they were fighting against the Japanese. Wars can create strange bedfellows. Then as well as now, security issues and geostrategic interests, not ideology, guide the behaviour of superpowers.

Today's China may not be behaving as aggressively as Japan did in the early and mid-twentieth century, but its influence is spreading rapidly and it is important to remember that any superpower dominance, Western as well as Asian, poses a threat to national sovereignty. And China is far from as peaceful as it purports to be, and its official policy of 'non-intervention' is little more than a smokescreen for an active involvement in the internal affairs of other countries, especially small and vulnerable ones. It also has a vast network of spies and agents of influence in major powers such as the US, Australia and Europe.[4]

Gui Congyou, China's former ambassador to Stockholm, was summoned by the Swedish foreign ministry no less than forty times for threatening local journalists, Swedish PEN and even the country's Culture Minister Amanda Lind with 'consequences' for raising the case of the publisher and bookstore owner Gui Minhai, a Swedish citizen of Chinese origin who was abducted in 2015 and is being kept incommunicado and without trial in Chinese custody. Gui Congyou has also been outspoken on other issues and, as a consequence, public opinion polls shows that two-thirds of Swedes hold negative views of China, while close to 80 per cent distrust the country.[5]

In Singapore in 2017, Chinese-American academic Huang Jing had his residence permit revoked after the city state's home ministry called him 'an agent of influence of a foreign country'.[6] And in New Zealand in 2017, the home and office of academic and China critic Anne-Marie

Brady were burgled, her car was tampered with, she received a series of anonymous phone calls and a threatening letter. It all came after she had published a paper on China's influence in the Pacific. Brady believes that she has become 'the target of a campaign of intimidation and "psy-ops" ... directed by Beijing towards her and her family.'[7] But 'the Chinese government has not responded to requests for comment,' *The Guardian* newspaper reported on 23 January 2019.[8]

From the time the People's Republic of China was established in 1949, it has fought wars in Korea in the early 1950s, against India in 1962 and Vietnam in 1979. China invaded Tibet in 1950, until then a de facto independent nation, and it attacked Taiwan militarily in the 1950s and continues to threaten the self-governing island, which has no desire to be 'reunited' with the authoritarian ruled mainland. China provided communist insurgents in Myanmar and Thailand as well as ethnic Naga and Mizo rebels in Northeast India with weapons in the 1970s. Beijing was also the only outside power that supported the dreaded Khmer Rouge when it was in power in Cambodia from 1975 to 1979.

Today, China is behaving belligerently in the South China Sea and along the line of actual control with India. Chinese-made weapons have been supplied directly or through middlemen to the United Wa State Army in Myanmar and to militants in Syria and Gaza. The rulers of China have brutally suppressed pro-democracy movements at home in China in 1989 and in Hong Kong 2019–2020. And they continue to rule the Tibetans and the Uighurs with an iron fist. China, under its present rulers, is hardly any ideal to follow, and there is undoubtedly rising discontent with China's policies in Myanmar, where Beijing is seen as a major supporter of that country's military dictatorship. Demonstrations have been held outside the Chinese embassy in Yangon, among the Balochis in Pakistan and, most recently as far outside the region as Ecuador.

A free-trade agreement between China and Ecuador was once hailed as a milestone for Beijing in Latin America but, in January 2024, demonstrators gathered outside the Chinese embassy in Quito holding banners with texts like 'Chinese companies get out of Ecuador'.[9] The main objection is that the agreement could have a severe impact on Ecuador's sensitive ecosystems. Mentioned as examples were the demand for balsa wood by China's wind turbine industry, which has already contributed to deforestation in Amazonian conservation zones, and the open-pit Mirador mega-mine—an undertaking run by the Chinese conglomerate CRCC-Tongguan Investment, which has devastated the surrounding environment.[10]

There is also the Coca Codo Sinclair hydroelectric dam, which was constructed by China's Sinohydro Corporation. The erosion from the dam has destroyed Ecuador's largest waterfall as well as nearby villages.[11] Over the years, China has provided Ecuador with loans totalling US$19 billion for the construction of bridges, highways, irrigation, schools, health clinics and dams, among them Coca Codo Sinclair. Unable to repay the loans, Ecuador has been forced to provide China with oil at a discount. By 2018, that meant that 80 per cent of the oil produced in Ecuador went to China.[12]

The rise of China and Xi's BRI have prompted other countries to launch more attractive and favourable alternatives. Japan was the first to react. In 2015, Japan designed a project called Partnership for Quality Infrastructure (PQI) with a five-year budget of US$110 billion. It was initially limited to Asia and the name referred to an emphasis on quality, in contrast to China's haphazard and often shoddy infrastructure projects launched with little or no consideration for the impact they would have on the environment.[13] In 2016, PQI became global and the budget was raised to US$200 billion.[14]

But as the European Parliamentary Research Service noted in 2021: '... the PQI has not been able to keep pace with the meteoric expansion of the BRI in quantitative terms at [a] global level despite Japan's strong foothold in Southeast Asia's infrastructure construction sector.'[15] But Japan has managed to establish a close relationship with India, a key partner capable of balancing China's rise to a global economic power. Japan's most high-profile project in India is the construction of a high-speed rail connection between Mumbai and Ahmedabad, a distance of 508 kilometres.[16] It was supposed to be completed by the end of 2023, but due to problems in acquiring land in Maharashtra, the project has been delayed and will probably open in 2027.

Under the 2009–2017 administration of President Barack Obama, the US launched the Power Africa public-private partnership to assist African countries in getting better access to electricity, the US–ASEAN Connect to enhance trade with Southeast Asia, and the Global Procurement Initiative to link American companies to infrastructure projects in developing countries.[17] And in 2018, Australia, the US and Japan announced a trilateral partnership called the Blue Dot Network Initiative for investment in infrastructure in the Indo-Pacific region.[18]

The interest in global affairs declined under Donald Trump's 2017–2021 presidency, but when the G7 countries met for a summit in Cornwall, England, in June 2021, he was gone and Joseph Biden had taken over. British Prime Minister Boris Johnson was the host and he as well as Biden received leaders from Canada, France, Germany, Italy and Japan. They agreed on a 'values-driven, high-standard and transparent infrastructure partnership' known as the Build Back Better World (B3W) initiative.[19] The European Union adopted a resolution calling for a 'global connectivity strategy […] in order to strengthen the EU's role as a geopolitical and geo-economic actor with a single narrative, and to broaden partnerships with democracies across the world that share the EU's fundamental values.'[20]

The Bay of Bengal Initiative for Multi-Sectoral Technical and Economic Cooperation (BIMSTEC), predates the BRI, but has come to play a role as a regional counterweight to China's influence in South and Southeast Asia. Originally founded in Bangkok in June 1997 and then called BIST-EC (Bangladesh, India, Sri Lanka and Thailand Economic Cooperation), it was enlarged when Myanmar joined in December 1997 and called BIMST-EC (Bangladesh, India, Myanmar, Sri Lanka and Thailand Economic Cooperation). When Nepal and Bhutan became members in 2004, no more first letters of countries could be added to the acronym, so the bloc adopted its present name, the Bay of Bengal Initiative for Multi-Sectoral Technical and Economic Cooperation without a hyphen between the T and the E.

A permanent secretariat for BIMSTEC was opened in Dhaka in 2014, and from then onwards it can be seen as an attempt to counterbalance China's influence in the region with horizontal linkages between South and Southeast Asia. India, the most energized member of the bloc, provides it with about a third of its funding and sees it as a key element in the 'Act East' policy, which Prime Minister Narendra Modi launched shortly after his first election victory in May 2014.[21] But, as the European Union's Parliamentary Research Service has noted, BIMSTEC needs a stronger leadership from New Delhi to make it a tool to enhance the economic growth and connectivity of members, which may otherwise be tempted to focus on the BRI.[22]

The countries that participate in what are in effect anti-China alliances, but which have never openly declared them to be that, are, like China, looking beyond trade and economic development. Regional and bilateral defence alliances have been formed as well. Naval cooperation between France and India is only one outcome of the rise of China in the new post-Cold War world order, and so is the fact that supposedly pacifist Japan has a military base in Djibouti. At any given time, China has six to seven warships, including submarines, deployed in the Indian Ocean, and that has prompted India and Japan to sign an agreement aimed at facilitating the ability of their respective navies to share critical information 'of mutual interest'.[23] Japan participates with India, the US and Australia in the annual Exercise Malabar, which is not confined to the waters around India but has also included naval exercises in the Arabian Sea, and off the coasts of Japan and the Philippines.[24]

Cooperation between India and Japan involves not only naval exercises but also land-based manoeuvres. In November 2018, a joint exercise called 'Dharma Guardian' between India and Japan was conducted at the Counter Insurgency and Jungle Warfare School at Vairengte in the north-eastern Indian state of Mizoram.[25] According to an official Indian statement at the time, the aim of the exercise was to carry out 'joint training of troops in counter-insurgency and counter-terrorism operations in [...] mountainous terrains.'[26] Dharma Guardian became an annual event and the 2019 exercises were held at Vairengte as well.

Why Japan's Self Defence Forces, the euphemism for their powerful military, would be interested in such operations in 'mountainous terrains' was not made clear, but the statement after the 2019 exercise said that, 'Exercise Dharma Guardian-2019 will further cement the long-standing strategic ties between India and Japan.'[27] Mizoram does not border China, but it is not far from areas of potential violence in the Himalayas.

The Covid-19 crisis interrupted active collaboration, but in February 2022, military personnel from India and Japan conducted their third Dharma Guardian exercise in a completely different part of India: at the Foreign Training Node in Belagavi near Belgaum in Karnataka. This time, they shared 'experiences gained during operations in order to enhance inter-operability in planning and execution of various operations in jungle- and semi urban/urban terrain.'[28] The fourth Dharma Guardian exercises were carried out in February 2023, but this time at Camp Imazu in Shiga prefecture in Japan.[29] According to a statement issued by the Indian Ministry of Defence: 'Exercise Dharma Guardian will further enhance the level of defence co-operation between [the] Indian Army and Japanese Ground Self Defence Forces, furthering the bilateral relations between the two nations.'[30]

Japan's post World War II constitution may still be pacifist in character, but, in essence, the Japanese Self Defence Forces (SDF) are like any other military in the world. And it is the threat posed by China that has made the Japanese become more active outside their own islands. The combined services of the SDF have nearly 250,000 active personnel and are equipped with the latest weaponry and technology procured mainly from the US, including a wide range of missiles, fighter planes and helicopters, as well as some of the world's most technologically advanced diesel-electric submarines and indigenously built battle tanks. According to the Stockholm International Peace Research Institute (SIPRI), Japan also has the world's tenth-largest military budget after the US, China, Russia, India, Saudi Arabia, Britain, Germany, France and South Korea.[31]

Then there are two regional alliances: the Quad, or the Quadrilateral Security Dialogue, which brings together the US, India, Australia and Japan, and AUKUS, a tighter grouping encompassing, as the name suggests, Australia, the UK and the US. AUKUS' focus is on military capability, while, in addition, there is 'the Five Eyes' intelligence-sharing alliance, which also includes New Zealand and Canada. New Zealand, though, cannot become a full member of AUKUS due to its anti-nuclear position.[32] But the security pact between the Solomon Islands and Nauru switching diplomatic relations from Taiwan to China have alarmed New Zealand and Canada as well, and prompted them to work more closely with AUKUS countries.[33] At a meeting in Melbourne on 1 February 2024, New Zealand's Foreign Minister Winston Peters said there had been '"external interest" in the Pacific because countries with traditional interests had "neglected" the region [and] when you have a vacuum being formed, it will be filled.'[34]

A statement issued after a meeting with Quad leaders in the White House in Washington in May 2022 stated that the bloc strongly supports 'the principles of freedom, rule of law, democratic values, sovereignty and territorial integrity, peaceful settlement of disputes without resorting to threat or use of force, any unilateral attempt to change the status quo, and freedom of navigation and overflight, all of which are essential to the peace, stability and prosperity of the Indo-Pacific region and to the world.'[35]

The Chinese have definitely got the message. At the sidelines of the annual National People's Congress in March 2023, Xi accused the US and other Western countries of trying to 'contain, encircle and suppress China.'[36] Xi no doubt had the Quad as well as AUKUS in mind when he made that statement. And he was not actually wrong. China under Xi is perceived as a threat that Western powers as well as India and Japan believe has to be dealt with.

However, AUKUS ran into trouble with France, an important ally, when Australia in 2021 decided to scrap a French contract worth US$65 million for the delivery of twelve conventional submarines and, instead, made a deal with the US to acquire and build a new class of nuclear-powered but conventionally armed attack submarines. France recalled its ambassadors from Canberra and Washington in protest, and the Chinese did not miss the opportunity to highlight the rift in the pact aimed against them. A columnist in the official paper, *Global Times*, quoting various Chinese spokespersons wrote that Trump's 'America First' and Biden's 'America is back' are 'just different measures serving the same goal of US hegemony [...] as long as it's in the interest of the US, they can betray anyone, even an ally like France.'[37] But the dispute was short-lived. In December 2023, France and Australia for the sake of regional security decided to patch up their differences and promised to grant 'enhanced' access to each other's military bases across the Indo-Pacific region as well as to increase the sharing of intelligence.[38]

The Chinese, on the other hand, have had more serious problems with their foreign relations. When Darius Rochebin, a Swiss journalist, was interviewing Lu Shaye, the Chinese ambassador to Paris, on French TV in April 2023 and said that the Crimea peninsula 'belongs to Ukraine according to international law,' Shaye stated that the former Soviet countries do not 'have effective status in international law'.[39] Representatives of the three Baltic states, Estonia, Latvia and Lithuania, complained; France and the European Union asked Lu to clarify what he had meant; and about eighty European lawmakers signed a letter calling on the French government to expel Lu.[40]

After the storm, the Chinese embassy in Paris issued a statement saying that Lu's remarks 'were an expression of personal views and were not a political statement [and] the remarks should not be over-interpreted.'[41] But the damage was done and former Soviet republics other than the Baltic ones had to be reassured of China's respect and support. In May 2023, Xi unveiled a grand plan for the development of the former Soviet republics in Central Asia—from building infrastructure to boosting trade. China is prepared to take on a leadership role in a region that has traditionally been a Russian sphere of influence.[42]

Xi called on China and the Central Asian republics to increase their trade in oil and gas, 'develop energy cooperation across industrial chains and boost cooperation on new energy,' including the 'peaceful use of nuclear energy.'[43] In the longer term, Xi said, the cooperation 'would strengthen the construction of transport hubs of China–Europe freight train services.'[44]

That 'cooperation' basically means that those countries have to export their oil and gas to China, perhaps in exchange for some favours in cash or in kind. In order to forge closer ties with the Central Asian republics, China has built a new, fancy sports stadium in Uzbekistan—with a loan from the Export-Import Bank of China.[45] A railway has also been built from China to Kyrgystan and Uzbekistan and, according to plans, will continue through Turkmenistan and the Middle East to Europe.[46]

According to the *Global Times*: 'In history, Tashkent, the capital of Uzbekistan, was once an important hub along the ancient Silk Road [...] the Silk Road Economic Belt under the China-proposed Belt and Road Initiative (BRI) has changed dramatically from its predecessors. One by one, major projects designed and built by China have left a unique and beautiful mark along the Silk Road in the new era.'[47] The symbolic value of such a well-developed trade corridor is important since the myth of an ancient Silk Road through those territories has to be kept alive.

China may be able to extract oil and gas from the Central Asian republics, but what the *Global Times* writers call 'the China–Central Asia–Europe transportation corridor' is unlikely to be operational within the foreseeable future. Russia's invasion of Ukraine in 2022 put an end to that dream. Now international flights have to go around Russia and Ukraine, and European trade boycotts and sanctions against Russia have made commercial movements of any kind along that route impossible.

The war in Ukraine has put China in a difficult dilemma. As Jingdong Yuan and Fei Su at SIPRI wrote in *Global Asia* in June 2022, by not taking sides, Beijing hopes it will avoid offending either side.[48] China, those two analysts argue, '... is in a bind in its relationship with Russia. China is clearly upset by Russia's invasion (although it has yet to formally characterize it as such) but has chosen neither to publicly condemn it nor join the West in imposing sanctions on Russia.'[49] China has also refrained from sending military material to Russia because that could lead to Western sanctions against the Chinese entities involved in such deals. Russia, therefore, has had to turn to North Korea to procure missiles and related equipment.

But completely deserting Russia now, Yuan and Su argue, could upset China's long-term strategic objectives. At the same time, a weakened Russia, which would remain in a strategic partnership with Beijing, would place China in a better position to expand its presence and influence in Central Asia, moves that Russia has so far resisted, and to cut better energy deals at a moment of limited options for Russia.[50]

In the Indo-Pacific region, China has more options and can operate more freely. The construction of ports is the most obvious sign of Chinese presence in the Indian Ocean, but China has another much more subtle approach to expanding its regional influence: submarine sales to Indo-Pacific countries, which come replete with training of naval personnel from the receiving countries and Chinese maintenance technicians at the actual sites, which would at least officially be under the control of the sovereign countries in which they are located. But if tensions escalate between China and rivals such as India and the US, Beijing could conceivably gain access to foreign naval bases where they already have a presence without having to establish any of their own. Such developments are underway to varying degrees in Ream in Cambodia, Kyaukphyu in Myanmar, Hambantota in Sri Lanka and Gwadar in Pakistan.

China has also tried to get permanent access to the Thai naval base at Sattahip east of Bangkok. China offered to sell a submarine to Thailand, but the deal did not materialize. Thailand has instead decided to use the money allocated to buy the submarine to procure a frigate from China.[51] The Thais had become wary of China's submarine policy and if the deal had gone through, China would have been able to send personnel to Sattahip, the largest Thai naval base, to train their Thai counterparts and provide repairs and upgrades.

Some training of Thai naval personnel has already taken place, but in China, and junior officers are learning Mandarin while they are there. And, in October 2017, the Chinese naval fleet commander rear admiral Shen Hao visited Thailand and oversaw a joint exercise of four ships with more than 800 officers and soldiers.[52] There have been further joint exercises, most recently the China–Thailand Blue Strike in the Gulf of Thailand in September 2023 and in November a joint training in which other Southeast Asian countries also participated. But that exercise was held in China's southern Guangdong province.[53] And that appears to be as far as the Thais are willing to go when it comes to interacting with the Chinese Navy.

In December 2021, the Myanmar Navy took delivery of a 2,100-tonne Type-35 Ming Class submarine from China. The event went viral on social media with videos showing the submarine moving up the Yangon river. It was unclear where the submarine was headed but it could have been docked at the old naval base at Monkey Point for maintenance and from there be transferred to one of the Myanmar Navy's bases on the coast of the Bay of Bengal. The delivery of the Chinese submarine came a year after India had refurbished one of its Soviet-era Kilo-class submarines and gifted it to Myanmar.[54] It was an obvious attempt by New Delhi to counter China's influence in the region, but China outdid India by giving Myanmar a more modern and more advanced submarine.

The competition between China and India is even more evident in Bangladesh where both Asian superpowers are committed to investing in the same port at Mongla, the country's second largest and second busiest seaport. India has selected Egis India Consulting Engineers to help upgrade the port, while China has agreed to include a parallel project at Mongla in its development plans and provide a government-approved loan to finance the construction of two container terminals and delivery yards. India has pledged to fund the construction of jetties, roads, parking lots, offices and, near the port, a residential complex.[55]

The China Harbour Engineering Company was instrumental in upgrading Bangladesh's largest port at Chittagong (now Chattogram). Work there began before Xi launched his BRI but it was subsequently listed as a BRI project. However, the company was blacklisted in 2018 for offering bribes to government officials in connection with a road construction project in another part of the country.[56] But China has not given up its interest in Chittagong's port. State-owned firms have offered to build a new 'Smart City' on reclaimed land near the port, a project some experts believe could adversely affect the environment.[57]

The main port facility at Chittagong is purely commercial, but next to it is BNS Issa Khan, Bangladesh's main naval base. In 2015, a Bangladesh government official said that his country 'has never hosted a naval ship from China and has no plans to.'[58] But in January 2016, three Chinese vessels—the guided-missile frigates Liuzhou and Sanya and the supply ship Qinghaihu—docked at Chittagong.[59] The five-day visit was the first of its kind in Bangladesh and came after China had launched a frigate specially built for the Bangladesh Navy. Bangladesh has also bought several frigates from China, and, in 2017, two Type-035G Ming Class Chinese diesel-electric submarines were delivered to BNS Issa Khan and with them came, as usual, agreements on training and regular maintenance by Chinese technicians.[60] And it should not be forgotten that China is Bangladesh's main source of military hardware, including anti-ship missiles, tanks and fighter aircraft.[61]

Bangladesh's turning to China for defence procurement, trade and investment is hardly surprising. Despite the fact that Bangladesh would not have been an independent nation had India not intervened in the 1971 fight for freedom—what many Bangladeshis see as constant interference in the country's internal politics has caused resentment among the general public. Bangladeshi politicians have used that resentment to gain popular support, which has resulted in a divide between the Awami League, which is perceived as pro-Indian, and the Opposition Bangladesh Nationalist Party (BNP), which is closer to China and, somewhat ironically, Pakistan, the enemy against whom the war of 1971 was fought.

That resentment has grown after a controversial election held on 7 January 2024. Prime Minister Sheikh Hasina's Awami League won a fourth straight term in office, while the BNP boycotted the polls.[62] Pinaki Battacharya, an exiled politician, launched a #BoycottIndia campaign on social media, which got thousands of followers, some with photos of Indian products crossed out.[63] Nurul Haque Nur, the leader of Gono Odhikar Parishad, a new and rising political party and BNP ally, said at a rally in Dhaka after the election: 'You people have seen how India interfered in our last general election. We all have to start an "India Out" campaign.'[64]

China, eager to maintain good relations with whoever is in power in Dhaka, stated that it will back the Bangladeshi government against 'external interference'.[65] Even if the Awami League is considered pro-India, many of its leaders have close relations with Chinese counterparts. The family of Salman Rahman, Sheikh Hasina's top adviser, owns Beximco, one of Asia's largest textile firms, which has significant business deals with China; and Zunaid Ahmed Palak, the minister of state for information and communication technology, has been accused of being too soft on the activities of Chinese companies in Bangladesh.[66]

Mohamed Muizzu's election victory in the Maldives in December 2023; the bewildering intricacies of Bangladeshi politics; and one crisis after another in Nepal in which the India–China rivalry is a constant denominator—mean that New Delhi now has serious issues with countries it once regarded as friends. Pakistan, of course, has always been China's principal ally in the region. All the neighbouring countries except Bhutan have joined the BRI, and those alliances, combined with China's growing naval presence in the Indian Ocean, have made India fear a potential strategic encirclement.[67] It is evident that the surge of Chinese influence across South Asia has reshaped the regional order.

However, India and its allies, Japan, the US, Australia and France, still maintain naval superiority in the Indian Ocean. But even there the race is on as India as well as China are expanding their respective aircraft carrier fleets. At present, the Indian Navy operates two aircraft carriers: the Russian-made *INS Vikramaditya* and the *INS Vikrant*, India's first home-built carrier, which entered into service in September 2022. On 9 October 2023, the chief of the Indian Navy, Admiral Hari Kumar, said that there are plans to build another Vikrant-class carrier.[68]

China, meanwhile, acquired its first aircraft carrier in 1998 by extraordinarily unconventional methods. Ukraine had inherited an unfinished aircraft carrier after the break-up of the Soviet Union, and wanted to sell it to anyone who was willing to buy it. It was eventually sold to an unknown 'leisure company' in Macau, then still a Portuguese territory. The firm, Agencía Turistica e Diversões Chong Lot Limitada, or the Chong Lot Tourism and Amusement Agency, said it was going to convert the aircraft carrier into a floating casino and discotheque.[69] The price was US$20 million. The plot thickened when local journalists in Macau found out that the company's registered address did not exist. Besides, it would have been impossible to park a 67,000-tonne aircraft carrier in the extremely shallow waters around Macau.

The 306-metre-long ship had difficulty passing through the Bosporus Dardanelles Strait, which connects the Black Sea with the Mediterranean. It was not until the Turks eventually allowed the aircraft carrier to be towed to China that it could leave. But it never went to Macau; it was towed to the Dalian naval shipyard in north-eastern China, where it was it was refurbished and upgraded. Initially called the *Varyag* after a warship which played an important, and supposedly heroic, role during Russia's 1904–1905 war with Japan, it became the Liaoning in China and was commissioned in September 2012.

By then, the true identity of the Macau-based company had also been revealed. Its boss was actually Chan Kai-kit, an infamous underworld character with links to the Chinese mafia, the so-called Triads.[70] The deal was typical of the way in which China sometimes conducts its overseas businesses; organized-crime figures are used to perform certain duties for the authorities and, in return, get protection for their other, more unsavoury activities. In this case, the deal would have caused too much attention from the outside world, and perhaps been stopped, if China had been the official buyer of the aircraft carrier.

China's second, and this time domestically produced, aircraft carrier was launched on 26 April 2017 and, after more work on it, was fully commissioned into service on 17 December 2019. Called the Shandong, it was built at the Dalian Shipyard and is a significant improvement on the Liaoning. A third aircraft carried, Fujian, has a displacement of over 80,000 tonnes and is the largest in China's current fleet. It is expected to be fully commissioned in 2025 and could play a role should China launch an invasion of Taiwan.[71]

This build-up of a navy is unprecedented in Chinese history. After Zheng He's exploits in the fifteenth century, China turned inwards and the Ming and Qing emperors saw no need for a fleet that would venture far away from the country's own shores. The priority was on having smaller vessels suited for the defence of China's coastal areas and to police inland routes like the Grand Canal, the world's longest artificial waterway that runs through the eastern parts of the erstwhile empire. After the last emperor, Puyi, was overthrown during the 2011–12 revolution and China became a republic, the navy remained small and poorly equipped. It was no match for the Imperial Japanese Navy and other Japanese forces when they invaded large parts of eastern China, including nearly all coastal areas, in the 1930s.

After the communist takeover in 1949, the Soviet Union provided assistance to China in the form of naval equipment and technology. But that support ended when the Chinese and the Soviets parted ways in the late 1950s and early 1960s. The Chinese Navy remained largely a riverine and littoral, brown-water force. It was not until the disintegration of the Soviet Union, and the adoption of an export-oriented economy during the time of Deng Xiaoping and his successors, that China's leaders began to develop a blue-water navy.

But, as the Australian defence expert David Brewster has pointed out, China's strategic vulnerability is a function of geography.[72] The Indian Ocean is largely an enclosed ocean with few entry points and vast distances between them. According to Brewster, China has no ability to exert control over any of those chokepoints, and China's vulnerability is reinforced by the scarcity of overland transport routes to the Indian Ocean.[73] Access to newly built ports and friendly relations with several island nations are not enough, if China aspires to become a truly powerful Indian Ocean power. In this maritime region, India, with its long east and west coasts, and islands in the Andaman Sea, holds a clear military advantage over China.

To make up for its shortcomings, China has placed a lot of emphasis on intelligence gathering. As for overland transport connections to the Indian Ocean, the China–Myanmar Economic Corridor down to Kyaukphyu is China's most important—in fact only—reasonably reliable access route to the Indian Ocean. It is, therefore, not surprising that a heated debate ensued when the London-based policy institute Chatham House published in 2023 satellite images of what appeared to be new military installations on Myanmar's Great Coco Island.[74]

But John Pollock, the author of the exposé and a Chatham House-affiliated analyst, also added words of caution. According to his commentary on the photographs: '... the most common allegation is that since the early 1990s Myanmar has allowed a Chinese signals intelligence facility on the archipelago. Little evidence exists for such a facility,' Pollock also said, '... bar a heavily weathered radar station, but recent satellite photographs have raised concern, especially in India.'[75]

The Coco Islands—Great Coco, Little Coco and some smaller islets—are separated from the northernmost of the Andaman Islands by the 40-kilometre-wide Coco Channel. The other side of the channel is the domain of India's strategically important Andaman and Nicobar Command, the only tri-service theater command of the Indian Armed Forces. The Indian media were quick to claim that China is behind the new constructions on Great Coco and, as *Hindustan Times* reported on 5 April 2023, that they aim at expanding the 'Chinese naval footprint in the region.'[76]

But all that could be said for certain, judging from the photographs gathered by Maxar Technologies, a private US-based company that specializes in satellite imagery, was that the 1,300-metre runway on Great Coco's airport has been extended to 2,300 metres. It has also been widened and new hangars have been built. A new, large pier is visible as well as a causeway connecting a cleared area on the southern tip of Great Coco with a smaller, uninhabited islet a short distance off the coast. South of the runway is a radar station, construction of which began in 2014 and was completed two years later. According to Maxar: 'Photographed in January 2023, the green dome covers the radar system to keep it protected from both the environment [...] and counter-surveillance efforts.'[77]

What Maxar and Chatham House appear to have overlooked is relatively new construction on the uninhabited, densely forested Little Coco: a huge building in the middle of the island with two nearby helipads, and a road connecting that place with the coast. Similar projects can also be seen on Preparis, a small island in the waters between Great Coco and the Myanmar mainland. There too, military-style buildings and two helipads away from the coast can be seen. As with the Cocos, Preparis is strictly off-limits to civilians.

On 10 April 2023, the foreign ministry in Beijing dismissed the reports of a Chinese-run spy post on Great Coco as 'complete nonsense',[78] while Major-General Zaw Min Tun, spokesman for Myanmar's ruling junta, called them 'absurd'.[79] But those statements did not allay fears of some substantial Chinese military or intelligence involvement in a very sensitive maritime area. The controversy—and speculation—actually began in the early 1990s when the Myanmar military launched a program to upgrade its navy and naval facilities. The prestigious defence journal, *Jane's Defence Weekly*, reported on 29 January 1994 that technicians from China were present on Great Coco installing Chinese-supplied equipment.[80] That revelation led to wild, often exaggerated coverage of the issue, especially in the Indian media.

Then came a report in the now-defunct Hong Kong-based weekly, *Far Eastern Economic Review*, on 30 January 1997, of an unpublicized visit to Beijing by General Maung Aye, the vice chairman of the then ruling junta, in October the year before. A deal had been finalized, under which China would 'train 300 Myanmar air force and navy officers in flying skills, naval duties, and the gathering of intelligence in coastal areas.'[81]

In contrast to those cautious and rather carefully worded reports, wild and exaggerated versions of what was happening in Myanmar appeared in the Indian media and on websites. China's security agencies supposedly operated electronic-intelligence and maritime-reconnaissance facilities on the two Coco Islands that were part of India and then said to have been transferred to Myanmar in the 1950s and leased to China in 1994.

In fact, the Coco Islands became part of British Burma in the 1880s. At that time, there was little more than a lighthouse on Great Coco. Burma became a province of India in 1886, but that did not change the status of the islands. When Burma was separated from India in 1937 and became a separate colony, the Coco Islands remained Burmese territory.

The Coco Islands never changed hands and they have never been leased to China.

Great Coco once served as a penal colony for political prisoners, most of them communists, and then became a base for the Myanmar Navy. What happened in the 1990s was that China helped Myanmar upgrade that base—as well as several naval bases on the mainland. Among other military equipment that China transferred to Myanmar at the time were four unspecified radars for the navy and twelve JLP-40 and JLG-43 radars, presumably for the air force and the army.[82] But those radars seem to have been meant for navigation and height finding rather than surveillance, and fit into the pattern of the paranoia of the generals in power in Myanmar, who have always feared an invasion from what it perceives as 'hostile, Western powers'.

There is hardly any doubt that radars and other equipment were installed on Great Coco in the 1990s, and that those which have been delivered more recently come from China. But the question is what use the Chinese would have for a 'ground station' on an island in the Bay of Bengal. Buildings and other installations that can be gleaned from Google Earth images appear to be too small for advanced operations such as monitoring missile tests on India's east coast, and that appears to be what the Indians fear the most.

China's advanced satellites and its Yuan Wang tracking ships would be far more useful for such intelligence gathering. Those ships have powerful satellite and missile tracking and surveillance capabilities, and they are regularly deployed to three major oceans—the Western Pacific, the South Pacific and the Indian Ocean. They are officially classified as non-military research vessels which support, track and control missions of China's Shenzhou spacecraft and spaceflight programs. They were initially nevertheless operated by the Chinese People's Liberation Army Strategic Support Force, which was the authority responsible for space, cyber and electronic warfare until it was disbanded in April 2024. In short, the Chinese vessels are spy ships packed with all sorts of communication and surveillance gear.

In November 2022, one of those ships, the Yuan Wang 6, entered the Indian Ocean, only three months after its sister ship Yuan Wang 5 had docked at Hambantota. The August mission by Yuan Wang 5 was widely publicized in India, where Press Trust of India reported the government was concerned about 'the possibility of Chinese vessels' hi-tech tracking systems attempting to snoop on Indian defence installations while being on their way to Sri Lankan ports.'[83]

After the November mission, the Sri Lankan website TheMorning.lk reported: 'This is not the first time that the Yuan Wang 6 has voyaged into the Indian Ocean, with one visit reported early in 2020 that lasted nearly three months.'[84] Then on 6 January 2022, an unidentified high-altitude balloon was spotted in the skies above the Andamans, only days after the Indian military had concluded an important tri-service drill on the islands.[85] It was never confirmed that it was a Chinese spy balloon, but the similarities with incidents in the US and elsewhere are striking. In February 2023, the US Air Force even shot down with great fanfare what Washington claimed was a balloon meant for spying. The Chinese have always insisted that the balloons are civilian research vessels.

A more plausible explanation for China's involvement in the upgrading of Myanmar's naval bases in the 1990s is that it was a goodwill gesture that would help Beijing secure and perhaps even expand its influence in the country. The radars that China delivered in the 1990s may not have been that sophisticated, though that is not to say that old and new installations on the Coco Islands cannot be used for some limited signals intelligence gathering from which the Chinese could benefit. But the Myanmar military's thoughts behind the projects, no matter how far-fetched it may seem, remain fear and paranoia. Myanmar's ruling generals still believe that a Western invasion from the sea may happen, and that they, therefore, need radars and signals intelligence posts along Myanmar's coasts and on its islands.

The Chinese probably view the issue more realistically, and with other considerations in mind. They want Myanmar to remain a close ally providing an easy and convenient access to the Indian Ocean. That is also why China is going ahead with its BRI projects in Myanmar, even after the February 2021 coup and the subsequent imposition of sanctions on the ruling junta by Western nations.

On the other side of the Southeast Asian peninsula, China is also facing challenges. Japan may have lost its once vast empire at the end of World War II, but its string of islands from Hokkaido in the north to Okinawa in the south form a natural barrier that would substantially hem in China during any future military conflict. As Japan seeks stronger ties with Taiwan, that line of island defence may be more robust than many analysts realize.

In the event of a sea conflict with the US, China would need access to wide and secure sea lanes in order to reach the Pacific Ocean, and even if Beijing has managed to establish close relations with several Pacific Ocean nations, it would not be easy to reach that maritime buffer between Asia and the Americas. Just before Kiribati and the Solomon Islands shifted recognition from Taipei to Beijing in September 2019, then US Secretary of State Mike Pompeo visited the Marshall Islands and Palau, two nations that continue to recognize Taiwan, and the Federated States of Micronesia, which has relations with China. He stated that, '… today, I am here to confirm the United States will help you protect your sovereignty, your security, your right to live in freedom and peace … I'm pleased to announce the United States has begun negotiations on extending our compacts … they sustain democracy in the face of Chinese efforts to redraw the Pacific.'[86]

In light of recent developments in the Indo-Pacific region, the US is strengthening its line of defence closer to China and the Asian mainland. That is part of the rationale behind Japan and Taiwan's emerging China containment wall. While neither Japan nor the US has official diplomatic relations with Taiwan, Washington is a major supplier of arms to Taiwan and Japanese lawmakers have stated that the Japanese and Taiwanese 'share fundamental values such as freedom and democracy.'[87] Japan is already a force to be reckoned with in the region and Taiwan is emerging as its closest, if understated, regional strategic ally. Although it has never been officially acknowledged, Japan and Taiwan—and the US—also share intelligence about domestic Chinese politics as well as security issues of common concern.

Japan and its outlying islands provide not only a base to monitor or interdict Chinese naval forces breaking out of the Yellow Sea and into the Pacific, but also to contain China's ally Russia, whose Far Eastern Fleet is based at Vladivostok on the opposite side of the Sea of Japan. Combined with developments in the Indian Ocean, the encirclement that China fears has become a strategic reality.

Xi's position as the most powerful politician in China was long beyond doubt. But the mishandling of the Covid-19 pandemic and the economic slowdown China has had to face after the worst of the health crisis was over, have made Xi's grip on power less secure. The BRI and China's worsening property crisis show how hubris and poor planning can have a devastating impact on a country's economy—and when it is a big country with a huge economy like China, the fallout can be very serious.

To remedy the situation, Xi has purged the civil service of tens of thousands of supposedly corrupt civil servants, including those involved in the procurement of military equipment, as well as high-ranking government ministers such as Defence Minister Li Shangfu and Foreign Minister Qin Gang—and, more significantly from a security point of view, nine generals in the armed forces were sacked in December 2023. As Reuters reported: 'The recent downfall of generals and military equipment suppliers, however, has punctured some of this aura, and raised questions over whether there has been adequate oversight over these massive military investments as China vies with the United States in key areas, including Taiwan and the South China Sea.'[88] And, it should be added, with India and allied forces in the Indian Ocean.

It is highly unlikely that the twenty-first century will, as Xi envisaged in 2013, be the Chinese century. Xi has more internal and external enemies now than he had when he assumed power and launched his ill-fated BRI. China is entering an era of political uncertainty and the rest of the world may have to pay the price for Xi's inflated dreams of power and China's greatness.

ACKNOWLEDGEMENTS

THIS BOOK IS BASED ON NUMEROUS RESEARCH TRIPS IN THE region and I have also benefitted from the writings of academics, researchers and journalists such as Li Jianglin, Roderick MacFarquhar, Frank Dikötter, Khoddadad Rezakhani, Akhilesh Pillalamarri, Probal Dasgupta, Nirupama Rao, Yang Jisheng, Rush Doshi, Tsering Shakya, Anne-Mary Brady, Ron Crocombe, John Garver, Nicholas Eftimiades, Maria Adele Carrai, Roger Faligot, Michael Schoenhals, Grant Evans, Andrew Selth, Mary Callahan, Philip Bowring, Sebastian Strangio, Wang Gongwu, Wasana Wongsurawat, Chiranan Prasertkul, Desmond Shum, Carol Li, Stephen Guettiera, Andrew Mertha and many, many others.

Lars Ellström, a renowned Swedish Sinologist, helped me translate documents and other writings in Chinese. Robert Keith-Reid, founder-editor of *Islands Business*, was my guide in Fiji, and Anna Powles, a renowned New Zealand academic, showed me around Honiara when I visited the Solomon Islands. Andrey Zabiyako, a local academic, took me on a tour of Blagoveshchensk across the Amur River from Heihe in China.

Local journalists and activists, who have asked to remain anonymous, helped me when I visited Mauritius, the Seychelles, Réunion, the Maldives, the Marshall Islands, the Northern Marianas, Papua New Guinea, the Solomon Islands, Vanuatu, Fiji, Samoa, Tonga, Tahiti and the Cook Islands. I also went to Bhutan, where I met security officials, and to Nepal, where I covered the Maoist insurgency. And I travelled to

Djibouti to find out what was happening at the Chinese base there. In India, I went to Arunachal Pradesh to visit the line where India meets China, and to the strategically important Andaman Islands in the Indian Ocean. Any mistakes or factual errors in this book are entirely my own for which my sources, written as well as oral, should not be blamed. And I am grateful to Simon Robson for proofreading the manuscript and tidying up my English.

NOTES

Scan this QR code to access the detailed notes.

INDEX

Act East policy of India, 192
Afghanistan, China's interest in mining, 120–121
aircraft carriers of China, 200–201
Ali, Choudhry Rahmat, 117
Allende, Salvador, 186
ambassador road, 16
Andaman and Nicobar Islands, 152
Anglo-Russian Convention (1907), 111
anti-Westernism, rise of, 44, 47
Ardern, Jacinda, 183
Artificial Intelligence (AI) Governance Initiative, 185–186
Arunachal Pradesh, 111, 114
Asian Infrastructure Investment Bank, 84
Assam, 111
Association of Southeast Asian Nations (ASEAN), 79, 84
Australia, 181; China's security threat to, 151–152; external territories, 151; and India, defence cooperation, 152

Ball, Warwick, 8
Balochistan, 116–117
Balochistan Liberation Army, 117
Bay of Bengal Initiative for Multi-Sectoral Technical and Economic Cooperation (BIMSTEC), 191–192
Belt and Road Initiative (BRI), vii–viii, 1, 15, 17, 19, 24–25, 52, 55, 70–72, 78, 82, 114, 122, 129, 145, 153, 175, 198, 208; branding with new slogan Small is beautiful, 185; challenges and problems faced by, 2–8; failure in Himalayan states, 105; fragmentation of, x; funding of, x; Health Silk Road, 21; international aid plan, 2; outcome of, 2; Silk Road Economic Belt, 1, 196; Silk Road Fund, x; strain in China and Maldives relations, 21
Bering Strait, 31
Bhagat, Premindra Singh, 112

Bhutan bilateral relationship: with China, 101–105; with India, 102–103
Biden, Joe, 4, 191; America is back, 195
bipolar world, 186–187
Blagoveshchensk, 32
Blagoveshchensk massacre, 36, 49
Boli city, 32
Bolshevik revolution in 1917, 35, 45
Bose, Subhas Chandra, 187
Boxer Rebellion, 34
Brazil, 48
Brooks, Henderson, 112
Build Back Better World (B3W) initiative, 191
Buryat, 54
Bush, George W., 79

Cambodia, 56; and China bilateral relationship, 75–78, 151
Central Treaty Organization (CENTO), 118
China–Central Asia–Europe transportation corridor, 196
China/Chinese (People's Republic of China), 56, 190; advanced satellites and Yuan Wang tracking ship, 205–206; capitalist China of 2024, 114; domestic problems in, 23; emphasis on intelligence gathering, 202–203; European coins unearthed in, 13; exports, hurdles in, 57–58; external environment for development, 23–24; fought wars with countries, 189; increase in exports to South Pacific, 164; mega-developments, ix; monolithic nation-state, 7; navy build up, 202; non-intervention policy, 188; population of, 6, ix; problems with foreign relations, 195; Southeast Asia as Great Golden Peninsula for, 91; strategic vulnerability, 202; Swedes negative views of, 188
China–India bilateral relationship, 131; 1962 war, 56, 111–114, 118; border dispute, 109; competition for Bangladesh, 198–200; Doklam stand-off, 104–105, 114; *Hindi Chini Bhai Bhai,* 107, 109–110
China–Myanmar Economic Corridor (CMEC), 115, 202–203
China Observers in Central and Eastern Europe (CHOICE), 145–146
China–Pakistan Economic Corridor (CPEC), 58, 115, 117, 119, 122
Christmas Island, 151–152, 203
Clinton, Bill, 79
Coca Codo Sinclair hydroelectric dam, 190
Cocos (Keeling) Islands, 151, 203–205
Cold War, 1–2
Commonwealth of Nations, 163
Communist Party of Australia (Marxist-Leninist), 57
Communist Party of Burma (CPB), 56, 59, 61–65
Communist Party of China (CPC), 23, 108; Communique of the Seventh Plenary Session of the 19th Central Committee, 6; state communism of 1931, 7

Communist Party of Malaya (CPM), 56
Communist Party of North Kalimantan, 56
Communist Party of Thailand (CPT), 56
Comoros, 138–140, 185; and China bilateral relationship, 141, 143
Cook Islands, 161
Covid-19 pandemic, ix–x, 21, 23, 44, 177, 193, 208
Cultural Revolution in China, 26

Dahal, Pushpa Kamal (alias Prachanda), 92, 94–95, 97
Dalvi, Brig. John, 113
da Sailva, Luiz Inácio Lula, 44–45, 47
Deng Xiaoping, 6, 15, 57, 63, 145, 202; market-oriented reforms, vii, 59
Didi, Muhammed Fareed, 130
Diego Garcia, 149–150

Eastern Siberians, 51
East Turkestan Islamic Movement, 117
Economic Corridors: China–Myanmar, 3–5; China–Pakistan, 3
Ecuador and China free-trade agreement, 189–190
Ellström, Lars, 15
Escobar, Pepe, 21–22
Estonia, 45
Eurasia, 12
European Russia, 37
European Union, viii, x, 46, 54, 67, 142, 191–192, 195
Export-Import Bank of China, 73, 84, 129, 196

Far East of Russia and China, 32, 50, 53, 55, 123, 186. *See also* Bolshevik revolution in 1917; Chinese ancestors treatment, 33; Chinese gangs establishment and its impact, 40–41; economic expansion into, 27–31; ethnic cleansing of, 36; ethnic Koreans in, 36; foreign investment, 38; harsh climatic conditions, 39; loss of economic independence, 39; loss of population, 29; rich in mineral resources, 38; withdrawal of Japanese, 36
Fiji: and China bilateral relations, 171–174; end of cooperation with China, 4, 183; military coups in, 162–163, 172–173; readmission to Commonwealth, 163; Silkroad Ark Hotel project, 165; violent attacks on Chinese, 173–174
Finland: Continuation War (1941–1944), 45; joined Eurozone, 46; member of European Union, 46; NATO membership, 46; Soviets naval bases in, 45; Winter War (1939–40), 45

Gayoom, Maumoon Abdul, 130–131
Germany, 2, 33, 47, 75, 124, 151, 169, 191, 193
global connectivity strategy of European Union, 191
Goulart, João, 186
Great Patriotic War, 47
Green, Nile, 13

Hailanpao, 32

Haishenwai (sea cucumber cliffs), 32
Hansen, Valerie: *The Silk Road: A New History*, 10
Hasina, Sheikh, 199–200
Hatta, Mohammed, 187
Huaqiao, 28
Hu Jintao, 94

Ibrahim, Anwar, 88
Illarionov, Andrej, 46
Indian Ocean, 180, 205; Australian external territories, 151; France's exclusive economic zone in, 150–151
Indian Ocean and China, 57, 200; and BRI, 125; Djibouti first naval base by China, 123–125; importance of, 123
Indonesia and China bilateral relationship, viii, 89–91
Indo-Pacific region, 146, 182, 186, 191, 194–195, 197
Industrial Workers of the World (IWW) (or the Wobblies), 35
International Monetary Fund (IMF), 71, 121

Japan, 3, 24, 28, 32, 35–36, 40–41, 47, 75, 87, 128, 132, 151, 155–157, 173, 183, 207; Djibouti overseas military base, 124; and India bilateral and defence relations, 190–193; invaded Burma and Andamans in 1942, 187; Japanese Self Defence Forces (SDF), 193; military budget, 193; Partnership for Quality Infrastructure (PQI), 190; presence on Taiping Island (known as Itu Aba), 80
Jiang Zemin, 37, 96
Johnson, Boris, 191
Johnson South Reef, 82

Kachin Independence Army (KIA), 59
Kang Sheng, 56–57
Karakhan, Lev, 35
Karakhan Manifesto (or the Karakhan Declaration), 35
Kazakhstan, vii–ix, 3, 82
Kenya, viii, 143
Khabarovsk, 32
Khan, Imran, 119
Khan, Kublai, 9–10
Khrushchev, Nikita, 26
Krasnoshchyokov, Alexander Mikhailovich, 35
Kremlin, 48–49
Kunwar, Padam, 95
Kyrgystan, viii, 3, 196

Lama, Dalai, 96, 103, 107–108, 110, 113
Laos and China bilateral relationship, 72–75, 186
Lenin, Vladimir, 6, 35
Liberation Tigers of Tamil Eelam (LTTE) (or the Tamil Tigers), 126–127
Li Keqiang, 53, 88
Liu Shaoqi, 63
Lord Palmerston, 48
Lyndon LaRouche movement, 22

Madagascar, 19, 138; and China bilateral relationship, 142–146;

joined BRI, 145–156; in pre-colonial era, 143–144; relations with other countries, 144
Malacca Strait, 84, 126
Malaysia: Bumiputera policy, 87; and China, bilateral relationship, 86–88
Maldives, 5, 18–19, 81, 153, 185; attacks by Islamists, 132; and China bilateral relationship, 128–130, 200; and India bilateral relationship, 131–132; joined BRI, 131; terrorism-linked incident of violence in, 132–133
Manchu Qing Dynasty, 31
Mao Zedong, vii, 6, 15, 26, 56, 59, 93, 107; Great Leap Forward, 113
Marape, James, 163
Marcos, Jr, Ferdinand, viii
Maritime Silk Road, 1, 17–18, 20–21, 128, 142
Marles, Richard, 183
Marshall Islands, 157, 180–181, 207
Marxism-Leninism, 6, 27
Mauritius, 133, 137, 143, 146; British colonial, 147; and China bilateral relationship, 148–149; Île de la Réunion, 147–148; Indians presence in, 147
Maxwell, Neville: *India's China War*, 112
McMahon, Henry, 110
McMahon Line, 110–111
Melanesia island, 155
Micronesia island, 155, 161, 180
Middle East, ix, 12, 17, 57, 82, 122–123, 128, 149, 196
Millward, James, 7

Mishustin, Mikhail, 53
Modi, Narendra, 131, 192
Mohamad, Mahathir, 88
Mossadegh, Mohammed, 186
Muizzu, Mohamed, 132–133, 200
Myanmar, 4–5, 16–17, 20, 22, 57–60, 187; Arakan Army (AA), 67; Arakan rebellion, 61; bama and myanma British colony, 60–61; Dohbama Asiayone (Our Burma Association), 60; Great Coco Island, 203–205; Lao People's Revolutionary Party (LPRP), 72; Myanmar National Democratic Alliance Army (MNDAA), 64–65, 67–68; National Democratic Alliance Army (NDAA), 64–65; nationalities in, 60–61; New Democratic Army-Kachin (NDA-K), 64–65, 67, 70; opium production, 64; State Administration Council (SAC), 71; Ta'ang National Liberation Army (TNLA), 67; United Wa State Army (UWSA), 64–69; upgradation of naval bases, 206; uprising for democracy in 1988, 67
Myanmar and China bilateral relationship, 186, 198; BRI projects, 207; China–Myanmar Economic Corridor (CMEC), 59, 70; China's long-term goal, 68; debt on Myanmar, 70–71; exports by China, 67; registered drug users in China and Myanmar, 68

Nasheed, Mohamed, 131

Nasir, Ibrahim, 130
National Liberation Front, 56
Nauru: Chinese aid to, 158–159; diplomatic relations with Taiwan, 159; recognized People's Republic of China, 159
naval cooperation between France and India, 192
Nehru, Jawaharlal, 106–107, 109; Forward Policy, 112
Nepal: Communist Party of Nepal (Maoist) (CPN(M)), 92–93, 95; Maoist insurgency in 1996, 92, 94; panchayat system, 94
Nepal and China bilateral relationship, 93, 186; agreement on highway construction, 94; BRI cooperation and debt trap, 96–99; BRI projects awarded to Indian companies, 100–101; increase in trade, 95; and India as Nepal's ally, 97; and India's northern border defence, 100; India's suggestion to build cross-border railway, 99–100; Sino-Nepalese Treaty of Peace and Friendship, 94; Xi's message to enemies, 96
New Caledonia, 178, 180
New Silk Road, 1, 23
New Zealand, 181, 183, 188–189
nine-dash-line, 81
Non-Aligned Movement, 113
North Atlantic Treaty Organization (NATO), 44–46
Northeast Frontier Agency (NEFA), 111–112
Nu, U, 61

Obama, Barack, 179, 191
Oli, K.P. Sharma, 96, 98
One Belt One Road (OBOR). *See* Belt and Road Initiative (BRI)
Outer Manchuria (Wai Manzhou), 31, 37, 39

Pacific Fleet headquarters, Vladivostok, 50
Pacific Ocean, xii, 4–5, 78, 152–153; aboriginals from Taiwan, 154; BRI projects in nations, 156, 184; China's growing influence in, 162, 179, 189
Pacific Silk Road, 21
Pakistan, 3, 25, 44, 58, 100, 114, 117; and China, bilateral relationship, 119–122, 186; debt trap, 71, 121–122; East Pakistan broke in 1971 war, 118–119; Gwadar port, 115–117; and India, hostility between, 118; meaning of, 117–118; political instability in, 58
Palau, 157, 180, 207
Pan Qi, 59
Papua New Guinea: Beijing's mission in, 167; and China bilateral relations, 156–157, 169–171, 175; corruption in, 163
Partai Komunis Indonesia (PKI), 56, 89
Patel, Vallabhbhai, 105–106
People's Liberation Army, 23
Pohiva, Akilisi, 165
Poland, 45
Polar Silk Road, 21, 38, 52–54
Polo, Marco, 9–10
Polynesia island and presence of

China, 155, 161, 177–180
Pompeo, Mike, 207
Putin, Vladimir, 22, 24, 29–30, 37, 43–44, 48–49, 54–55; pivot to the east policy, 38; role models, 46–47

Quadrilateral Security Dialogue (Quad), 194

Rabuka, Sitiveni, 183
Republic of Kiribati, 159, 161, 164, 180; and China bilateral relations, 159, 182; Tarawa station, 181–182
Republic of Palau, 161
Rezakhani, Khodadad: *The Road That Never Was: The Silk Road and Trans-Eurasian Exchange*, 11
Rini, Snyder, 166
Rome and China, trade during ancient times, 8
Russia and China bilateral relationship, 24, 26, 39, 48, 53–54. *See also* Far East of Russia and China; China's plunder of natural resources, 50; joint declaration in 2023, 52–53; new world order, 43, 49–50; Russia-China investment fund, 38
Russian Eastern Military District, Khabarovsk, 50
Russian revolution, 6

Sakhalin, 32
Samarkand, 11
Samoa and China, bilateral relations, 176–177, 185
sea routes, 19
Seneca the Younger, 11–12

Seychelles, 133–138
Sharif, Nawaz, 58
Shatra, Lama Lönchan, 110
Sikkim, 110–112
Siliguri Corridor (Chicken's Neck), 104
Silk Road, 8–14, 21; first used in China in 1989, 15; southern, 15, 17; in West, 15
Singapore, 3, 73, 84, 87–89, 128, 130, 188
Singapore and China bilateral relationship, 88–89
small island nations: forced to borrow money from China, 164–165
Solih, Ibrahim, 131–132
Solomon Islands, 160, 162, 175, 181–183; anti-Chinese sentiment in, 166; diplomatic relations with Taiwan, 166
South China Sea, 57, 80, 82, 152, 189, 208
Southeast Treaty Organization (SEATO), 118
Soviet Union, 26–29, 45, 56; collapse of, 45–46, 52, 79, 186
Sri Lanka and China bilateral relationship, 186; BRI projects, 2, 126; China as main supplier of military hardware, 127–128; debt trap, 71, 126–127; financial distress, 126; Hambantota port construction, 126–127
Stalin, Josef, 26; Great Terror in 1930s, 36
Strait of Malacca, 57
Sukarno, 187
Sun Yat-sen, 7

Suu Kyi, Aung San, 71, 187
Swe, Ba, 109

Taiwan, 24, 47, 75, 80, 166–167;
   cheque-book diplomacy
   with China, 158; and China
   unofficials relations, 157–158;
   ouster from United Nations, 158
Taliban and China relationship,
   120
Tang Code of the Emperor Taizong,
   12–13
terrorist attacks on 11 September
   2001, 124
Thailand and China bilateral
   relationship: BRI in, 82–84,
   86; China's efforts to access
   naval base, 197–198; Sino-
   Thai community, 84–85; trade
   relations, 85–86
Thavisin, Srettha, 84
Theory of Three Represents, 6
Third World, 114
Thondup, Gyalo, 108
Tibet, 7, 94, 96, 98–100, 103; and
   China bilateral relationship, 107,
   110; China's invasion in 1950,
   105; Lhasa uprising, 107–108,
   113; official recognition by India
   in 1954, 106
Tobgay, Tshering, 101
Tonga and China, bilateral
   relations, 159–160, 167–168,
   175–176
trade between southern China and
   Southeast Asia, 16
Trans-Siberian railway, Chinese
   labour participation in
   construction of, 33–34

Treaty of Nerchinsk, 31
Treaty of Peking, 31
Triads, 201
tribute road, 16
Trotsky, Leon, 35
Trump, Donald, 191; America First,
   195
Tuvalu, 157

Uganda, viii, 134
Uighurs in Xinjiang, China's
   treatment of, 47
Ukraine–Russia war, ix, 23–25, 44,
   49, 53–54; and China's dilemma,
   196–197
United Nations Educational,
   Scientific and Cultural
   Organization (UNESCO),
   142–143
United Nations High Commissioner
   for Human Rights, 119
United States, India, Australia and
   Japan (AUKUS), 194–195
US, vii, 2, 84; Central Intelligence
   Agency (CIA), 107–108; Hawaii
   military installations, 180–181;
   -led invasion of Iraq in 2003,
   44; Marshall Plan, vii–viii, 1–2;
   military intervention, 186; Power
   Africa public-private partnership,
   191; strengthening of defence
   closer to China and Asian
   mainland, 207; and Taiwan
   diplomatic relations, 207
Uzbekistan, ix, 3, 11, 36, 196

Valdai Discussion Group, 46
Vietnam, 56; and China, bilateral
   relationship, 78–82; reunification

in 1976, 80; Vietnam–China Comprehensive Strategic Partnership, 78
Vladikavkaz, 32
Vladivostok, 32

Wen Jiabao, 94
Wild-West capitalism, vii
Win, Ne, 61
Wuchi Route, 17

Xi Jinping, xi–xii, 20, 22, 38–39, 43–44, 49, 52, 58, 78–80, 91, 96–97, 105, 114, 128, 132–133, 148, 163, 165, 179, 185, 190, 194, 198; on China and Central Asian republics trade in oil and gas, 195–196; dream to make China great again, 2; imperialist policies, 186; One Belt One Road, 1; single nation-state, 6; on South Pacific region, 154; third revolution under, 6; third term of, 23

Yameen, Abdulla, 131
Yellow Sea, 208
Yeltsin, Boris, 29, 37
Yihequan (secret society), 34

Zhang Qian, 15
Zheng He, 18–19
Zhou Enlai, 94, 106–110, 113

ABOUT THE AUTHOR

Bertil Lintner is a Swedish journalist, author and strategic consultant who has been writing about Asia for nearly four decades. He was formerly the Myanmar correspondent of the *Far Eastern Economic Review* and the Asia correspondent for the Swedish daily *Svenska Dagbladet*, and Denmark's *Politiken*. He currently works as a correspondent for Asia Times. He has written extensively about Myanmar, India, China and North Korea for various local, national and international publications in over thirty countries. He mainly writes about organized crime, ethnic and political insurgencies and regional security. He has published several books, including *China's India War* and *Great Game East*. In 2004, Lintner received an award for excellence in reporting about North Korea from the Society of Publishers in Asia and, in 2014, another award from the same society for writing about religious conflicts in Myanmar.

HarperCollins *Publishers* India

At HarperCollins India, we believe in telling the best stories and finding the widest readership for our books in every format possible. We started publishing in 1992; a great deal has changed since then, but what has remained constant is the passion with which our authors write their books, the love with which readers receive them, and the sheer joy and excitement that we as publishers feel in being a part of the publishing process.

Over the years, we've had the pleasure of publishing some of the finest writing from the subcontinent and around the world, including several award-winning titles and some of the biggest bestsellers in India's publishing history. But nothing has meant more to us than the fact that millions of people have read the books we published, and that somewhere, a book of ours might have made a difference.

As we look to the future, we go back to that one word—a word which has been a driving force for us all these years.

Read.